Heinemann
Advanced
Music

Pam Hurry and Mark Phillips

with Mark Richards

Heinemann

Heinemann Advanced Music

Heinemann is an imprint of Pearson Education Limited, a company incorporated in England and Wales, having its registered office at Edinburgh Gate, Harlow, Essex, CM20 2JE. Registered company number: 872828

Heinemann is a registered trademark of Pearson Education Limited

Text © Pam Hurry and Mark Phillips with Mark Richards, 2001
First published in 2001

10
9 8 7

Copyright notice

British Library Cataloguing in Publication Data
A catalogue record for this book is available from the British Library

ISBN 978 0 435812 58 4

Typeset by Halstan & Co. Ltd., Amersham, Bucks., England.
Picture research by Thelma Gilbert
Printed and bound in Malaysia, KHL

Acknowledgements

The authors and publishers would like to thank the following for the use of copyright material:
The Rite of Spring – Igor Stravinsky © Copyright 1912, 1921 by Hawkes & Son (London) Ltd. Reproduced by permission of Boosey & Hawkes Music Publishers Ltd, on pp. 96-7 and 98-9; *Suite für Klavier* (extract) by Arnold Schoenberg, Copyright 1925 by Universal Edition. Copyright renewed 1952 by Gertrude Schoenberg. Reproduced by permission of Alfred A. Kalmus Ltd, on p. 103; *Classical Symphony in D, Op. 25* by Prokofiev © Copyright 1926 by Hawkes & Son (London) Ltd. Reproduced by permission of Boosey & Hawkes Music Publishers Ltd, on pp. 106-12; *Dance Suite* (extract) by Béla Bartók, Copyright 1924 by Universal Edition. Reproduced by permission, on pp. 116-21; *Symphony Op. 21* (extract) by Anton Webern, Copyright 1929 by Universal Edition. Copyright renewed 1956 by Anton Webern's Erben. Reproduced by permission of Alfred A. Kalmus Ltd, on pp. 124-6; *Structures II* by Pierre Boulez, Copyright 1967 by Universal Edition. Reproduced by permission of Alfred A. Kalmus Ltd, on p. 128; *Kontakte* by Stockhausen, Used by permission of the Stockhausen-Verlag, on pp. 130-2. CDs and scores are available from Stockhausen-Verlag, 51515 Kürten, Germany; *Sequenza I for Solo Flute* by Berio © 1958 Edizioni Suvini Zerboni, Milano. By permission of Edizioni Suvini Zerboni, on pp. 135-7; *In C* by Terry Riley, Used by permission of Terry Riley. www.terryriley.com, on pp. 138-9; *St Louis Blues* Music by W.C. Handy © 1914 Handy Brothers Music Co Inc., USA. Francis Day & Hunter Ltd, London WC2H 0EA. Reproduced by permission of IMP Ltd, on p. 144; *All the Things You Are* Words by Oscar Hammerstein II, Music by Jerome Kern © 1939 T.B. Harms & Company Incorporated, USA. Universal Music Publishing Limited, 77 Fulham Palace Road, London W6. Used by permission of Music Sales Ltd. All Rights Reserved. International Copyright Secured, on p. 149; *One Note Samba (Samba De Una Nota So)* Original Words by Newton Mendonça, Music by Antonio Carlos Jobim, English Words by John Hendricks © Copyright 1961, 1962 & 1964 Duchess Music Corporation, USA. Universal/MCA Music Limited, 77 Fulham Palace Road, London W6 for all English speaking territories. Used by permission of Music Sales Ltd. All Rights Reserved. International Copyright Secured, on p. 151; *Higher and Higher* Words and Music by Gary Jackson, Carl Smith and Raynard Miner © 1967 Chevis Publishing Corp/Warner-Tamerlane Publishing Corp/Unichappell Music Inc Warner/Chappell Music Ltd, London W6 8BS/EMI Music Publishing Ltd, London WC2H 0EA. Reproduced by permission of IMP Ltd, on p. 157; *All Day and All of the Night* Written by Ray Davies. Published 1964 Edward Kassner Music Co. Ltd. for the World. Used by permission, on p. 160; *Don't Look Back in Anger* Words and Music by Noel Gallagher © Copyright 1995 Oasis Music, Creation Songs Limited & Sony/ATV Music Publishing (UK) Limited, 10 Great Marlborough Street, London W1. Used by permission of Music Sales Ltd. All Rights Reserved. International Copyright Secured, on pp. 169-70; *Eastenders* by Leslie Osborne and Simon May © Copyright 1985 ATV Music, Sony/ATV Music Publishing (UK) Limited, 10 Great Marlborough Street, London W1. Used by permission of Music Sales Ltd. All Rights Reserved. International Copyright Secured, on pp. 173–4; *'Something's Coming'* from *West Side Story* by Leonard Bernstein (music) and Stephen Sondheim (lyrics) © Copyright 1956, 1957, 1958, 1959 by the Estate of Leonard Bernstein and Stephen Sondheim. Copyright renewed. Leonard Bernstein Music Publishing Company LLC, Publisher. Boosey & Hawkes, Inc., Sole Agent. International Copyright Secured. Reproduced by permission of Boosey & Hawkes Music Publishers Ltd, on pp. 177–9; *Fourth String Quartet* by Schoenberg © Copyright 1939 (Renewed) by G. Schirmer, Inc. International Copyright Secured. Reprinted by permission, on pp. 302-3; Piano Phase (extract) by Steve Reich, Copyright 1980 by Universal Edition (London) Ltd, London. Reproduced by permission on pp. 307-8.

The authors would like to offer special thanks to Jim Hurry and Nicola Phillips, Benjamin and Henry Phillips, Sue Walton and Nicola Haisley for their encouragement and support.

Additional thanks are offered to David Motion, Debbie Nicholls, Lynsey Brown and students at Harlington Upper School for support and for trialling materials.

The publishers would like to thank the following for permission to use photographs:
Corbis on pp. 122, 127 and 144; Kobal Collection on p. 154; Les Productions Mille-Pattes on p. 180; Mary Evans Picture Library on pp. 10, 21, 94 and 114; Redferns/Paul Bergen on p. 171; Redferns/William Gottlieb on p. 176; Redferns/Michael Ochs Archives on pp. 146 and 158; Redferns/David Redfern on p. 166.

The publishers have made every effort to trace the copyright holders, but if they have inadvertently overlooked any, they will be pleased to make the necessary arrangements at the first opportunity.

Tel: 01865 888058 www.heinemann.co.uk

Contents

Listening and Understanding

Introduction 5
How to use this book 5
Listening and understanding 5
Composing 5
Performing 5
Integration 6

Renaissance 7
Sacred music in the Renaissance 8
Secular music in the Renaissance 13
Looking towards a new era – music
    from Venice 16

The Baroque 19
The birth of opera 20
Baroque forms 24
Baroque national styles 38

The Classical Period 1750–c.1820 39
Musical style – the transition from
    Baroque to Classical 42
The symphony 49
Music for small ensembles 65
The concerto 67
The sonata 68
The art song 73
Sacred choral music 73

The Romantic Period 76
The symphony 80
The concert overture 84
Opera 86
The lied 89
Piano music 89
Concerto 90
Sacred music 90

The Twentieth Century 92
Impressionism 93
Expressionism 94
Inventing new languages, reinventing
    old ones 100
Neo-classicism 104
Nationalism and folk music 113
A new direction 122
More new directions 128
Aleatoricism and the absurd 133
Minimalism 137

Pop, Rock and Jazz 141
The Blues 143
Jazz 147
Rock 'n' roll in the 1950s 153
Gospel meets rhythm 'n' blues:
    sweet soul music 155
The British beat and The Beatles 158
The modern sound of 60s Britain 159
Guitar greats of the 60's and 70s 161
Heavy rock, heavy metal and grunge 162
Folk rock and protest songs 162
Reggae 164
1970s disco, 1980s house 165
Fusion and funk 166
Glam and glitter 166
Punk rock 167
The 1980s and new technology 168
Rap and hip hop 168
Britpop 169
Dance and club styles 172
Television signatures 172
Film music 175
The musical 176
Folk music today 180

Composing

Composing Renaissance Vocal Counterpoint   181
Approaches to writing Renaissance vocal counterpoint   184

Composing Two-part Baroque Counterpoint   188
Approaches on how to start writing two-part Baroque counterpoint   193

Composing Chorales in the style of J.S. Bach   197
Approaches on writing your own harmonisations   206

Composing String Quartets in the Classical Style   209
Writing string quartets in the Classical style   210
Approaches on how to start composing a string quartet   211
Characteristic features of Classical string quartets   221

Composing Variations   238
Writing variations   240
Approaches on how to start writing variations   241
Identifying compositional techniques   241

Composing Piano Accompaniments in Early Romantic Style   261
Approaches on how to start writing piano accompaniments   263

Characteristic features of piano accompaniments   269

Composing Romantic Miniatures   284
Writing Romantic miniatures   284
Chopin   285
Analysis of Chopin's style   286
Schumann   293
Grieg   297
Approaches on writing for the piano   298

Composing Using Serial Techniques   300

Composing Using Minimalist Techniques   306

Composing in Popular Musical Styles   309
Using ICT to help you compose   313

Choosing a 'free' Composition Topic   315

Performing   316
Preparing your recital programme   316
Constructing your recital programme   316
Programme notes   318
Performing   318
Assessing performances   320
Performing improvisations   320
Performance investigation   321
Ensemble playing and recitals   323
Performing your own composition   325

Introduction

How to use this book

This book has been specially written for students studying advanced music courses for AS and A level. While based on the components for the new advanced music specifications, the broader aim of the book is to help expand horizons of music knowledge and understanding, and to stimulate opportunities for further creative and performing experiences. Throughout, the emphasis is on an integrated musical study of the three component areas: listening and understanding, composing and performing.

The book is organised into three main sections. The first section, listening and understanding, acts as a foundation for the whole course of study by providing a valuable background from which to explore music further. The second section, composing, comprises the main composition techniques and styles required for AS and A2 level. The third section, performing, offers guidelines for the whole of the performing spectrum. To support this book there is also a *Teacher's Resource File* with tasks to help you practise listening and compositional skills, plus two audio CDs containing the extracts mentioned in this book and in the tasks file.

Listening and understanding

The listening and understanding section is divided into different periods or styles, progressing chronologically from Renaissance through the Baroque, Classical and Romantic periods to twentieth century and popular music styles. Each section broadly sets the musical style in cultural and historical context and provides detailed information on key musical characteristics, key genres and the balance between continuity and change, and the role of significant composers in the development of genres. The sections also provide clear, musical analyses of extracts of music which illustrate important features and which are supported by two audio CDs. The music has been especially selected to help you in your studies of specific topics, prescribed works and in responding to questions in the listening paper.

To help you broaden and deepen your interests and understanding of particular genres or styles, the sections also offer suggestions for further work and listening.

Composing

The composition section is very much practical 'hands-on' advice on how to approach your compositions, how to work out and develop musical ideas, and how to compose to achieve a stylistically convincing and musically successful piece. Progressing chronologically from *Composing Renaissance vocal counterpoint* to *Composing in popular musical styles*, each section first provides a brief introduction of the style from a composer's view-point and offers suggestions for further explorations of different compositional techniques. All the sections then provide key composing considerations with analyses of music which illustrate characteristic composition techniques and strategies. While clear links can be made to the analyses in the listening and understanding section, these analyses are specifically geared to composing techniques. As well as illustrating detailed technical strategies, the analyses also show and explain important composing elements such as how a composer has created a sense of direction, built up to a particular tension point, or developed or varied a musical idea, or cajoled a poignantly expressive musical moment.

Performing

In this section all aspects of performing are discussed – from planning and constructing your recital programme, effective practice to full performance and how to prepare for different performance situations. Advice is also offered on improvising in performance. The section also provides details of how performances are assessed using the common criteria categories, accuracy, interpretation and communication.

To help you develop fully as a performer, *Performance investigation* suggests ways in which you can actively broaden your performance horizons. Advice is given on ways of evaluating performances, responding to different interpretations and performing styles, building up your knowledge of professional performers and performance practices and writing about and discussing music. Practical guidelines for successful ensemble work include directing and playing in ensembles and working effectively with your accompaniment.

Integration

In using this book, the emphasis throughout is on studying music in an integrated way. Try to avoid compartmentalising your studies into listening, composing and performing, or viewing your musical activities outside of the classroom as somehow different and separate from your AS and A2 level music work. All your playing, exploring, listening to and reading about music needs to be synthesised into a fusion of broad musical knowledge, understanding, appreciation and enjoyment.

A good way to use this book is to first read quickly through the sections that particularly interest you or that you already know a bit about. Link the cultural and social contexts of music styles with your general knowledge of history, art, literature, politics, geography and so on. This will help you grasp a solid understanding of the broad background and also give you a deeper understanding of how styles change over time – which particular features continue and which evolve to eventually transform one style into another – changes which have often been set in motion by social, cultural and historical changes. Then, as you begin more concentrated study carefully follow through the different sections. You may like, for example, to read about Romantic music in the listening and understanding section, following carefully the analyses in the section, then begin exploring a Romantic miniature piano piece. Such study could be further enhanced by then learning or playing through pieces written in the Romantic period.

Different sections from the book can be cross-referenced to others. For example, analyses of music extracts in the listening and understanding section can be drawn upon for composing. Similarly, information about particular genres can be used as a basis for composing. For example, the section on film music can be used as a starting point for composing music for a film. Having a practical knowledge of, and therefore being able to recognise, compositional techniques characteristic of particular styles can greatly help listening work. Background knowledge of styles discussed and analysed in the listening and understanding section can valuably benefit performance interpretations.

Most importantly, the book has been written by musicians for all musicians. Have fun!

A new era

The word Renaissance means, quite literally, 'rebirth'. This gives an indication as to why scholars (and examination boards!) consider the Renaissance to be a good place for us to start the study of our western art music tradition. It is not that there was a lack of music before the Renaissance period. However, it was during this era that music, art, science and literature – in fact, every area of human endeavour and achievement – underwent an accelerated rate of development. The development of printing during this period – which started in Italy in the fourteenth century and had spread to the whole of Europe by the sixteenth century – did much to aid the spread of ideas and to promote and drive the efforts of some remarkable philosophers, artists, writers and composers. Art, architecture, literature and music of this period is characterised by graceful line, rich colours, attention to detail and depth of thought.

Sacred and secular

Music in the Renaissance fell into two broad types – music composed for the church, and secular music. Within these two areas, there were a number of variations of style that can be attributed to regional or national differences, or more local contextual factors. However, any study of Renaissance music should start with a short exploration of the modes that formed the basis of musical developments before the seventeenth century.

Modes

Before the major/minor diatonic system was established in the Baroque period – about which, more later – music was modal. The seven authentic modes, in their Greek names, were:

The Ionian mode is, clearly, exactly the same as what we know as C major. However, the other modes do not fit exactly into any major/minor key pattern – the Aeolian coming closest, being the descending A minor melodic scale. Each one of the modes had an individual pitch organisation, and therefore each mode had its own distinctive flavour.

Two modal melodies to perform

Try performing these two modal melodies. The first is a sacred, plainsong chant thought to have been composed in the twelfth century. The second is a secular ballad thought to have been composed by a French 'trouvère' (a 'wandering minstrel'), also in the twelfth century.

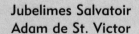

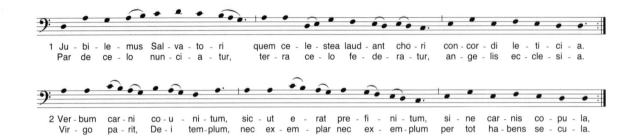

You will have noticed that both of these extracts appear to be monophonic – that is, they consist of a single melody line with no accompaniment. In practice, the melodies may well have had an improvised accompaniment. The trouvère melody may have been accompanied by a simple harp or psaltery playing sporadic, punctuating chords, whilst the plainsong may have been sung with an organum accompaniment – that is, another voice doubling the melody at a 5th below.

There is also a difference in the approaches that the two pieces take to rhythm – the plainsong has a fluid, unmetred approach whilst the trouvère song has more metrical accents.

The plainsong is in the Dorian mode; the trou-vère song in the Aeolian mode. You can tell this from the 'resting' notes at the ends of the final phrases, which are the key notes of the modes. These notes are known as the 'final' notes (as opposed to the 'tonic' notes of major/minor keys).

Sacred music in the Renaissance

During the Medieval period plainsong melodies such as *Jubelimes Salvatoir*, developed from being single monophonic lines into more textually substantial works. This was done through organum, and through imitation and layering. These practices probably started through performance practice, although in time composers began to incorporate performance practices into their written compositions.

By the time of the Renaissance, composers of sacred (church) music were composing texturally complex works for three and four voices. Their music was still based around the plainsong chants, and the music was still modal, but it included musical imitation of the plainsong ideas between the voices and, as the interweaving voices came together in the musical texture, the resultant harmonies – almost entirely what we would refer to today as root position and 1st inversion chords – gave the music a new depth and dimension. Although the rhythms of the polyphonic works became more regular, the smooth melodic and rhythmic movements characteristic in plainsong were maintained.

Musica ficta

The new harmonies that were created by the combining of three or four modal lines in a polyphonic texture presented Renaissance composers with some challenges. The coincidence of some lines was creating what would sound as dissonance to the Renaissance ear. For example:

- If a modal melody leapt by four or five notes, the interval might sound as a tritone, rather than a perfect 4th or perfect 5th. To Renaissance musicians, this interval was known as *diabolus in musica* – the devil in music – and was to be avoided (especially in church music!). What was happening in practice was that singers were flattening or sharpening one of the notes in the interval to make it perfect, thus avoiding the devil's interval. Recognising this, composers began to add accidentals to their scores in appropriate places.
- If the final chord of a piece contained a minor 3rd, then the 3rd was omitted by the performers or even changed to a major 3rd – the practice that we know today as the 'tierce de picardie'. Again, composers recognised this performance practice by writing appropriate accidentals into their scores.

These practices would, over the course of the sixteenth century, lead to the amalgamation of the modes into what we now know as the diatonic major/minor system.

Purity and perfection

Important composers of sacred church music included the Netherlanders Josquin and Lassus and the English composers Tallis, Byrd and Gibbons. However, the greatest of all the Renaissance church music composers was Palestrina, whose work is generally considered to be the purest and most perfect example of the style.

Palestrina (c. 1525–1594)
'Agnus Dei' from Missa Papae Marcelli

About this piece

As Choirmaster of the Julian Chapel at St.Peter's, Rome, Palestrina worked at the heart of the Roman Catholic Church. This piece is taken from one of some 100 Mass settings that he composed as part of his job there. The 'Agnus Dei' is the fifth of the five prayers in the *Ordinary of the Mass*, the others being the 'Kyrie', 'Gloria', 'Credo' and 'Sanctus'.

Palestrina's music is the Renaissance church style at its purest. Other composers used similar techniques, but because of local factors and the fact that they did not work at the centre of operations in Rome, their music was flavoured with other influences. However, the broad principles of the polyphonic style were to have a great influence on many of the musical forms that were continued into the Baroque period and beyond.

How to study Palestrina's style

The best way to start your study and analysis of this piece is to sing it! Once you've mastered the complexities of the different voice entries, look for the following stylistic points that are so typical of this style of *a cappella* Renaissance church music and notice:

- the way that the initial idea in the tenor line (middle stave) is taken up and imitated in turn by the other voices (known as a point of imitation)

- the way that the vocal phrases are long, but also vary in length and the parts overlap with each other
- the way that the melodic lines move mostly by step, and when there is a leap the next note usually returns to within that leap
- the harmonies formed by the coincidence of the melodic lines are concordant, forming root position or 1st inversion chords
- where there is a clash of notes – i.e. where there is what we would refer to as a suspension – Palestrina always takes great care to prepare and resolve the note in the same vocal line
- how this movement is in the Ionian mode, but there are points where chromatic alterations are made in accordance with the conventions of *musica ficta*
- how all of these factors combine to create a distinctive, calm and restful 'wall of sound'.

Giovanni Palestrina

'Agnus Dei' from Missa Papae Marcelli
Palestrina

Secular music in the Renaissance

Secular song forms

In the same way that plainsong melodies had developed into the three- and four-part Masses and motets of the Renaissance, so the songs of the trouvères and troubadours in France, the Minnesingers in Germany, the Spanish Cantigas, and the English minstrels, developed into more sophisticated forms.

The madrigal

The principal type of secular vocal composition in the Renaissance was the madrigal. Originally an Italian genre, an English school of madrigal composition developed after 1588 when a collection of Italian madrigals was published in England. The madrigal proper was, in many ways, close in style to Renaissance church music in its use of polyphonic textures and imitative techniques. However, because of the secular nature of the words – and the secular context in which the music was performed – composers generally took many more liberties with the treatment of dissonance, including suspensions, and the observance of the *musica ficta* conventions. Often, composers used dissonance and chromaticism deliberately in their madrigals when they wanted to match the meaning of the words with the music used to set those words – what we now call 'word painting'.

The frottola, the ballett and the lute song

A lighter form of madrigal was the frottola, or its English counterpart the ballett. These songs were generally much lighter in texture and were usually homophonic, with dance-like rhythms. Frottolas and balletts were strophic in form – that is, there were a number of verses all set to the same music – so there was much less word painting than in the madrigal proper. In the English ballett, a distinctive feature was the 'fa-la-la' chorus. The principle theme of Italian and English madrigals was love. In the case of some English madrigals and especially balletts, the lyrics contained a number of *double-entendres* or *conceits* – the 'fa-la-las' implying ' . . . *and you can guess what happens next . . .*'!

Another form of vocal music that became popular in England during the Renaissance was the lute song – a work for solo voice accompanied by a lutenist. Again, the main subject of these songs was love. The main composer of lute songs in England was John Dowland.

Instrumental music

Before the Renaissance, instruments were used both to provide music for dancing to, and to accompany vocal performances. In the latter case, the instruments more often than not merely doubled the vocal parts. Sometimes, the pieces would be performed solely on the instruments and composers would sometimes write the instruction 'Apt for voices or viols', indicating that the music could be performed in a variety of ways.

During the Renaissance, composers began to take an interest in composing bespoke instrumental compositions. Instruments were organised into ensembles, or consorts, of related instruments such as recorders and shawms (which continued from the Medieval era) and newer instruments that developed from the Renaissance, such as viols.

Dance music

Secular dances were organised into pairs and groups, foreshadowing the Baroque dance suite that would follow in the seventeenth century. These dances often took a homophonic texture, with sections being repeated in a more ornamented form. As keyboard instruments developed, these dances formed the basis for sets of keyboard variations which were especial-

ly popular with English composers like Byrd and John Bull, and the Dutch organist Sweelinck.

Contrapuntal forms

Following the practice of instruments playing music originally composed for voices, many of the new compositional genres developed for instruments in the Renaissance bore strong structural resemblance to vocal genres. The ricercare was very similar to the contrapuntal style of church music, with points of imitation and long-breathed phrases. The ricercare was the precursor of that great Baroque instrumental form, the fugue. The canzona was built out of shorter sections, and often included more homophonic textures. In turn, the canzona would pave the way for the development of the instrumental sonata and concerto forms.

Thomas Weelkes (c. 1576–1623)
'Late in my Rash Accounting'

This is a ballett, rather than an English madrigal proper, being in strophic form and having the 'fa-la-la' type of refrain.

Notation in Renaissance music

Of particular interest is the key notation of this piece. There is only one flat in the key signature, but the piece is clearly in what we would regard as the key of G minor. Looking through the score, we can see that E♭s and F♯s are indeed often added to the lines, confirming our suspicions of G minor. In terms of Renaissance modal structures, however, the piece is actually in the Dorian mode – D–D on the keyboard – transposed up a 4th to start on G. This necessitated a B♭ at the start of the stave, in order to preserve the pitch patterns of the Dorian mode. The sometimes F♯s and E♭s during the course of the score are there due to the requirements of *musica ficta*. If all of this seems complicated and rather fussy, you can see why in due course composers began to write all the necessary accidentals at the start of the stave in a key signature!

'Late in my Rash Accounting'
Thomas Weelkes

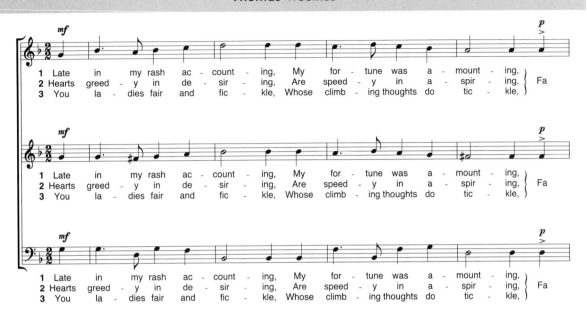

Learning from your performance

Enjoy performing the ballett – the words are full of conceits that leave little to the imagination, but have the most effect when sung without inference! As you sing through, note the following key stylistic points:

- the verses have a wholly homophonic texture, adding to the directness in the deliverance of the words, whilst there is some limited imitation in the refrains
- the cross-rhythms and off-beat accents in these refrain sections
- the change of metre in the second refrain section, giving a dance-like rhythm to the music
- the juxtaposition of F♮ and F♯ in bar 15 (soprano and alto parts) – an effect of *musica ficta*. This device is known as a 'false relation'.

Further work and listening

- Compare and contrast the musical style of this ballett with an English madrigal proper – try 'The Silver Swan' by Orlando Gibbons.

Looking towards a new era – music from Venice

The importance of context

One of the things that makes the study and analysis of music so fascinating is that it is often impossible to categorise composers or works exactly into a certain style or era. When analysing music of any style or genre, knowledge of the context in which that music was composed and first performed is always helpful towards gaining a real understanding of how and why the music 'works'.

Both of these thoughts apply particularly to the music that was composed in and around St Mark's Cathedral in the latter half of the sixteenth century. The works by the two Gabrielis – Andrea and his nephew Giovanni – brought new innovations to the Renaissance polyphonic church music and instrumental music traditions which would point the way towards the new Baroque style in the seventeenth century. Furthermore, the innovations came about because of Venice's geographical position in Italy and in Europe.

Sixteenth century Venice

Certainly, Venice's situation was quite different to that of Rome, where Palestrina was working. Rome's importance was due to the power of the Roman Catholic Church that, even after the Reformation in 1517, was immense. Venice's power, on the other hand, was due to its position as the major trading port for the Euro-Asian spice and salt trade, and the city amassed considerable wealth in the centuries leading up to the Renaissance. This gave Venice a rather more worldly and secular outlook than Rome, and whilst Palestrina was composing his pure, *a cappella* vocal Masses and motets for the Papal chapel, music at St Mark's Cathedral composed by the Gabrielis was becoming spectacularly colourful and with an increasingly flamboyant outlook.

St Mark's Cathedral

St Mark's Cathedral itself was – and still is – a rich, colourful building with gold mosaics covering floors, walls and ceilings. Furthermore, the church authorities were so well-resourced that they were able to employ a variety of musicians on diverse instruments to accompany the music at services. In turn, they built a second organ in the cathedral, with a second choir loft to go with it – this meant that they had to employ a second organist, and a second choir! The two organs/choir lofts were placed facing each other, on opposite sides of the cathedral build-

ing, in a primitive kind of stereo arrangement.

These fantastic resources provided opportunities for the Venetian composers to produce music that matched the richness and extravagance of the environment in which they worked. Instruments – brass, woodwind and strings – were used to accompany the singers. Exploiting the special architectural properties of the cathedral, with two organs and two choir lofts, the Gabrielis wrote antiphonal ('question and answer') passages in their music, where the two choirs/groups of instrumentalists would alternate.

Antiphony and the concertato style

It is this antiphonal aspect of Venetian music that pointed the way to the Baroque style. As we shall see, one of the major principles of Baroque music is *concertato*, seen best in the concerto grosso (where a small group of solo instruments alternates with a larger group of instruments). The antiphonal writing of the Venetian composers led the way for this development.

Another important textural feature of Venetian music was the fact that much of the music – particularly the sections where all of the forces are performing – was homophonic. The sheer logistics of the cathedral – with the players in different locations – required such a texture, for practical reasons if not for sheer musical impact. There are plenty of polyphonic passages in the Venetian music, of course, and the principles governing points of imitation are followed. There are also sections for soloists, accompanied by keyboard instruments. But the grand homophony – coupled with the often (secular) dance-like rhythms that accompanied these textures – pointed the way towards the harmonic progressions and textures of the Baroque.

Rigatti (1615–1649)
'Dixit Dominus' from
Messa e salmi parte concertati

Listen to the extract on CD1, track 1.

Rigatti was one of the school of composers that followed immediately after Giovanni Gabrieli in Venice. Throughout the short extract you will hear a number of musical features typical of the Venetian school.

- The extract opens with a homophonic section performed by all of the forces (singers and instruments) in stately common time.
- This is followed by an antiphonal section for the two choirs. Each choir is singing homophonically, but the antiphonal texture gives a different aural effect. Note the dance-like, quicker triple rhythms in this section.
- The third section continues with the quicker rhythmic idea, but only a small group of soloists are singing at the start. The texture here is imitative polyphony, with an organ and strings accompaniment. Towards the end of the extract, as more singers and instruments join in, the texture goes back to the antiphonal style.
- This extract ends as it began, with all voices singing homophonically in stately common time.

Further work and listening

- If you were asked to produce a performance of this piece, how would you stage it and how would you prepare/rehearse your performers?

The Baroque

Time and perspective

All of the labels that we apply to periods of musical style – Renaissance, Baroque, Classical, Romantic, Impressionist, Expressionist and so on – are also terms used in other art forms such as painting, literature, and architecture. The term 'Baroque' was originally used in connection with the art and architecture of seventeenth century Europe, and it was later applied to music from the period approximately from 1600–1750. As we have already intimated, it is impossible to draw clear boundaries between adjacent music styles like the Renaissance and the Baroque. The changes in musical style between the two eras happened over a period of time and during this time, the following developments took place that brought about the change in styles. It is, of course, impossible to separate or to place these developments chronologically – they happened simultaneously.

Renaissance ➡ to ➡	Baroque
• Music was fundamentally modal, although the modality was modified by the conventions of *musica ficta*.	• The *musica ficta* conventions became standardised and modes evolved into what we now know as major and minor keys.
• There were distinctive sacred and secular vocal styles, including imitative polyphony and expressive homophony with word painting.	• There was increasingly less distinction between sacred and secular vocal styles.
• Composers thought linearly, in terms of individual lines.	• As homophonic textures gained more importance in all kinds of music, composers thought vertically in terms of harmonies, as well as linearly.
• Polyphonic instrumental compositions were modelled on (if not copies of) vocal pieces.	• Bespoke instrumental compositions took on their own importance. The ricercare developed into the formal and highly organised fugue. This, and the canzona da sonar developed into the sonata, again a more highly structured form.
• Homophonic (mostly secular) instrumental ensemble pieces took the form of dances.	• Dance suites were composed for ensembles and keyboard instruments. The dances became longer and more formally organised.
• Non-keyboard instruments were largely inherited, unchanged, from the Medieval period.	• Non-keyboard instruments became more refined, particularly string instruments which developed into the modern violin family. As performers' technique improved, composers began writing virtuosic pieces for them to play.
• Arrangements of ensemble instrumental pieces were made for keyboard instruments, along with extended pieces in variation form.	• With the development of the major/minor system and the continuo, keyboard instruments took on an important role in the texture of Baroque music.

The birth of opera

We have seen how aspects of the work of the Venetian composers paved the way for the change from the Renaissance into the Baroque musical style. At around the same time as the Gabrielis were composing their polychoral music, separate developments in another part of Italy were to play an equally important role in bringing about the new era in music.

'The Florentine Camerata'

In Florence, a group of composers and academics – known as 'The Florentine Camerata' – was engaged in a lively debate about how words should be set to music. Some musicians, such as Artusi – who, not surprisingly, was employed by the church – had published papers supporting the view that the beauty of music was everything; that the words that were set to music were not of importance. Artusi took as his model of perfection the polyphonic style as exemplified by the works of Palestrina.

The Florentine Camerata took an opposing view, stating that music should always be the servant of the words and that, rather than compose music that conforms first and foremost to music 'rules' and conventions, vocal music should be composed according to the dictates of the words set both in terms of natural rhythms and meanings.

The Camerata, led by Vincenzo Galileo (father of the rather more famous astronomer), were a secular group. They put their theories into practice by composing short vocal pieces called monodies. This was where the singer was given a melodic setting of a text supported by a single keyboard or fretboard instrument that provided a simple chordal accompaniment over a bass line. Because of the small number of performers involved, this meant that the singer was at liberty to sing the rhythms of the monody with a certain amount of freedom in accordance with the natural rhythms of the text – as if reciting a poem. This style of singing became known as *recitativo*. A further development led to these recitatives being introduced into the pastoral plays that were popular in Italy at the end of the sixteenth century.

Monteverdi's *L'Orfeo* of 1607

As with many developments and innovations in the arts, the development of this new vocal style took place over a number of years and involved a number of musicians, all of whom played their part. However, the major breakthrough in what was to become opera was made by one man who was really the catalyst for the birth of the true Baroque musical style – Claudio Monteverdi. What made Monteverdi so important to the birth of the Baroque style is that, like Mozart in the Classical period, he worked in all of the major genres of the day: he composed madrigals, instrumental pieces and church music. Significantly, he was employed by St Mark's Cathedral in Venice and wrote some stunning polychoral music.

Monteverdi's *L'Orfeo* of 1607 is considered to be the definitive first opera. What makes it a true opera – and the model for all operas since – is that as well as containing recitatives and other solo vocal numbers in the monodic style, it also contains choruses as well as instrumental dance and interludes. Some of these interludes were reoccurring throughout the points in the opera, and these became known as *ritornelli*, pointing the way towards the *rondo* and *ritornelli* forms used in mature Baroque instrumental music.

Claudio Monteverdi

Monteverdi (1567–1643)
'Recitative' from L'Orfeo, Act I

Listen to the extract, which is on CD1, track 5. As you listen, note how:

- the bar lines on the score – which is a modern edition – are there for reference only. In performance practice, the bars are of lengths determined by the way in which the singer delivers the text
- Monteverdi has given the accompanying instruments just the bass note as guidance – the keyboard/fretboard instruments would be required to realise ('work out') the chord to be played from the bass note. In practice, this would usually be a root position or first inversion chord.

'Recitative' from L'Orfeo, Act I
Monteverdi

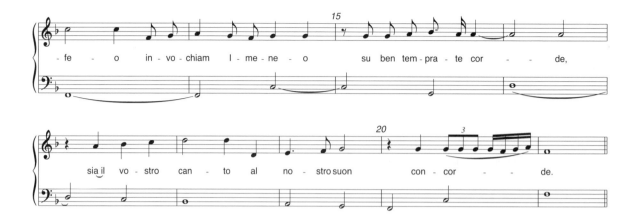

-fe - o in - vo - chiam I - me - ne - o su ben tem - pra - te cor - - de,

sia il vo - stro can - to al no - stro suon con - cor - - de.

Translation of text:
Muses, honour of Parnassus, love of heaven, gentle
consolers of a weary heart, may your sounding citterns
rend from every cloud the dark veil; and while today propitious to our
Orpheus I invoke Hymen on well-tuned strings,
let your songs with ours be concordant.

The continuo

As we saw in the extract from *Orfeo*, the key-board/fretboard players – who became known as the continuo – had to rely on a single bass note upon which to realise the accompanying chords. As the Baroque style – and the major/minor key system – developed, the requirements of composers for more complex harmonies led to the development of a notational 'shorthand', where composers would add figures below the continuo bassline to indicate the harmonies that were required. This system is known as 'figured bass', and the art of translating this figured bass in performance is known as 'realisation'.

Figured bass

The principle of figured bass is that the figures given refer to the notes to be played in addition to the bass note. Thus, a bass note C with a 5 and 3 written below it indicates that the composer requires the notes C, G (a 5th above C) and E (a 3rd above C) to be played. Whether a 3rd is major or minor depends on the key of the music. In C major, a $\frac{5}{3}$ above C would produce the chord C/E/G. In E♭ major, a $\frac{5}{3}$ above C would produce the chord C/E♭/G.

An 'at-a-glance' guide to bass figurings

Figuring	Description of chord
$\begin{smallmatrix}5\\3\end{smallmatrix}$	This figuring is given to a root position chord. More often than not, it is not necessary to write this figuring at all – if a bass note has no figuring, it is assumed that it is a root position chord.
$\begin{smallmatrix}6\\3\end{smallmatrix}$	This figuring is given to a 1st inversion chord. More often than not, it is sufficient to write just the figure 6 – this indicates that it is a 1st inversion chord.
$\begin{smallmatrix}6\\4\end{smallmatrix}$	This figuring is given to a 2nd inversion chord. Both figures are given to indicate the chord and position.
$\begin{smallmatrix}7\\5\\3\end{smallmatrix}$	This figuring is given to indicate a 7th chord in root position. It is sufficient only to give the figure 7 – if this is the case, then the 5th and 3rd above the bass are assumed.
$\begin{smallmatrix}6\\5\\3\end{smallmatrix}$	This figuring is given to indicate a 7th chord in 1st inversion. It is sufficient only to give the figures 6 and 5 – if this is the case, then the 3rd above the bass is assumed.
$\begin{smallmatrix}6\\4\\3\end{smallmatrix}$	This figuring is given to indicate a 7th chord in 2nd inversion. It is sufficient only to give the figures 4 and 3 – if this is the case, then the 6th above the bass is assumed.
$\begin{smallmatrix}6\\4\\2\end{smallmatrix}$	This figuring is given to indicate a 7th chord in 3rd inversion. It is sufficient only to give the figures 4 and 2 – if this is the case, then the 6th above the bass is assumed.
$\sharp$	A sole sharp sign under a bass note indicates a root position chord in which the 3rd above the bass is sharpened a semitone above the note indicated by the key signature.
$\begin{smallmatrix}6\sharp\\\sharp\end{smallmatrix}$	This figuring indicates a 1st inversion chord in which both the 3rd and 6th above the bass are sharpened above the note indicated by the key signature.
Accidentals	The basic rule is that a sharp, flat or natural sign next to any note in a bass figuration indicates that that note above the bass should be altered against the note indicated by the key signature.
Suspensions	$\begin{smallmatrix}4\\3\end{smallmatrix}$, $\begin{smallmatrix}7\\6\end{smallmatrix}$ and $\begin{smallmatrix}9\\8\end{smallmatrix}$ over a bass note indicate suspensions; for details see the section on composing in the Baroque styles.

Baroque forms

As the length of vocal and instrumental pieces increased, composers began to use more formal structures for their pieces. With the major/minor key system becoming more established, composers used the principle of key relationship to build these structures.

The main forms used by Baroque composers were:

Binary form **AB**	Binary form is the simplest of the Baroque forms. It was used primarily for the various dances in the suite. A binary form movement has two sections, usually separated by a repeated double bar. The two sections usually share thematic (melodic) material. The main contrast between the sections is tonal. Section A usually starts in the tonic key and, by the end of the section, has modulated to the dominant/relative minor key or rests on the dominant/relative minor chord. Section B starts where Section A left off, and then works back to the tonic key, perhaps via other keys such as the subdominant.
Ternary form / da capo aria form **ABA**	Ternary form has three sections. It was commonly used by Baroque composers for arias in operas and oratorios. It was customary for Section A to be in the tonic key, with Section B modulating, and ending on chord V of the tonic key in preparation for the return to Section A. This form is also sometimes known as 'da capo' form – this name reflecting the Baroque convention of only writing out the first two sections and ending Section B 'da capo' ('to the head', indicating that the performers should return to the start of Section A).
Rondo form / Ritornello form **ABACA**	Rondo (or, in the French spelling, rondeau) is a form where one section keeps returning, or coming around again and again. The middle sections usually contrast with the A idea through tonality, instrumentation, melody, or a combination of features. The A sections are known as the *rondo theme*, whilst the middle sections (B, C, etc) are known as the *episodes*. The term *episode* is also used in fugue – don't get the two confused! Ritornello is much the same as rondo, in that one main theme keeps recurring. The sections in ritornello movements tend to be shorter and more abundant than in rondo form. Ritornello form is commonly found in the movements of concerti grossi and solo concerti.
Variation form **AA^{1}A^{2}A^3**	Variation form was a favourite with the Renaissance keyboard composers, and the form continued into the Baroque period. In performance, solo singers and instrumentalists were quite used (and often expected) to vary a repeated line or section by adding ornaments or scalic passages, embellishing the line written in the score.

Further developments in Baroque opera

Following the success of *Orfeo*, *The Return of Ulysses* and *The Coronation of Poppea* – all by Monteverdi – opera gained much popularity throughout Italy. The first public opera house was built – not surprisingly – in Venice in 1637, to be followed by many others throughout Italy. As the seventeenth century progressed into the eighteenth century, numerous composers contributed to the development of the genre, including Legrenzi and Alessandro Scarlatti (father of the rather better known Domenico).

Two types of recitative

Later Baroque composers developed Monteverdi's operatic innovations in a number of ways. Firstly, they introduced two types of recitative – the *recitativo secco* ('dry' recitative) and the *recitativo accompagnato* ('accompanied' recitative). The *secco* variety of recitative was accompanied only by the continuo instruments – keyboard and bass, and the sparseness of texture meant that long sections of dialogue or dramatic action could proceed quickly and, indeed, that the singer could take more liberties with matters of rhythmic delivery. In contrast, the *accompagnato* variety of recitative required tighter rhythmic control from the singer, because of the forces involved, but also provided the composer with more dramatic opportunities.

The aria

A further type of solo vocal operatic form that developed during the Baroque period was the aria. The aria was similar to the *recitative accompagnato* in that it was scored for solo singer, continuo and orchestral instruments. Unlike the recitative, the aria was in a regular metre with exact rhythmic requirements. The aria also had a clear form, which was later to become known as *da capo* form, as we have seen. Sometimes, the *da capo* aria accompaniment had a solo instrumental line that acted as a foil to the voice. This line is known as the *obbligato* – that is, one is obliged to have the instrumental line playing with the singer. If you are performing an *obbligato* aria with a piano reduction of the orchestral score for accompaniment, you should try to engage an instrumentalist to play the *obbligato* line – it really is your obligation!

An aria is often a reflective moment in an opera, where a single character is alone to share his/her thoughts and feelings with the audience. In this respect, the aria is very much like a soliloquy in a play.

Opera in the rest of Europe

During the mid-sixteenth century, Italian opera became fashionable throughout Europe, through performances by Italian opera companies in Germany, Austria, France and England. In Germany, the popularity for opera encouraged the development of the German *Singspiel* which was characterised by spoken dialogue in place of recitative. Similarly, in England, the *Masque* was a popular form of entertainment that featured a series of songs, choruses and instrumental dances rather than a continuously conceived musical entity. The only proper and substantial English opera from the Baroque era is Henry Purcell's *Dido and Aeneas* in 1689.

Opera in France

Ironically, the country outside Italy where opera underwent its greatest development in the late-Baroque era was France, where there had previously not been as much interest in opera as there had been in Germany or England. And the double irony was that the composer who acted as the catalyst for the rise of French opera was an Italian – Jean-Baptiste Lully.

Lully

Lully was appointed by King Louis XIV to the court at Versailles where there was already a long and excellent tradition of entertainment featuring ballet, drama and choral singing. There was also a tradition of high decoration in the architecture of the palace and, indeed, in the manners of the French aristocracy itself. The

'Sun King' was the centre of much adulation, and there was a great sense of French national pride and supremacy. Lully's skill was to include all of these features, together with his own (albeit tenuous) Italian background, creating the tradition of French opera. Of course, French and Italian are different languages, and recitatives in French operas generally have a softer, more lyrical feel to them. For his part, Lully was extremely careful about his score writing, and even in recitatives did not allow the flexibility of tempo and/or rhythm that is found in recitatives from Italian operas. By all accounts, Lully was a rather imposing musician, both as a composer and conductor which, perhaps explains the high level of detail in his scores.

The overture

One of Lully's most important contributions to the development of music in the Baroque era was the *ouverture* – an instrumental movement that was used not only to signal the start of an opera, but also the opening movement of a dance suite, a sonata or a concerto. Later, in the Classical period, the French overture principle would develop into the 'slow introduction' used by some composers for the first movements of symphonies.

Typically, a French overture was laid out in a bipartite form:

A	homophonic slow tempo characterised by a dotted rhythmic motif
B	contrapuntal, sometimes fugal faster tempo sometimes ends with a more homophonic, slower cadential passage

The French overture form was used by composers throughout Europe including J. S. Bach (in his keyboard and orchestral suites), and Henry Purcell.

The sonata and the concerto

At the end of the Renaissance era, a number of important trends had emerged in instrumental music. These included:

- bespoke instrumental compositions being produced, albeit modelled on vocal forms
- in secular music, dances were often grouped together in pairs, such as the 'Pavane and Galliard'
- in Venetian church music, instruments taking a much larger and much more colourful role
- Venetian church music exploiting new textures in music, most notably the antiphonal style.

We have also seen that, through the development of the monodic vocal style, keyboard and fretboard instruments were assuming a new importance. The principle of the continuo became established in instrumental as well as vocal music.

Music for church and chamber

In the early seventeenth century, Italian composers began to extend instrumental composition for both church and secular contexts. Instrumental dances and instrumental compositions such as the canzona and ricercare were put together to form works of (usually) four or five movements which were contrasting in tempo. As the principles of tonality became established, these movements became linked by key – they were either all in the same key, or in closely related keys, thus giving an overall unity to the work. The name 'sonata' (literally, music 'to be sounded') was applied to the works that were designed to be played by a small group of instruments. Works for larger instrumental ensemble were called 'concertos' (literally, music 'to be played together' by a group).

There was a further distinguishing label applied to these early sonatas and concertos. Some were given the suffix 'da Chiesa' and others the suffix 'da Camera'. This indicated that some were in a style suitable for performance in church, whilst some in a style more suited to a secular context (quite literally, 'chamber' music). At first, the musical styles of these two types was clear, with the 'da Chiesa' forms tending to favour more learned, serious styles such as the ricercare, and the 'da Camera' forms having a lighter feel to them with movements in homophonic dance styles. However, as the Baroque era progressed (and as with opera/oratorio styles), the distinction between the 'da Chiesa' and the 'da Camera' forms narrowed. By the end of the seventeenth century, the suffixes had gone, and works were either called 'sonata' or 'concerto'.

The terms 'da Camera' and 'da Chiesa' may have become blurred during the course of the Baroque era, but throughout the period two distinct types of concerto were evident. As with so many genres, the concerto grosso and the solo concerto developed in two regional centres, and their development was much a consequence of locational circumstances.

Concerto grosso and solo concerto

As far as the two types of concerto are concerned, the concerto grosso is characterised by two groups of instrumentalists – the *concertino* group, containing a number of soloists, and the *ripieno* group, made up of the remaining (orchestral) players. The continuo usually served both groups. The origins of the concerto grosso texture can be seen in the antiphonal style of the Gabrielis, Monteverdi, and their successors. There are other practical origins to the concerto grosso too – at Saint Petronio's

church in Bologna (also in northern Italy) composers wrote concerti that could be played together by the small group of professional musicians employed by the church (who became the *concertato* group) and a group of slightly less able but enthusiastic local amateur musicians.

The solo concerto, on the other hand, featured just one solo instrument, with ripieno. Antonio Vivaldi, who was one of the greatest and most prolific composers of solo concerti in the mature Baroque, was not only a priest but also director of music at the Piéta Conservatoire in Venice, an all-girls school where, by all accounts, there was a large orchestra. Vivaldi was also working at a time when the great masters of Italian violin making – such as Stradivari and Guarneri – were at the height of production. Certainly, some of Vivaldi's solo violin concerti (including the famous *Four Seasons*) reflect a high level of technical virtuosity and showmanship.

There were a number of Italian composers who made important contributions to the development of the concertos and sonata forms, particularly Vivaldi (primarily in the solo concerto) and Corelli (in both the sonata and the concerto grosso). Later in the era, the forms were taken up by the German Baroque composers, especially J. S. Bach, Handel and Telemann.

Further work and listening

- Consider how the terms 'sonata' and 'concerto' have taken different meanings in the Baroque, Classical, Romantic and twentieth century eras.
- Listen to sonati and concerti by Vivaldi, Corelli, Torelli, Telemann and Bach. Compare and contrast their compositional styles and approaches to the genres.

The suite

If the sonata and concerto forms had their roots in Baroque Italy, then it was in Germany and especially France that the stylised suite of dances had its homes. Dancing was a central part of the culture at the courts of the kings of France, and the court composers arranged sets of dances for performance and entertainment. It should be stressed that the dance suite started very much as functional music, to be used as accompaniment to dancing. However, in time, the suites became common items in musical concerts.

There were four main dances that served as the basic framework of the suite – each with their own tempo, metre and rhythmic characteristics.

Dance	Metre	Tempo	Special characteristics
Allemande	$\frac{4}{4}$	Moderate	The allemande – a dance of German origin –started with an anacrusis of three semiquavers and then continued with continuous semiquaver movement in the texture.
Courante	$\frac{3}{2}$	Moderate	The French courante – there was an Italian version, too – was characterised by the cadential metre changing to $\frac{6}{4}$, creating a hemiola effect.
Sarabande	$\frac{3}{4}$	Slow	The sarabande was a slow Spanish dance with characteristic dotted rhythms and accents placed on the second beat of the bar.
Gigue	$\frac{6}{8}$	Fast	A dance originating in Britain, the 'jig' was always in compound time with a lively 'skipping' rhythm.

To these standard four dances, composers would sometimes add one or more additional dances.

Dance	Metre	Tempo	Special characteristics
Minuet	$\frac{3}{4}$	Moderate	The minuet had origins as a rustic French country dance, although in the dance suite it was rather more restrained and refined.
Gavotte	$\frac{4}{4}$	Moderate	Similar in style to the minuet, the gavotte had a characteristic two-crotchet anacrusis.
Bourrée	$\frac{4}{4}$	Moderate	Similar in style to the minuet and the gavotte, the bourrée had a characteristic one-crotchet anacrusis.
Polonaise	$\frac{3}{4}$	Moderate-slow	Originating from Poland, the polonaise had a stately, almost martial feel to it.

Many of the dances were of foreign extraction – the French court was very cosmopolitan!

Couperin (1668–1733)
'Les Moissonneurs'

About this piece

This descriptive piece – called 'The Reapers' and presumably meant to represent the rustic antics of French farm workers at harvest-time – was included in Couperin's second volume of *Piéces de Clavecin*, published in 1717.

Form and genre

Although it is not called as such, this is a gavotte, characterised by the two-crotchet anacrusis. The entire piece is in rondeau form, with four statements of the rondeau theme and three episodes (called by the French term 'couplet').

The couplets are distinguished from the rondeau theme in two ways. Firstly, the first two couplets feature contrasting thematic material, with the third couplet developing the thematic material of the rondeau. Secondly, they feature modulations to keys other than the tonic, the rondeau theme staying in the tonic key throughout. The form and pattern of modulations in the piece is as follows :

A	B	A	C	A	D	A
B♭	➡F	B♭	➡Gm	B♭	➡Cm	B♭
Rondeau	Couplet 1	Rondeau	Couplet 2	Rondeau	Couplet 3	Rondeau

Ornamentation

A glance at the score of 'Les Moissonneurs' gives a clear indication that this is music from the French Baroque. Like French art, architecture and, indeed, manners of the period, French Baroque music is characterised by a high level of ornateness and embellishment. You will notice that a number of the ornamental signs used by Couperin are not in common use today.

The French Baroque composers used a particular code of ornamentation, which they called 'les agréments'. In his book *L'Art de toucher le clavecin*, published just a year before 'Les Moissonneurs', Couperin gave precise and definitive instructions on how to perform these ornaments. There are three types of agrément in this piece:

Agrément	Name	Performance Notes
┼	*Pincé*	The *pincé* corresponds to what musicians today would refer to as a mordent. The length of the ornamenting notes is proportional to the length of the note being ornamented.
∧∧	*Tremblement*	The *tremblement* is something of a cross between an inverted mordent and a trill. The *tremblement* starts on the upper note (unlike the modern trill) and, again, the length of the ornament should be in direct proportion to the length of the ornamented note.
∨	*Aspiration*	The *aspiration* is a precise form of staccato mark, indicating that the note should be shortened by three-quarters of its value.

If you can, play through this piece and try to use the correct, authentic ornamentation.

'Les Moissonneurs'
Couperin

Oratorio

At around the same time that opera was emerging in Italy, similar developments were taking place in religious music. At the Oratory of St Philip Neri in Rome – where the oratorian sect of the Roman Catholic Church was founded – dramatic performances of musical settings of religious texts were performed, with soloists, chorus and orchestra, much like the early operas of Monteverdi. Originally, these performances had scenery, costumes and dramatic action but these were soon abandoned in favour of purely musical performances.

By the time of the late Baroque, oratorios were being composed for and performed in theatres and concert rooms as well as in churches. Stylistically and formally, Baroque oratorios have a great deal in common with Baroque operas, with use of recitatives (secco and accompagnato), arias (including the da capo aria), choruses, and orchestral accompaniment.

Probably the best-known composer of oratorios in the Baroque period was Handel, whose oratorios The Messiah, Judas Maccabeus and Israel in Eygpt are among his best-known works.

The chorale and the cantata

In the German Lutheran Church, a central element of any church service was the chorale – a simple hymn which could be sung by the whole congregation. (Martin Luther, the great church reformer and founder of the Lutheran Church, wanted a greater congregational involvement in church worship, in contrast to the often remote and hierarchical practices of the Roman Catholic Church.)

As an employee of the Lutheran Church in Arnstadt, Mulhausen and, most notably, Leipzig, J. S. Bach was often called upon to write harmonisations of these chorale tunes for the choir to sing in four parts with the congregation. The style and language of Bach's chorale harmonisations is still the basis on which we learn harmony today, and the composing section of this book gives you guidelines for composing harmony in the style of J. S. Bach.

Bach extended his harmonisations and use of chorale melodies in the Chorale Preludes and Cantatas that he composed, also for use in church. The Chorale Preludes were composed, initially, through improvisation in all probability – for Bach to play himself at the start or end of a service. A chorale tune – one which would be sung by the congregation during the service itself – would be the basis through which virtuoso, florid counter-melodies would weave, disguising the original chorale tune as some kind of 'hidden melody'.

Similarly, Bach developed the cantata – a smaller scale version of the oratorio – around the chorale. A cantata would contain recitatives, arias, and choruses, much like an oratorio. However, Bach also included within the cantata one or more chorale melodies – which could be joined in with by the congregation – and these chorales might also provide motifs for other movements.

Fugue

As we saw through the extract from Palestrina's Missa Papae Marcelli, Renaissance composers took a highly organised approach to polyphonic compositions, using points of imitation to create a unified style to their work. In instrumental compositions, such as the ricercare, they took an equally organised approach.

These textural forms and principles continued in use throughout the early Baroque, and, as the major/minor tonal system took the place of modes, contrapuntal compositions took on an increasingly more sophisticated organisation. By the time of Bach, the fugue (as this advanced form of ricercare had now become known) was a highly complex and tonally-structured form.

The structure of a fugue

The form of a fugue is usually in three parts, called the exposition, development and final section.

The exposition is the section at the start of the fugue where each of the voices enters, in turn, with the subject/answer idea. This section is usually centred around the tonic and dominant keys of the fugue.

After all of the voices have introduced the fugal subject and the tonic/dominant keys, the fugue moves on to the central development section. Here, the main motives from the subject and countersubject are tossed about between the voices, usually involving sequences and journeys into more distant keys.

In the final section, we re-hear the subject, played with some emphasis and sometimes in *stretto*, and the music returns to the tonic key to round off the piece.

There are a number of key terms and phrases that we use when analysing a fugue:

Voice — Each melodic line in the fugue is called a voice, whether the fugue is sung or played. There may be three, four or more voices in a fugue. In a four-voice fugue, it is conventional to call the voices soprano, alto, tenor and bass.

Subject — The subject is the first theme that is played in the fugue. The subject is played by one voice, usually as a monophonic line. This is called the first fugal entry. The subject is usually in the tonic key.

Answer — When the first voice has played the subject, the second voice enters the musical texture. The theme played by the second voice is called the answer. The answer usually has exactly or almost the same rhythm and interval patterns as the subject, but it is usually in the dominant key.

The entries of a fugue usually alternate between the subject and answer, tonic and dominant. So,

the entries in a four-part fugue exposition would be

Subject (tonic) –
Answer (dominant) –
Subject (tonic) –
Answer (dominant)

Countersubject

When the first voice has completed the subject, and the second voice is playing the answer, the first voice usually continues by playing a new theme that is called the countersubject. The countersubject usually contrasts with the subject/answer phrase shape.

Free (derived) material

Once the first voice has finished playing the subject, and then completed the countersubject, the voice moves on to play what is loosely called 'free material' – i.e. neither subject or countersubject but, rather, contrapuntal padding. However, this material may derive some motifs from the subject or countersubject.

Episode — An episode is a passage where all of the voices are working with free (derived) material. These passages are most often found in the development section, but can come between entries of the subject/answer in the exposition.

Stretto — In the exposition, when the initial entries are made, a regular pattern for entries is established – i.e. the subject lasts for four bars, and the answer only enters at the end of that four-bar phrase. In the final section of a fugue, in particular, this pattern may be broken – i.e. the answer may enter two bars into the subject, thus creating an overlap of entries. This overlap is known as a *stretto*.

In many fugues, the subject, answer, counter-subject and free (derived) material all share motif material. This is one of the things that makes fugues such complex and sophisticated works of musical organisation. Fugues **are** complex and the best way to understand how the fugal structure works is through analysis and, of course, by playing through a fugue yourself.

J. S. Bach (1685–1750)
'G minor Fugue' from The Well Tempered Clavier, Book 1

Listen to the extract, which is on CD1, track 6.

About this piece

With the major/minor key system and the principle of keyboard 'equal temperament' now firmly established, J. S. Bach composed two sets of preludes and fugues, each set containing one pair of pieces for each of the major and minor keys. This fugue is from Book I of the *Forty Eight*, as the pieces are known. The fugue was composed by Bach in about 1720.

Form

This fugue is in the standard three-part form. The form and tonal scheme is as follows:

Exposition	Development	Final Section
Bars 1–8	Bars 9–28	Bars 28–34
Gm / Dm	*B♭ / Cm / Gm*	*Gm / Tierce*

Material

The fugue gives good, plentiful and easily identifiable examples for all of the key terms and phrases that we have already identified and defined. Trace them through on your score of the fugue.

Subject

The subject is two bars long. Each bar has a different interval and rhythmic characteristic. The first bar has the angular interval of the 6th and is in crotchets and quavers. The second bar features stepwise movement and includes semiquavers. Both halves of the subject start with a quaver rest.

Note that the subject starts on the dominant note (D), but it is firmly in the tonic key of G minor.

Answer

The answer has the expected resemblance to the subject. Note, however, that the start of the answer is metrically displaced – it starts halfway through the bar, whereas the subject started at the beginning of the bar. Also note that the answer is one beat shorter than the subject, the extra note in the subject overlapping with the start of the answer.

The answer starts on the tonic (and the first three notes outline the tonic triad), then modulates to the dominant area of D minor. Because the interval patterns in the answer are not exactly the same as the subject, this is known as a tonal answer. (If the subject and answer were exactly the same in interval patterns, then the answer would have been a real answer!)

Counfor Countersubject

Countersubject

Note the ingenious way in which Bach has created a seemingly different countersubject by reversing and inverting ideas from the subject/countersubject.

Free (derived) material

Free (derived) material

Basically, anything that is not wholly identified as the subject, answer or countersubject. The problem is that Bach is so economical, ingenious and cunning with his writing that almost everything in the fugal texture seems to be derived from an interval or rhythm in the exposition material!

Stretto

Stretto

There are some marvellous stretti in this fugue. Just one example is at the start of the final section (bars 28–29), where there are three overlapping entries of the subject in the space of just 1½ bars.

Exposition framework

To help you trace the working of the fugal exposition, follow this chart along with your score.

Bar	1	2	3	4	5	6	7	8
Soprano			Answer		Countersubject / Free (derived) material			
Alto		Subject		Countersubject / Free (derived) material				
Tenor							Answer	
Bass					Subject		Countersubject	

This section is a small episode

'G minor Fugue' from The Well Tempered Clavier, Book 1
J. S. Bach

Further work and listening

- If you are able to, play through this fugue, or make a sequence of it. Doing so will give you a much deeper understanding of how the structure works. You might even like to make an arrangement for four melody instruments – four different timbres will certainly help to bring out the individual components of the fugue.

- Listen to other preludes and fugues from Bach's *Forty Eight*. Do you agree with the thought that, even though the interval patterns in every major/minor scale are the same, each key has its own timbral characteristic?

- Draw out a plan for the whole of the 'G minor fugue', similar to the one provided for the exposition. Map out as many entries, episodes and stretti as you can.

Baroque national styles

Throughout our survey of music in the Baroque era, you will have noticed that there were regional variations in composers' approaches to both instrumental and vocal music. Whilst the basic language and message of Baroque music was the same throughout Europe, there were a number of important regional musical accents in Italy, France, and Germany.

Country	Composers	Favoured forms and features
Italy	Monteverdi Corelli Torelli Vivaldi Alessandro Scarlatti Domenico Scarlatti	Opera Concerto grosso Solo concerto Trio sonata Virtuoso solo writing, particularly for strings
France	Lully Rameau Couperin	Dance suite (French) Opera French ouverture High levels of ornamentation, particularly in keyboard music
Germany	Buxtehude Telemann Handel Fux J. S. Bach	*Singspiel* Concerto grosso Suite Fugue Oratorio Solid, thoroughly worked out contrapuntal textures

The importance of J.S. Bach.

Of all these Baroque composers, the most important was J.S. Bach. His music not only covers nearly all of the major genres of the period (except opera), but his compositional style brings together influences from the German, Italian and French Baroque. And lastly, but by no means least, J.S. Bach's sons Johann Christian and Carl Philipp Emanuel were major composers in their own right, their music drawing from the Baroque traditions of their father but also pointing the way towards the new Classical era.

The rise of the Classical style is closely linked with significant historical events and powerful political, cultural and social forces which led the way for new trends to emerge. These events were the breakdown of the absolute power of the old European system of monarchy which erupted in the terror of the French Revolution, the rise to power of the middle classes or *bourgeoisie*, and the spread of the liberal and national beliefs typical of the movement known as the Enlightenment. It was a time of enormous change, with new currents sweeping away the old styles and substituting others. The age was tinged with revolutionary spirit, new dynamism, a sense of tension, conflict, and the real prospect of social mobility.

The Enlightenment

The Enlightenment movement challenged authority of any kind. It was in favour of humanitarian ideals and the freedom of the individual, against privilege, and in favour of equal rights and universal education. The doctrines of the French writers, Voltaire and Rousseau, on the inequality of privilege and the rights of the individual, exerted immense influence in driving the movement forward and promoting social change. Philosophers and intellectuals of the Enlightenment sought rational answers for the difficulties that confronted them in politics, religions, social life and art. At the core of the movement was the belief that all questions could be answered by reason and knowledge. Humanitarian ideals of the Enlightenment embraced the concepts of belief in the individual, regardless of birth, and the virtues of tolerance and brotherly love. Human brotherhood was embodied in the movement of Freemasonry, of which Mozart was a member.

Cosmopolitanism

The eighteenth century was also a cosmopolitan age. Foreign-born rulers abounded, composers travelled abroad frequently, taking up posts in countries other than their own, and incorporating national styles into their music.

There were an amazing number of composers around at this time, all writing about and discussing each others' 'craft' of composition. Concert life in the major cities flourished, in particular Paris, Leipzig, London, but especially Vienna – the eighteenth-century cultural centre.

Popularising of the arts

The growing wealth and increased influence of the middle classes led to a popularising of the arts and a demand for a universal language – musical as well as literary – that could be understood and appreciated by all. Novelists and playwrights altered their language to depict emotions which related as much to the everyday world of ordinary people as to the aristocratic court. It also led to the emergence of a modern public music audience whose demand for public concerts began to rival the older private concerts and the academic system.

The rise in the number of public concerts inevitably led to an increase in **amateur** performances. These in turn prompted a growth in **music printing**. There were no copyright laws at the time and works were often published without the composer's knowledge, altered, or had movements omitted. The bulk of the music printing was geared towards amateur performance. At the same time, methods devoted to teaching the amateur to play or sing in 'ten easy lessons' flooded the market.

The emphasis on literature and the arts at this time also stimulated a new public interest in reviewing, discussing and writing about music. This led to the emergence of music **journalism**, and the beginnings of the appearance of the critic's review in newspapers. The general increase of learned and casual discussions, the spread of public concerts and the new momentum of published music meant that, by the end of the eighteenth century, the relationship between the composer and the public was very different from what it had been at the beginning of the century. This was the start of the Romantic notion of the composer as a creative artist, his art being omnipotent, and of his obligations being to the art itself and not to society.

Key characteristics

Key genres
- symphony
- chamber music
- concerto
- piano sonata
- opera
- sacred choral music
- art song

Continuity and change

The Classical age was predominantly an instrumental age. Significant genre changes from the Baroque period are:
- the Italian opera overture developed into the Classical symphony
- the concerto grosso became gradually displaced by the symphony as the dominant orchestral form
- the trio sonata was gradually displaced by the emergence of new forms, most notably the string trio, string quartet, piano trio, and piano quartet/quintet
- in keyboard music, the suite was displaced by the sonata
- the only instrumental genre to survive the transition from Baroque to Classical was the concerto for solo and orchestra, mainly through the works of Mozart
- in the early eighteenth century there was a reaction to the structure of *opera seria* which later was again challenged when a lighter comic opera emerged. Comic opera, or *opera buffa*, rose from humble beginnings to flourish alongside *opera seria*, reaching its heights in the operas of Mozart
- the oratorio, cantata and mass continued but in a much more contemporary accent.

The orchestra

The major change in the Classical period was not so much in the instruments themselves (although there were some changes) but in the new roles of the instruments:

i) The continuo, which was still present in some early Haydn symphonies, gradually disappeared. The practice of the conductor sitting at the keyboard and also conducting progressed to the leader of the violins assuming increased responsibility. This led to orchestras eventually having a conductor with a baton.

ii) The delicate tones of the viols gave way to the fuller sounds of the violin, viola and cello. Wind instruments such as the recorder, limited in dynamic variety, also disappeared, as did the florid Baroque trumpet parts; new instruments were eventually added, notably the clarinet.

iii) There was a shift in the balance of the Baroque orchestra between wind and string instruments, in favour of strings. A clear division was made between melodic instruments and those which sustained the harmonies. The instruments became more clearly divided into sections as we know them today: strings, woodwind, brass, percussion. In general, the higher strings and the woodwind were used melodically and the other instruments were used harmonically. The woodwind and brass were at first used more to sustain the harmonies than to play melodies because of the limited number of notes at their disposal.

iv) The core of the early Classical orchestra was the violin family, along with two oboes and French horns. Gradually an increasing number of woodwind instruments was added, along with timpani, trumpets and flutes, and later, trombones.

The Mannheim orchestra was the most progressive and forward-looking orchestra at the time. The Mannheim musicians were highly-trained players. Under the leadership of their conductor, J. Stamitz, the orchestra was famous for its new dynamic range, and its ability to build dramatic crescendos and shade diminuendos. A popular gesture of Stamitz was to begin a concert with opening forte chords from the orchestra, followed by a long steady crescendo from pp to ff, during which all the instruments would gradually enter, as the music slowly climbed up the scale – an effect calculated to thrill the audience. This was Mannheim's main 'party trick'.

The range and standards of players improved through the period. High-class virtuosos toured Europe displaying the new techniques of their improved instruments.

Keyboard

Due to the introduction of dynamics, the instruments that remained from the Baroque period were either adapted or became obsolete. The organ was adapted so that it could produce crescendos and diminuendos. The harpsichord was incapable of any gradation between *forte* and *piano* and gradually became obsolete. The clavichord, which was well suited to the ornamental and expressive style of the early Classical period, was limited in volume and capable of only a small dynamic range. It gradually became superseded by the piano around 1775. This was perhaps the greatest single event of this period with the greatest implications.

Form

Sonata form was the most important formal design in the Classical period. It developed in the last part of the eighteenth century, notably with Haydn and Mozart, and later with Beethoven in response to the needs of a new kind of texture. While Baroque music was essentially structured on long flowing lines within complex polyphonic textures, sonata form was fundamentally based on a vertical rather than horizontal scheme. This emphasised harmony rather than polyphony, keys and key changes and more simple melody–harmony texture. Contrast in sonata form was achieved by the sharp juxtaposition of keys and melodies, by clear sectional divisions and by textural contrasts.

Sonata form is a particular design on which movements of instrumental works – symphonies, concertos, trios, chamber works as well as sonatas – are built. Although most commonly found as the structure for first movements, composers also used the form for second, third or fourth movements of works.

Sonata form is basically ternary in outline – A-B-A – the different sections being called *exposition*, *development* and *recapitulation*. To this structure, composers often added an introduction at the beginning and a coda at the end. In the Classical symphony, the exposition is usually repeated. The basic design is that the melodic material is first stated in the exposition, developed in various ways in the development, and restated in the recapitulation. This design is treated in a huge variety of ways by composers, notably through contrasting melodic material; the tonality and number of key changes (sometimes called the tonal design); ways in which they develop their material; textural contrasts and actual changes to the sonata form structure. The basic plan is as follows:

The exposition

First subject: this is usually a strong, motivic theme in the tonic key.
Bridge passage: this functions as a passage for modulation from the tonic key to another key – usually the dominant or the relative major if the tonic is a minor key – to reach the second subject. Second subject: usually a more lyrical, cantabile melody in the new key.

The development

In this section the composer develops the thematic material of the exposition. The themes are often fragmented, and motifs from the melody are used for development, such as a particular intervallic leap, or rhythmic pattern. These motifs work through the entire texture of the section. The main point of the development is the often rapid key changes, which frequently build to a strong, dramatic climax point, after which the music 'travels' back to the home key. The tonal journey can be fairly straightforward, modulating through closely-related keys; or it can take sudden unexpected turns and shifts to move into far-reaching keys.

Recapitulation

The composer now restates the exposition section, usually adding some small variations. The main point about the recapitulation is that the bridge passage is altered, so that the second subject theme remains in the tonic key instead of modulating as in the exposition.

Coda

A coda is often added, summing up the movement, usually using themes already heard.

Further work and listening

- Listen to the first movement of a symphony or sonata by Haydn or Mozart. In the exposition, how does the second subject contrast with the first? What key does it modulate to? Which theme, or part of a theme, is developed in the development? Compare the recapitulation with the exposition – are there any changes, and if so, what are they? How does the composer end the work?

Musical style: The transition from Baroque to Classical

The change in musical style from Baroque to Classical closely reflects the social changes of the age. The change was gradual, and for some time the old style juxtaposed the new. Signs of the new style can be seen from about 1720 onwards, particularly in the works of Couperin, Pergolesi, D. Scarlatti, C.P.E. Bach, J. C. Bach, and in a range of pre-Classical styles, detailed below, that flourished in around 1730.

Rococo

The rococo (*rocaille* or rockwork) style was a reaction to the heavy grandeur, power and formalities of the Baroque period. The style embraced playfulness, refined wit and elegance. The less formal, more intimate social atmosphere of the salon became preferable to the imposing formality of large court entertainment. The simplicity of the pastoral scene, very characteristic of the rococo style, was a stark contrast to the heroes and mythological scenes characteristic of the Baroque. In music, as a reaction to the complex contrapuntal lines of the previous era, the rococo style was light and decorative. One of the main stylistic characteristics was graceful, melodic ornamentation.

Style galant

A French term implying 'elegant', 'courtly'. The style emphasised a pleasing, entertaining and 'natural' style of music, as opposed to the elaborate counterpoint and severe lines of the previous era. Melodies were made up of short phrases, often repeated with simple accompaniment and transparent harmonies with frequent cadences. The galant style can be found in the works of Pergolesi and G.B. Sammartini.

Pergolesi (1710–1736)
La Serva Padrona (The Maid as Mistress)

Listen to CD1, track 15 and follow the score opposite.

La Serva Padrona (The Maid as Mistress)
Pergolesi

This opera is a good example of *opera buffa*, or comic opera in the *galant* style. Comic opera enjoyed great popularity at this time as the music was easy to listen to. The arias were shorter and simpler in structure than those of Baroque opera, the vocal ranges were modest and the melodies often suggested folk song or a popular melody. Accompaniments were light, allowing the melody to be heard clearly. The bass voice was now added to ensemble singing, having been more or less excluded in Baroque opera. Importantly, the operas were sung in the language of the country.

Pergolesi's opera *La Serva Padrona* was immensely successful during his lifetime and is still performed today. The plot is easy to follow, sometimes sentimental, but above all, amusing and entertaining. It depicts characters in everyday life, rather than myths and legends characteristic of *opera seria*. In this opera there are only three characters, one of which is mute throughout. The opera is based on six tunes with recitatives to hold them together.

The opera is about a maid who induces her boss to marry her, a plot which stands as well today as it did in Pergolesi's time. In this extract, the good-looking maid, Serpina, wants to know how to attract her master and, hopefully, soon-to-be-lover, Uberto (bars 1–6); and better, how to scorn (bars 7–33). In the opera, Uberto is depicted as a wavering, somewhat irate man, unused to female attention.

Melody

The melodies are short, catchy and involve much repetition. They fall into regular two- and four-bar phrases. There is a bubbling excitement and a hint of wit throughout.

Harmony

The harmonies are straighforward, very simple tonic-dominant, in the key of A major. The key modulates to the dominant E at bar 17. The cadences are frequent, occurring at two- and four-bar intervals.

Orchestration

The scoring of violins I and II and violas, supported by the continuo is simple but effective. Generally, the instruments support the vocal line. Violins I and II often play in unison or thirds while the violas provide a counter-melody. The continuo part fills in the harmonies and also adds melodic figurations to complement the vocal line.

Listen particularly for:

- the catchy, simple melodies and rhythms
- the short, repetitive phrases
- the way that the music portrays the attractive character of Serpina
- the transparent, simple harmonies and frequent cadences
- the musical wit and bubbling excitement.

Further work and listening
- Listen to other works in the *galant* style, such as the instrumental music of G.B. Sammartini. Identify the *style galant* features in the music.

Empfindsamkeit stil

The name of this style comes from the North German word for 'expression'. This is a deeper, more expressive style than the *style galant*. It aimed to portray human emotions and states of mind. This style can be recognised by the expression of a variety of sentiments or moods in rapid succession, often designed to draw tears of melancholy. When composing in this style, composers sought a singing, expressive style, without excessive ornamental embellishments. The ideals are characteristic of the music of C.P.E. Bach.

C.P.E. Bach (1714-1788)
Württemberg Sonata No. 1

In this sonata, the expressive passion and melancholy character of the *empfindsamkeit* style is conveyed through subtle nuances and harmonic shadings. The flexible improvisatory nature of the music was intended to suggest the composer writing in an emotionally sorrowful state; it was considered especially suited to conveying the many changes of mood of the style. C.P.E. Bach preferred the light, gentle tone of the clavichord to the harsher tones of the harpsichord as it sounded more delicate, more refined and could create the subtle dynamic shadings needed.

Notable features of this piece include:

- the constant dynamic changes to express mood changes
- the free, improvisatory, speech-like melody
- the singing, expressive style combined with constantly fluctuating rhythmic patterns
- the frequent turns of harmony.

Württemberg Sonata No. 1
C.P.E. Bach

Sturm und drang (Storm and stress)

This developed from the *empfindsamkeit* style and is characterised by dramatic emotional intensity and passionate, violent outbursts. Several composers of the age combined lyric, expressive styles with the bold, robust *Sturm und drang*, for example, C.P.E. Bach, Gluck, Haydn and Mozart.

These styles served as a bridge between music of the Baroque and Classical ages, and were subsequently absorbed into the Classical style.

Further work and listening

- As you work through the analyses of the different Classical genres in this book, trace the way that these pre-Classical styles became absorbed into the Classical style.

- Listen to C.P.E. Bach's *Württemberg Sonata No. 6*. Listen out for these characteristics of the style:

  i) bold, robust passage work

  ii) elements of surprise and sudden dynamic changes

  iii) sudden shifts of harmony

  iv) unusual and often swift melodic turns.

Change and continuity

Baroque characteristics	Early Classical characteristics
Melody Continuous melodic line without obvious cadences. Melodies frequently built on motivic and sequential repetition; often a compact pattern repeated in a self-perpetuating manner. No regular periodic structures; regularity was often disguised through melodic extensions, irregular or dovetailed cadence points	Melody is important. Simpler melodies based on triads, scales, with definite rests; relatively short clear-cut phrases; often lyrical phrases, balanced, sense of proportion; regular phrase lengths of eight bar measures often split into 4+4
Texture Texture more complex and subtle, very much based on counterpoint, with some homophonic passages	Texture clearer and less complicated. Clear distinction between melody and accompaniment. Use of typical accompaniment patterns, for example, *alberti bass* – chords of the harmony broken up into short patterns. Steady bass patterns in orchestral music which give the rhythmic drive to Classical music, compensating for the energetic drive of the Baroque bass continuo line
Mood One mood (affection) throughout an entire section or movement	Deliberately composed for emotional contrasts and varied moods within a movement, with one mood juxtaposed against another. A much stronger sense of drama, contrasting moods, tension and relaxation. The pacing of climaxes and their dénouement was very important. Audience's emotional experiences are kept in a greater state of flux
Dynamics Limited use of dynamic contrasts; sudden contrast from f to p.	Deliberate use of dynamics for contrast and surprise. Haydn frequently tried to surprise his audience with sudden 'surprise tactics'. More explicit instructions for the performer eg: f, p, mf, mp. Dynamics now much more an integral part of the music
Harmonic pace Quick harmonic pace with regular pulse. Continuous energetic harmonic motion driven from the basso continuo (walking bass)	Harmonic pace generally slower. Pace more crucial now to the impact of a movement – more varied, playing a definitive role in the ebb and flow of the music. Modulations less adventurous in Early Classical period
Harmonic foundation Harmonic foundation provided by figured bass (harpsichord and bass); other instruments played parts continuing the melodic interest; florid, ornamental; 'gap' between subordinate bass and florid melodic lines. Basso continuo (walking bass) was a principal force – everything was based on this	Harmony/tonality – most popular keys: D, F, G and Bb majors. Much more simple. Initially predominantly tonic, dominant, sub-dominant harmonies, progressions often based on a circle of 5ths; repeated bass lines; increasingly chromatic harmonies; tonality and far-reaching modulations intensified
Harmony and tonality Rich harmonies, quick harmonic pace, bold chromatic harmony, rich dissonances, great use of the minor keys	More emphasis on blending and balance; orchestra became more closely divided into melodic and harmonic instruments; fundamental harmonies given notably to brass and woodwind

The symphony

Introduction

The symphony is an extended work for orchestra, usually in three or four movements. Its origins can be traced to the late seventeenth-century Italian opera overtures (*sinfonias*), which were usually in three movements – fast:slow:fast. These overtures had no musical connection with the operas they introduced and came to be performed as separate concert orchestral items without any reference to the opera. Their inclusion as orchestral works in concert programmes laid the foundations for the development of the genre.

The main musical centres in this flourishing period were Milan, Berlin, London, Mannheim, Paris, and Vienna. Reputations travelled widely as composers and virtuosi travelled extensively. Musical entertainment was immensely popular, and the new symphony form flourished.

Milan: G.B. Sammartini (1701–1775)
Symphony No. 13 in G major

Sammartini wrote over 70 symphonies and was a leading figure in the change from the Italian opera sinfonia to the Classical symphony. He led the way with structures and texture, defining first and second subjects and introducing lyricism into second subject themes. Sammartini wrote in the galant style and his music marks a halfway point between Baroque and Classical styles.

Listen to CD1, track C16.

Symphony No. 13 in G major
G.B. Sammartini

This symphony, composed around 1740, shows several early Classical features. Listen particularly for:

- the clear first subject. In the early symphonies, the first subject was most important and dominated the first movements
- the writing for strings. Violins I take all the melodic interest with the other instruments accompanying
- the semiquaver repeated patterns
- the Baroque features – the continuo part, chains of suspensions and, in places, a walking bass style
- the definite modulation to the dominant, D major, for the second section at bar 18. Although the music remains the same as the opening section, this second section eventually became the development section. Here it is basically a short travel from A-B and back to A. This, and other similar rudimentary first movements, set the foundation for the later full exposition, development and recapitulation structure of first movement sonata form.

C.P.E. Bach

C.P.E. Bach was one of the most influential composers of the age. He was associated with the *empfindsamkeit style*; his symphonies show the gradual emancipation of the orchestra from its dependence on the continuo. He was the link between the contrapuntal style and forms of his father and those of Haydn and Mozart.

Mannheim: J. Stamitz (1717–57)
Symphony in G major Op. 3 No. 1

It is often said that the symphony was born at Mannheim. This is due to the musical developments occurring there and, most especially, the development of the Mannheim orchestra, founded by J. Stamitz. In 1746, Stamitz also firmly established the sections of sonata form in a way that others were able to improve on and refine. His first themes are bold and vigorous, and his second themes very contrasting. His contribution to the growth of the symphony is considerable. Although he was not the first to introduce it, the four-movement symphony plan was firmly established at Mannheim. His *Symphony in G major Op. 3 No. 1* was composed around 1750.

Vienna: The cultural centre

Vienna was an international centre of cultural activity in the eighteenth century. Leading Italian and French poets and composers of the day held prominent arts positions in the city, influencing the direction of the new cultural scene. The vibrant cultural climate of Vienna attracted a constant stream of travelling musicians from neighbouring countries. The most influential musician in Vienna was Salieri, who held the post of imperial court composer and conductor of Italian opera for 36 years. Although none were originally from Vienna, the fact that Haydn, Mozart and Beethoven lived in the city firmly established it as the home of classical instrumental music.

Monn (1717–1750)

Monn is important in the early development of the Classical symphony as he contributed to shaping the symphony form, notably by including a minuet as the third of the four movement form. His works show evidence of contrasting themes, a style of composing which emphasised short motivic ideas with changes of harmony, and a use of dynamics characteristic of the *empfindsamkeit* style.

Wagenseil (1715–1777)

Although his significance later dwindled, Wagenseil was an important composer and keyboard virtuoso of the time. He contributed particularly to shaping the four movement form of the symphony, and influenced Mozart with lyrical style. His *Symphony in D major* was originally the overture to his opera *La Clemenzo di Tito* (1746), an earlier version of Mozart's later opera.

Haydn (1732–1809)

In many ways Haydn arrived on the musical scene at a most favourable time for him. He was influenced by the works of Stamitz, Sammartini and C.P.E. Bach who were drawing on features of the rococo, *sturm und drang* and *empfindsamkeit* styles. Gradually this mix of styles, along with the international cross-currents fused to form the Classical style. It was Haydn who took several major steps to firmly establish the style. He is recognised as the first major Classical composer.

Haydn gave new dimensions to the symphony form. He established the sections of the sonata form of the symphony, beginning with three movements in his earliest to four definite contrasting movements in his later symphonies. His imagination and inventiveness for thematic development, his constant desire to experiment, and his amazing productivity affected the development of the symphony profoundly. Haydn's development of the symphony form can be summarised as follows:

Early symphonies (No. 1: 1759–No. 31: 1766)

Haydn wrote for the day and to suit his orchestral players at the court of Esterhazy. Many of his early symphonies are in concerto grosso style, with concertante parts recalling Baroque *concerto grosso* style. The works show a great variety of form and instrumentation, with perhaps a predominance of wind instrumental sound. He used the harpsichord in his symphonies for continuo support until around 1770, often conducting from the harpsichord. His slow movements show the continued use of Corelli-like chains of suspensions. Structurally, the first movements were the most important: the andantes were usually in two parts, the minuets and trios broke away from the typical courtly dance style after *Symphony No. 8*, and were subsequently composed in a more rustic style. The finales of the earliest symphonies, in 3/8 or 6/8 metre, were eventually considered too light to act as fitting conclusions and gradually changed to 2/4 or 4/4 time, in sonata or rondo form. They can be characterised as compact, gay, witty and full of typical Haydn surprise tactics.

Late symphonies (No. 88 1787–No.104 1795):

Haydn's late symphonies, composed from 1787, are all on a much grander scale. They are much longer, and often have majestic slow introductions and large-scale sonata form first movements with a great deal of development of thematic material, particularly of first subject themes. His codas are often similar to a second development. Many of these symphonies show brilliant orchestration and an expanded harmonic range. They have an intensified rhythmic drive and highly unified yet varied movements using themes characteristically limited in range and carefully balanced in phrase structures.

Haydn
Symphony No. 6, 'Le Matin'

Haydn's *Symphony No. 6* (1761) is the first of a trilogy of symphonies – *Nos. 6, 7 and 8* – called 'Le Matin' (the morning). It is the first symphony Haydn composed at Esterhazy. This symphony still contains some Baroque features but importantly establishes the symphony foundations, fusing pre-Classical styles with Haydn's own compositional style.

Listen to CD1, track 17 which features the first movement of the symphony. Listen particularly for:

- the opening slow introduction – said to depict the sun rising – beginning in French overture, dotted style, acting as a slow archway to the Allegro
- the variety in the scoring; for example, the flute takes the first theme instead of the usual violins
- the harmonic pace of generally one or two changes per bar, presented by a characteristic repeated bass notes structure
- the sudden dynamic contrasts, particularly the *sfz*s
- the octave arpeggio passagework at the end of the first section
- Haydn's marvellous ability to develop themes imaginatively, creating unity as well as variety
- the continuous changes of texture and material. This contrasts with earlier and

contemporary composers who would have kept the same material throughout
- harmonically, a more adventurous harmonic scheme than his predecessors.

Further work and listening
- Listen to the rest of the movement, particularly noting:
i) the first movement's development section which explores more distant keys
ii) the touch of genius at the entry of the recapitulation where a surprise horn entry plays the opening bars of the main theme just before the recapitulation proper begins with the main theme. These features place Haydn over and above many of the Classical composers of his day.

Mozart (1756–1791)

Mozart's symphonies show the influence of Sammartini and Haydn. Mozart had an operatic approach to symphony writing, characterised by a greater amount of thematic material. His themes were generally more lyrical and expressive, and his harmonies richer and often more chromatic than Haydn's. Although the latter's harmonic surprises, such as startling modulations and abrupt changes of key, are not as frequent in Mozart's mature works, a melodic chromaticism is more evident. Mozart was capable of beautiful orchestral scoring, elevating writing for the woodwind to an equal with the strings. His symphonies show a greater textural complexity and brilliant contrapuntal skill in contrasting themes.

Further work and listening
- Listen to symphonies by early Classical composers, for example, Monn: *Symphony in E♭* (1740); C.P.E. Bach: *Symphony in E minor* (1773); J. Stamitz: *Symphony in E♭* (1750); Sammartini *Symphony No. 13 in G major* (c.1740). These are good examples of the early

Classical style. Focus your listening on the early Classical features such as the short motivic themes, a less complicated texture, contrasting first and second subjects and the use of dynamics alongside continuing Baroque features such as the inclusion of the harpsichord.

Beethoven (1770–1827)

Beethoven was one of the most disruptive influences in the history of music. He came on the musical scene at a time when new and powerful forces were radically sweeping Europe. He is regarded as being part of the culmination of the Classical style and at the same time opening the gateway to Romanticism. His music reflects much of the social atmosphere of the time: optimism, the feeling of a new age, of revolutionary spirit and of liberated energy. His music is rich in sheer sound mass, abrupt dynamic shadings, robust, urgent rhythms and is intensely emotional in a Classical sense.

With Beethoven's symphonies we see the beginning of the 'great art work'. Earlier in the eighteenth century, audiences went to the opera or concerts to hear 'the latest new works', considering those composed even the previous year to be old. The symphony was thought of as an attractive new form of concert entertainment, and was expected to last no more than 30 minutes in length. The symphonies of Beethoven, however, established a permanent change in attitude and the status of the symphony rose to one of an 'art work', written to last for posterity. This change can be seen in the declining number of symphonies written by individual composers. As the status of the symphony rose, the number fell: Haydn wrote 104, Mozart 41 and Beethoven 9 symphonies.

Beethoven extended the length of the symphony through extensive development of themes. He had an extraordinary ability to 'milk a theme dry', using extremely economic material. He was a master of formal design and structural balance; his symphonies are based on large tonal designs, a wider harmonic palette and longer development and coda sections. Unlike in Haydn's earlier symphonies in which the first movement is by far the most weighty, in Beethoven's symphonies every movement contributes to the length and compositional significance; slow movements are deeply expressive, substantial movements, scherzos developed into fully fledged one-in-a-bar movements and finales into full, weighty movements.

Although the actual orchestra for which Beethoven composed was the same size as that of Haydn, there is a sense that a larger orchestra should be used because of the increased depth, expressiveness and wider dynamic range. Occasionally Beethoven added trombones for extra weight and other instruments such as the piccolo and contrabassoon. In general, the instrumental parts are more technically demanding than in earlier symphonies.

Beethoven had an enormous imagination, evident throughout all his symphonies, from the large-scale innovations to intricate thematic development techniques. Examples of his large-scale innovations include his use of voices in Symphony no. 9 and his use of programmatic material in the *Pastoral Symphony*, a form in which a descriptive programme had not been used before.

Beethoven's works are often divided into three periods:

First period (to 1802): *Symphonies Nos. 1* and *2*, *String Quartets Op. 18*, the first ten piano sonatas (up to Op. 14), *Piano Concertos Nos. 1, 2* and *3*.
Second period (up to 1816): *Symphonies Nos. 3–8*, the opera *Fidelio*, *Piano Concertos Nos. 4* and *5*, the *Violin Concerto*, *String Quartets Op. 59* (*Rasumovsky Quartets*), *74* and *95*, and the piano sonatas up to and including *Op. 90*.
Third period: *Symphony No. 9*, the last five piano sonatas, the *Diabelli Variations*, the *Missa Solemnis*, *String Quartets Op. 127, 130, 131, 132, 135*, and the *Grosse Fuge* (*Grand Fugue*) for string quartet, *Op. 135*.

Beethoven
Symphony No. 3 in E♭, 'Eroica'

Composed in 1803, Beethoven's *Symphony No. 3* marks a significant advance over his first two symphonies, which were considerably influenced by the symphonies of Haydn and Mozart. It stands out as a landmark in the development of the form. The whole symphony distinguishes itself from earlier symphonies by its dramatic qualities and personal expression of optimism, sheer dynamism and energy. It also predicts a new world of heroic greatness, as it was composed with the spirit and ideals of his hero – Napoleon – in mind, who was to have attended the first performance.

The symphony is longer and more complex than any previously written, and marks the first of Beethoven's immense expansion of the form. The size of the first movement sections, for example, are *exposition* – 154 bars, *development* – 244 bars, *recapitulation* – 158 bars, *coda* – 130 bars. The length, not only of this movement, but of all the movements is due to the large-scale tonal designs, often modulating to remote keys, and his genius in thematic development.

Listen to CD1, track 18.

Symphony No. 3 in E♭, 'Eroica'
Beethoven

Analysis: 1st movement (bars 1–45)

Themes and motifs

All the material developed in this movement is presented in the first 36 bars. The opening two chords dramatically announce the beginning of the movement, followed by the main theme. This theme is in characteristic Classical vein, based on the tonic Eb chord. It is a lyrical theme and is presented in a romantic mode, being played by the cellos. The C# at the end of the theme, which has the effect of instantly destabilising the Eb tonality, opens up opportunities for endless directions for development. The theme is heard for the second time at bar 15, this time played by the horns, and continued by the strings. Note how the C# is now changed to a Db, preparing the way for modulation. The theme appears a third time at bar 35 in a full orchestral rendition, marked *fortissimo*. Note the change to the theme ending as the previous Db is used to pass again to further modulations.

The syncopation, introduced almost immediately in bar 7 by violins I is a central dramatic feature of the whole movement. Characteristically, it begins almost unobtrusively here at the beginning of the movement.

Bar 45 introduces the second theme, which is actually derived from the rhythm in bars 6–7 of the main theme. Note how the motif is passed through the instruments. This is typically a more lyrical, gentle theme, accompanied by flowing alberti bass quavers.

Harmony

Although the movement is in Eb, Beethoven sets up a conflict throughout between the tonic Eb and the dominant Bb. Note how Beethoven firmly establishes the tonic with the two dramatic chords at the opening, followed by the main theme based on the tonic arpeggio of Eb, followed shortly by a perfect cadence, marked *sf*, emphasising the Ab in bar 10, and again at bar 13. No sooner has he emphasised the Eb tonic than he sets it up in conflict in a very dra-

matic way: bar 18 gives hints of the supertonic minor – F minor, a characteristic Beethoven tonal side-stepping technique – then the composer builds the excitement and tension to Bb, reinforcing the key conflict through powerful dramatic syncopated chords played by the full orchestra. The harmonies used in this phrase include tonic, dominant 7th and augmented 6th chords, the chromatic chords creating a high level of tonal conflict between Eb and Bb. The re-establishing of the tonic Eb at bar 37 asserted by the fortissimo full orchestral main theme is immediately dislodged and the phrase finally arrives at F major for the second subject at bar 45.

Rhythm

Powerful rhythmic variety and energy is one of the main features of Beethoven's music. In this extract we can hear:

- how the relentless drive is achieved through the continual quaver movement and tremelos interrupted only by dramatic syncopated passages
- the force of the syncopation passages emphasises the second beat of the bars, almost losing the sense of the 3/4 metre of the movement
- the rhythmic contrast at bar 45 for the typically more lyrical second subject, now accompanied by a more lilting quaver pattern, in contrast to the repeated quaver patterns up to this point.

Further work and listening

- Listen to and study the first movement of the 'Eroica' symphony. How is the thematic material introduced in bars 1–36 developed in the rest of the movement?
- Listen to the other three movements. The slow movement entitled 'Funeral March' is a processional march in C minor, full of tragic grandeur and pathos. Beethoven replaces the traditional third movement Minuet with a

Scherzo (literally 'joke'), a fast one-in-a-bar movement. The fourth movement is a set of remarkable variations on a theme of his own (ballet music from *Prometheus*). Analyse the characteristic features in these movements, looking particularly at the way they are a significant development, both in terms of his earlier symphonies and those of Haydn and Mozart.

- Compare and contrast a late symphony by Haydn with a Beethoven symphony. In what way was Beethoven influenced by Haydn and how did he break new ground? Study development techniques, tonal scheme, the use of the orchestra, surprise tactics, dynamic sharpness, and the overall expansion of the form.
- Compare and contrast a Mozart symphony such as *Symphony No. 41 'Jupiter'* (1788) with a Beethoven symphony such as *Symphony No. 5* (1806–8), pointing out some differences in style and impact.

Music for small ensembles

String trio

A string trio is a work for three stringed instruments, either two violins and cello, or violin, viola and cello. After 1770 the latter took precedence over the former – an outgrowth of the Baroque trio sonata which was a work for continuo (bass and harpsichord) and two violins.

Piano trio

A piano trio is a work for piano and two other instruments, usually violin and cello. In Haydn's piano trios, the cello often doubles the piano bass line. The trios of Mozart and Beethoven are much more substantial works; for example, Beethoven's *'Archduke Trio' Op. 97*. Other combinations include Mozart's *Trio for piano, clarinet and viola K498* and Beethoven's *Trio for piano, clarinet and cello Op. 11*.

String quartet

A string quartet is a composition for four solo stringed instruments, usually two violins, viola and cello. The quartet evolved from the Baroque trio sonata to become one of the greatest art forms of communication between the composer and a musical medium. It is popularly, though controversially, thought that string quartets were originally composed for outdoor entertainment – the harpsichord being too difficult to carry about, it was therefore abandoned and a viola brought in.

Haydn

The most significant force in the development of the string quartet is Haydn. He brought on the form from its crude beginnings to a situation of personal communication with his mature quartets. In his hands the quartet has been likened to 'a bird taking flight'. Haydn's early quartets, *Op. 1, 2* and *3* (1760) had very simple parts for the second violin, viola and cello. All the interest lay in the first violin melody. With his *Op. 9* quartets, a four-movement scheme was established with developed instrumental writing showing increased independence of parts. The *Op. 17* quartets show a greater variety and richness in the individual string parts and a deeper, more personal level of communication than in his earlier quartets which tended more towards entertainment.

Haydn's *Op. 33* quartets (1781) represent a revolution in style. Haydn himself claimed that the quartets were written 'in an entirely new and special style'. Whereas previously there had been a clear textural distinction between the melody – usually played by the first violin – and accompaniment lines, in these quartets the accompaniments and melodic lines flow freely between all four instruments, creating a much richer texture. The six quartets show tremendous variety of texture, brilliant handling of the four instruments; and mature motivic developments. They are light-hearted and full of wit. The *Op. 77* quartets (1799) represent the summit of Haydn's quartet writing.

Mozart

It was not until Mozart composed his set of six quartets (1782–5), dedicated to Haydn and known as the 'Haydn' Quartets, that he showed mature mastery of the quartet medium. They are not mere imitations of Haydn's style but reveal Mozart's individuality, particularly the chromatic harmonies, the lyricism, the lightness and textural combination of harmony and counterpoint, and the increased virtuosity in the violin I writing.

Beethoven

The quartet was Beethoven's spiritually intimate medium. His early *Op. 18* quartets (1798–1800) show the influence of Haydn, particularly in the art of developing motifs and animating the texture by means of counterpoint. Beethoven's individuality, however, shows through in the sheer depth of their emotional intensity; the dynamic, relentless sense of forward direction combined with a sense of symmetry and formal Classical balance; his integral sense of tonal design; his use of Baroque styles and contrapuntal techniques; the tense, robust energy; his ability to drive the music forward and suddenly leave it hanging in excited anticipation; the biting agitation; sudden pauses; the pathos; the unexpected turns of phrases; the increase in technical demands.

Beethoven's *'Rasumovsky' Quartets Op. 59* (1806) have a position in the growth of the quartet similar to his *'Eroica'* symphony, and show the composer's mature style and characteristic manner of expression in this medium. They are full of emotional fire, boldness of formal treatments, and are strikingly original. So great was their novelty that musicians were slow to accept them at first. In these quartets, the sonata form is expanded considerably through the development of numerous themes, often characteristically concise and simple in their original statement. Along with this expansion, Beethoven deliberately conceals the structural dividing lines between the various parts of the movement; recapitulations are disguised and varied, new themes grow imperceptibly out of previous material and the progress of the musical idea has a dynamic propulsive character that adds tension to the symmetrical patterns of the Classical era. There is more equality of interest among the string parts making the texture more complex and sonorous.

Beethoven's late quartets, *Op. 127–Op. 135* (1824–6), are revolutionary in every way. Haydn could not have envisaged what was to become of his 'invention', and there is nothing quite like them in the subsequent repertoire until Bartok. The immense spirituality and emotional intensity of these works, and the sheer extent of structural, textural, thematic and expressive originality puts these quartets in a position in the growth of the quartet medium which far exceeds those of his contemporaries. The Russian Prince Galitzin summed it all up by describing them, and Beethoven: 'Your genius is centuries in advance'.

String quintet

A string quintet is a composition for five stringed instruments, usually two violins, two violas, and cello. Outstanding examples are Mozart's Quintets *K515 in C major* and *K516 in G minor*. The addition of the second viola makes for a texture that is fuller, darker and warmer than in a string quartet and it is conducive to increased emotional intensity.

Piano quintet

A piano quintet is a work for piano and four other instruments. The main significant Classical piano quintets include Mozart's *Quintet for piano and wind instruments K452* and Beethoven's *Quintet Op. 16*.

Further work and listening

- Listen to an early and a later Haydn string quartet, for example *Op. 9 No. 4* and *Op. 33 No. 2*. Listen particularly for the differences in the strings writing.
- Listen to one of Mozart's 'Haydn' Quartets, perhaps *K421 in D minor* or *K465 The 'Dissonance' Quartet in C major* – a marvellous example of Mozart's expressive harmony, and his *String Quintet in C major K515*. Compare the differences in string quality and texture between a quartet and a quintet.
- Compare and contrast the use of harmony and tonality in a Haydn and a Beethoven string quartet.
- Listen to a movement from an early, middle and late Beethoven string quartet, such as *Op. 18 No. 1*, *Op. 59 No. 1* and *Op. 131* or *Op. 132*. Listen particularly to the ways that the genre develops in Beethoven's hands.

The concerto

The solo concerto became popular in the Classical age, displacing the Baroque *concerto grosso*, as it fulfilled the public demand for concert performances that would provide entertainment. As public concerts increased, the ability of outstanding virtuoso performers to attract large audiences assumed greater significance. As a concert item, the solo concerto remains a popular form to this day.

The Classical concerto form of Haydn and Mozart has three main features which separate it from other genres of the time:

i)   It has three movements instead of four.

ii) It originally derived from the fast-slow-fast solo concerto of the type composed by Vivaldi.

iii) First movements have a double exposition and include a cadenza which is usually placed at the end of the recapitulation, followed by a short orchestral coda. Cadenzas were not written out, but left to the performer to write out or to improvise in the concert. Initially, when the performer was also the composer, the content of the cadenzas was based on themes integral to the movement and acted as a special kind of coda in which the principal ideas of the movement were presented again in a new light of virtuoso display. However, during the Classical era, the increase in public performances meant that the composer was not always the performer. In the hands of virtuoso performers, the value of the cadenza tended to decline and in some cases became no more than a vehicle for virtuosic display. Some composers, including Mozart and later Beethoven, wrote down cadenzas for their soloists, to give guidelines and so avoid meaningless display.

Mozart

The concerto was more important in Mozart's output than in that of any other composer of the second half of the eighteenth century. Mozart's enthusiasm for the then new piano inspired him to write more concertos for the piano than any other instrument. They are amongst his finest works, and represent the very essence of the Classical concerto. They are recognised as key works in the development of the concerto.

Mozart cultivated the form throughout his life, significantly influencing its deflection from the violin to the piano, and the change from the harpsichord to the piano. He established the Classical concerto form with a double exposition, and mastered the balance between the soloist and orchestra, changing the relationship of the soloist and the orchestra to one of combined duality in a dramatic context. He expanded the power and sonority of both solo and orchestra parts to a new level. His *Concerto in D minor K466* (1795), is one of only two concertos that Mozart composed in the minor key and is amongst the greatest masterpieces of the form. The historical importance of the work lies in its character: a mature, dramatic work, written at the height of Mozart's creative power, and connecting with the dramatic and turbulent spirit of the age. It is the concerto that Beethoven played and wrote cadenzas for.

Beethoven

Beethoven's treatment of the concerto was dramatic and rugged. He retained the three-movement plan but expanded the framework, collapsed the double exposition and intensified the genre. Beethoven's piano style is founded on the explosive nature of the instrument; he typically used sharp dynamic shadings, sudden *sfz*s, and he explored the extreme ranges of the piano. The solo virtuosity is more marked is his concertos than in Mozart's, often including double trills, 3rd scales, thick chords, leaping left hand passages, parallel octaves and so on. He contributed greatly to the change of emphasis from the aristocratic salon to the public concert hall.

Further work and listening

- Compare and contrast the relationship between the soloist and orchestra in a Mozart and a Beethoven piano concerto; for example, Mozart's *Piano Concerto in A major K488* (1785) and Beethoven's *'Emperor' Piano Concerto No. 5* (1809). Listen out particularly for:
  i) contrasting passages
  ii) passages of dialogue or conflict
  iii) the balance of thematic material between soloist and orchestra
  iv) the musical and dramatic effect of the soloist's cadenza
  v) the different technical demands in the writing for piano.
- Listen to one of Mozart's violin concertos (1775–7) and his *Clarinet Concerto* (1791) – an instrument favoured by Mozart. Look carefully at the balance between soloist and orchestra.
- How was the concerto shaped and developed by Haydn, Mozart and Beethoven? Identify the contributions that each made to the growth of the genre.

The sonata

In the Classical era, sonata was the name given to a work in several movements for one or two instruments only; for example, a piano, or violin and piano. The overall sonata scheme of a four-movement work contrasting in tempo and character is also common in symphonies, and chamber music.

In the early Classical period, keyboard sonatas were written for clavichord, harpsichord and piano. The clavichord was well suited to the ornamental and expressive style of early Classic music, but it was very limited in volume of tone. The harpsichord became obsolete around 1775, and after this time most pieces for solo keyboard – apart from the organ – are primarily for the piano, not the harpsichord. Although much keyboard music was printed with the heading 'For pianoforte or harpsichord', this was a device to attract the largest possible number of purchases.

The piano

Although Christofori made the first pianoforte in 1709, it was not really taken seriously until the 1740s, when J.S. Bach gave it his seal of approval. Later, the main thrust of piano development by the German, Silbermann, concentrated on developing the piano along the lines of the clavichord. This led to the invention of the 'Viennese action', developed particularly by the Stein family. The action was matched to the light frame and stringing of the early pianos. The touch was light and shallow and almost as sensitive as a clavichord. In addition, the light hammers gave a blow which sustained stringing, giving a singing tone of great beauty.

The English piano, developed first by Backer in the 1770s and later by the Broadwood firm, was bass heavy. On the English piano, the heavy touch meant that the keys sank deeper and consequently the return of the hammer and note repetition was not as quick. Improvements to the piano around 1800 concerned increasing the string tension, and designing the frame which would stand heavier performance weight without collapsing. In 1825, the piano was further improved, reshaped, enlarged to seven octaves and strengthened by metal plates. It was then capable of greater tension and its thick strings provided a fuller, more ringing tone.

From Baroque to Classical

The traditional Baroque keyboard forms had been suites, sets of variations, toccatas, fugues and preludes and fugues. Baroque sonatas were of two kinds; the *sonata da camera* (chamber sonata) and *sonata da chiesa* (church sonata). Each of these kinds could be expressed in two different kinds of instrumentation:

i) the popular trio sonata with two solo parts accompanied by a figured bass. The figured bass was played by the continuo player on the cello, viola da gamba or string bass and realised, that is, the chords played, by the harpsichord player. Although four players were actually needed to play trio sonatas, the 'trio' stands for the three melodic lines of the score.

ii) the rarer solo sonata, performed by three players – soloist, continuo player and keyboard player. The harpsichord was, as usual, included to play the continuo, but not as a solo instrument.

Both kinds of sonata usually consisted of four movements – slow – fast – slow – fast – all in the same key. While strings were the most common

medium, other instruments such as the flute and oboe, were used increasingly in the late seventeenth and early eighteenth centuries. All the movements are relatively short compared with Classical sonata movements. Corelli was the most influential composer of the Baroque sonata.

In the early eighteenth century, the desire for greater opportunites to give solo performances of sonatas led to a trend of transforming the trio sonata into the solo sonata. In the transformation one player maintained one solo part, the other solo part being played in the right hand of the harpsichord player and the figured bass realised in the left hand. J.S. Bach's *Six Sonatas for Cembalo* (harpsichord) *and Violin* are striking examples of the old trio texture performed in the new way. This type of solo sonata offered more opportunities for soloists to reveal virtuosic skills, and thus the parts for soloists became more technically demanding. In particular, the violin sonatas were filled with arpeggios, double stops, and other technical devices that added variety and brilliance.

D. Scarlatti

The harpsichord sonatas of D. Scarlatti show similar technical demands for the harpsichord player and in many ways they establish a link between the Baroque and Classical forms of sonata. Scarlatti composed around 550 sonatas for solo harpsichord. Unlike earlier sonatas, these are single movement works. They are full of original features and represent a significant point in the development of the solo sonata. They explore the full possibilities of the harpsichord and include dazzling runs, wide leaps, agile repeated notes and demanding passages which require crossed hands.

C.P.E. Bach

Composers were divided in their preferences for the different keyboards available at the time. The most characteristic examples of the early Classic sonata are those of C.P.E. Bach. His keyboard sonatas show the thin harmonies and decorative and expressive features of the rococo style and the robust passagework of the *sturm und drang*. C.P.E. Bach's treatise, *Essay on the True Art of Playing Keyboard Instruments* (1753–62) had a tremendous influence in his own time and for years later. Beethoven knew it well. Although he accepted the piano as being on equal terms with the clavichord and harpsichord, C.P.E. Bach continued to prefer the clavichord. J.C. Bach, however, embraced the piano wholeheartedly and contributed greatly to the popularising of the instrument, giving the first public performances of music on the piano in London.

Haydn

Haydn's 49 sonatas cover a long span of the composer's life. His early works show a great variety of style, and also the intended medium: either clavichord, harpsichord or piano. Many are in *style galant* – gay, simple, without being ornate or sophisticated, with characteristic *sturm und drang* features, notably his *Sonata in C minor*, with its continual dynamic changes and irregular shaped melodic lines. His late sonatas, written deliberately for piano only, show the greater breadth and dramatic vigour associated with his symphonies. They form a link to the sonatas of Beethoven. Equally significant are his dazzling piano trios which show some of his most imaginative and inspired writing for the piano.

Mozart

Sonatas for various instruments account for almost a quarter of Mozart's instrumental works, a larger proportion than in Haydn's instrumental works. Mozart was the first of the great pianist/composers and he was also an excellent violinist. Although all instruments were available to him, he favoured the piano, and in particular the light Viennese action piano with its capacity for an expressive singing tone. His works are significant and constitute an important position in the repertoire. In addition to his sonatas there are numerous variations, rondos, and fantasies.

> ## Mozart
> Piano Sonata in C minor K457

This sonata, composed in 1784, is recognised as one of Mozart's finest. It is also interesting because it served as the model for Beethoven's *Sonate Pathétique Op. 13* which he composed in 1798.

Listen to CD1, track 19.

Piano Sonata in C minor K457, 1st movement
Mozart

Analysis: 1st movement (bars 1–30)

Form

The form of the first movement is, of course, sonata form. The first subject is stated at the opening, in C minor, followed by the bridge passage in which the key modulates to E♭ for the second subject at bar 23.

Themes

The first subject sections, bars 1–8, comprises a typically strident arpeggio motivic theme based on the tonic key. First themes are generally strong and emphasise the tonic key. However, this is not totally characteristic of Mozart, who generally was more inclined to more lyrical opening melodies. Mozart balances this opening motif with an answering phrase – a delicate two-bar phrase, which is basically an imperfect cadence, marked *piano* in a higher register. In the second four-bar phrase, the motifs are the same but now based on the dominant G. The answering phrase now moves to a perfect cadence, to balance the previous imperfect cadence.

The second subject or theme appears at bar 23 and is of a more lyrical, cantabile character. Note how the alberti bass accompaniment gives a more gentle, song-like character, contrasting with the powerful octaves and octave pedals that we have heard up to this point. The theme is a beautifully simple, balanced melody, 2+2+4, varied on the repetition, ending in B♭.

Harmony

Generally, the harmonic pace is at a rate of one harmony per bar. Mozart quickens the pace in the transition or bridge passage to two chords per bar, moving the music forwards. The chords throughout are predominantly tonic and dominant with dominant and diminished 7ths at cadence points, and cadential sequences. Note the very typical Classical cadential progression at bars 17–19 of I, IIb, Ic, V7, I. Note, too, the dominant pedal in the transition section.

Interesting features

- The continual textural changes create variety and vitality. For example, the opening bare octave motif contrasts texturally with its answering phrase, which in turn contrasts with the powerful dominant pedal and chromatic lines of the transition.
- Authors often refer to unity and variety being achieved in a piece through a composer's technique of developing themes. This means taking a theme, or motif, or part of a melody and developing it in different ways. For example, in this extract the octave opening motif returns in the upper register only at bar 19 – leading us to expect a return of the full opening four bars – only to change direction and go on to present the octave motif in the left hand, change the key to E♭ to prepare for the second subject and introduce a rhythmic triplet accompaniment motif in the right hand.
- The dynamics emphasise the contrasting material and texture, often moving dramatically from $\boldsymbol{f}$ to $\boldsymbol{p}$.

Further work and listening

- Listen to the rest of this movement. Study how Mozart develops the material stated in the first 30 bars.
- Compare and contrast this sonata with Beethoven's *Sonate Pathétique*. Look particularly at the different ways the composers develop themes and motifs.

Beethoven

The sonatas, variations and other piano works of Beethoven occupy a similarly significant position in his output. Beethoven was influenced at first by the works of Clementi, and is known to have introduced his students to Clementi's *Introduction to the Art of Playing*. The character of his piano music, particularly his thirty-two sonatas, of exploring new structural and tonal harmonic territory; of enormously energetic dynamics; his improvisatory style; his fondness for 'swarming over the piano' contrasted him sharply with the polished, balanced style of the Viennese composers. It also made a great impact on Viennese audiences, particularly when he broke strings in performance!

Further work and listening

- Listen to a whole, or part of sonatas by C.P.E. Bach, Haydn, Mozart and Beethoven to get an overview of the different stylistic differences, for example:
- i) C.P.E. Bach: *Sonata No. 3 in E major, 1st movement* – contrasting themes in a single movement; *Sonata in C Minor* (1771) – fusion of rococo and *sturm und drang* elements; *Württemberg Sonata No. 6, 1st movement* – the emergence of C.P.E. Bach's 'dramatic' side; he contrasts louds and softs very effectively and makes full use of the power of the instrument.
- ii) Haydn: *Piano Sonata No. 52 in E♭ major* (1794) – a tempestuous work, very characteristic of Haydn.
- iii) Mozart: there are numerous to choose from – try *Piano Sonata in B♭ major K333* (1783), *Violin Sonata in D major K306* (1778), a brilliant concerto-like sonata.
- iv) Beethoven: again, numerous works to choose from – First Period: *Piano Sonata Op. 2 No. 1 in F minor* (1795); *Op. 13 Sonate Pathetique* (1799); Second Period: *Op. 53 in C major 'Waldstein'* (1804); *Op. 57 in F minor 'Appassionata'* (1805); *Violin Sonata Op. 47 'Kreutzer'* (1803).
- Compare and contrast the ways in which these composers write for the piano. Look particularly at the technical features, not only types of demanding passagework but also cantabile, expressive sections
- Compare the harmonic and tonal plans of the first movements of a Haydn, Mozart and Beethoven sonata.

The art song

Although the art song was not central to the work of the Classical period composers, some songs stand out as worthy of inclusion in any vocal repertoire. They are also valuable in that they show the lead-up to Schubert *lieder*. Early eighteenth century songs show the influence of the *empfindsamer stil*, and those of C.P.E. Bach are particularly interesting. Songs were simple, light and easy to sing. Their mood was unpretentious and they were often written on two staves only. During this time the art song was thought of as music for the home, often written for friends and small social gatherings and did not carry the weight and importance of the larger classical forms. Significant key points to consider are the relationship of the words and music and the impact of the developing piano and its new, expressive possibilities.

Haydn's songs are often simple in form, with basic text settings, with his early songs set on just two staves. The texts were not significant and some display a clear lack of concern with text-music relationships. Many carry a simple folk-like quality, typical of Haydn's style. Melodies are often triadic, diatonic, folk-like, not overly lyrical. The canzonets are superior to the songs. Many are longer, more substantial and varied, conveying a more expressive musical language. Characteristic surprise tactics can be discerned throughout, often typically in the form of abrupt changes of harmony, sudden *sfzs* and pauses.

The intimate art song with keyboard accompaniment occupied Mozart occasionally and briefly throughout his life. His songs include stylistic elements of Italian canzonettas, French *opera comique*, German sacred music and his operas.

Beethoven's *An Die Ferne Geliebte* is probably the most noteworthy of his song compositions. The work is a cycle of songs clearly showing traits of continuation from one song to the next. It is an extraordinary work and had a deep and genuine influence on the music of composers of the Romantic era.

Further work and listening

- Listen to some songs and canzonets by Haydn; for example, from his two sets of songs *Original Canzonettas* (1794 and 1795), in particular, the songs 'Fidelity' – a substantial song with changes in tempo, key and accompaniment patterns, and 'Despair', with its eloquent melodic line and careful dynamic markings suitable for the piano, the keyboard instrument Haydn now preferred. Listen out particularly for characteristic stylistic features.
- Listen to songs by Haydn's contemporaries, for example Zumsteeg and Reichardt. Reichardt set many of his songs to texts by Goethe. Compare Reichardt's setting of Goethe's 'Veilchen' with that of Mozart's, set several years later. Similarly, compare Reichardt's 'Erlkonig' (1794) – a simple, strophic song typical of the period – with Schubert's 'Erlkonig'.
- Investigate the text-music relationship in the art songs of the period, noting the differences between songs in which the text and the music show little correlation and those in which the music and text are inextricably bound.

Sacred choral music

Sacred music includes music used for the church service – for example, masses, motets, litanies, hymns, offertories, vespers and cantatas – and music with sacred words used for special occasions, for example, requiems and oratorios. Oratorios and masses were the most elaborate and important musically in the eighteenth century.

Mass

Haydn composed twelve settings of the mass (the Roman Catholic liturgy); Mozart composed nineteen (including a requiem) and Beethoven two. Haydn's most important masses are all large-scale festive works using full orchestral forces, often with horns and trumpets, and four solo vocalists. At the time, the sheer scale and exhuberance of his masses were occasionally criticised by the clergy for not being in the spirit and showing the decorum suitable for religious works. Haydn, however, justified his flamboyant writing by explaining that he thought it was appropriate for him to compose cheerful sacred music.

Unlike Baroque, Classical sacred music is characterised by the juxtaposition of musical styles – the Classical melody-harmony and the polyphonic style imitation and fugue. There is also an emphasis on the chorus and orchestra, the solo parts or ensembles for soloists occurring mainly as sections of the choruses. In some masses the orchestra plays a role at least equal to that of the voices, notably in Mozart's *Requiem*. As in the vocal writing, there is a blend of the old vocal polyphony and symphonic development.

The masses of Haydn and Mozart served as models for the early nineteenth century. Beethoven regarded his second mass, the *Missa Solemnis, Op. 123* as his greatest work in this form. It is recognised as difficult to sing and to interpret, and too long and elaborate for ordinary liturgical use.

Oratorio

An oratorio is an extended musical setting of a sacred, usually non-liturgical text. The forms and styles are similar to opera but without scenery, costumes or action. The most significant oratorios of the Classical era are Haydn's *The Creation* and *The Season*. Haydn was much influenced by the oratorios of Handel, and like Handel he uses recitatives and arias, duets, trios – sometimes larger ensembles – choruses and orchestra. The musical style and texture is that of the Classical era with fugue and fugato sections in the choruses alongside homophonic sections. A special feature of Haydn's oratorios is the way they depict scenes of nature.

Opera

An opera is a musical dramatic work which combines words, music, drama and scenery, costume and acting, with music normally playing a dominant role.

Gluck (1714–1787)

The opera reforms of Gluck paved the way for opera development in the Classical period. Particularly significant is his work, *Orfeo and Eurydice*. Gluck aimed to make the music bring out the expression of sentiments in the text, rather than dominate the poetry or interrupt the text for unconventional orchestral ritornellos, or for a display of ornamental pieces just to satisfy the demands of the singers. He also stressed that the overture should be relevant to the drama and the orchestration should suit the text. He aimed to break down the sharp contrast between recitative and aria and allow more integration and flow between movements and the dramatic action.

Opera buffa (comic opera)

The dominant position of *opera seria* was challenged in the early eighteenth century by opera buffa or comic opera. Pergolesi was particularly significant in this change with the phenomenal success of *La Serva Padrona* (see page 43). Above all, this opera could be understood because it had genuine dramatic qualities and because it was amusing. It was also characteristic of the reaction to the Baroque opera seria and of the new spirit of the later eighteenth century. Pergolesi created a distinct new genre which was subsequently imitated by composers after him, who extended the genre by increasing the number of characters (Pergolesi's *La Serva Padrona* has only three characters and one is mute), and the number of acts.

The greatest composer of opera buffa was Mozart. His works *Le Nozze di Figaro* (1786), *Don Giovanni* (1783) and *Cosi Fan Tutti* (1790) were all based on librettos by Da Ponte. He raised the opera buffa form to a higher plane by giving greater depth to the characters, and by highlighting serious social tensions and issues in a humorous, appealing way. The many ensembles and extended finales of these operas also brought a new emotional weight to comic opera.

Opéra comique

The French comic opera, or *opéra comique*, again modelled on Pergolesi, emerged as a reaction to the grand and complex operas of Lully and Rameau. Despite resistance from older supporters of French grand opera traditions, changes to French opera were given impetus by support from influential writers such as the philosopher, Rousseau – in his celebrated *Letter on French Music* (1753) he condemned French music.

The subject-matter of French comic opera was basically the same as Italian comic opera, being concerned with pastoral, peasant, middle-class and everyday life. Examples of French *opéra comique* include Grety's *Richard Coeur de Lion* (1784).

Singspiel

German comic opera, called *singspiel* was founded in the English ballad opera, notably *The Beggar's Opera*. As in England, spoken dialogues were interspersed with simple, folk-like songs and dances. Examples of the developed *singspiel* style are Mozart's two operas, *Die Entführung aus Dem Serail* (The Abduction from the Harem – 1782) and *Die Zäuberflute* (The Magic Flute – 1791). Beethoven's opera *Fidelio* (1805) is also based on the German singspiel.

Further work and listening

- Listen to and study Gluck's *Orfeo and Eurydice*. Look particularly at the use of the instruments of the orchestra, including the exceptional trombones; the choruses; and the combination of expressive style and the *sturm und drang* style with its powerful string figuration, leaping motives and tremelos.
- Try to go to see a Mozart opera, for example, *The Marriage of Figaro*, or *The Magic Flute*, noting especially how Mozart portrays the personalities of the characters and the social tensions of the time.

It is important to remember that the Classical and the Romantic are not clear-cut periods of music history. The word Romantic is simply a label by which music written in the nineteenth century is defined. Romantic traits in music go back much earlier than this, and Classical stylistic characteristics continued throughout the nineteenth century.

The Romantic spirit

Nineteenth century Romanticism in music reflected the spirit of the age which was one of intensity of feeling and of emotional communication. The Romantics valued freedom, remoteness and strangeness, passion, striving, endless pursuit of the unattainable, yearning, emotions, impulses. The Romantic age also had a strong interest in legends, exotic far-off lands, myths, the irrational world of the unconscious and the dream.

Music and words

The Romantic age is one of many contradictions. Instrumental music was considered the ideal romantic art – a pure art form, free from the burden of words. However, literature and poetry played an equally central role, and the lyricism of the lied strongly influenced instrumental music of the age. Many nineteenth century composers were very interested in literary expression. Berlin, Weber, Schumann and Liszt wrote distinguished essays on music. Leading novelists and poets of the time wrote about music with a deep love and insight. The lied was an important force in music for the intimate salon. The composers Schubert, Schumann, Brahms and Hugo Wolf reached new levels of intimacy with this particular union of poetry and music.

Programme music

The conflict of the Romantic ideal between pure instrumental music to communicate emotions and the strong literary emphasis was resolved in the concept of programme music. This is music which describes pictures by means of imaginative suggestion through the power of music. This differed from the rhetorical means of musical figures of the Baroque era, or of imitating natural sounds, reminiscent of the Classic era. The beginnings of programme music has its roots in Beethoven's *Pastoral Symphony*. It was later taken up by Mendelssohn, Schumann, Berlioz and Liszt.

The composer and the audience

The Romantic age also saw a changing relationship between the composer and the audience. There was a transition from relatively small, cultured audiences of the Classic era to huge diverse and relatively unprepared middle-class public audiences of the nineteenth century. Composers felt they had to strive to be heard and understood and to reach their vast new audiences. With the emphasis being very much on the individual, the picture arose of the composer 'struggling in his garret', a lone heroic figure, writing under artistic inspiration, working against a hostile environment, separating himself from society. This image of the struggling hero lent composers' music a quality of excitement which stimulated the audiences of the age.

Public concerts

The nineteenth century was a time of enormous population growth, which led to a rapid expansion of the major cities. Musical life flourished in the cities and they became thriving centres of musical activity with their public opera houses, large concert halls, choral societies and festivals.

As the number of concert halls increased, publishing houses and music stores expanded and provincial orchestras were established, with resident and touring conductors. With this expansion the distinction between the professional and the amateur grew sharper. A division emerged between the virtuoso performer, dazzling his audiences on the concert stage, and the intimate drawing room setting for piano solos, duets, lieder, and the family music-making evenings amongst amateur musicians.

Music and nature

The rapid population growth meant that many people moved to the ever-expanding cities for employment. Consequently the majority of the population lived in large impersonal cities rather than small villages. The more people's daily lives became separated from nature, the more they began to look towards it and hankered after it. Much music at the time had, or was given titles concerning nature; for example, Beethoven's *Pastoral Symphony*, Schumann's *Spring* and *Rhenish Symphonies*, Mendelssohn's overtures, for example *The Hebrides Overture*.

Nationalism

Nationalism was also an important feature of Romantic music. In the nineteenth century there was conflict between the growth of nationalism and the beginnings of the socialist movement and the writings of Karl Marx (1867). Some composers reacted to the threat of domination by German influences by incorporating their own national styles in their music. The main nationalist composers included the Russian 'Five', amongst them Mussorgsky, Borodin and Rimsky-Korsakov; Smetana and Dvorak in Bohemia; Grieg in Norway; and Sibelius in Finland. Although other Romantic composers such as Brahms, Chopin and Liszt included nationalist traits in their music, they were really only surface features.

Music of the past

Romanticism also had a revoltionary tinge to it. It was seen by some as a revolt against the lim-itations of Classicism. With the belief that music was now written for the future, for posterity, the concept that art had a history arose, bringing with it an interest in reviving music of the past. The desire for authentic source material led to the publication of critical editions of older composers, among them, Bach, Handel and Palestrina. One of the outcomes of this interest was the revival by Mendelssohn of Bach's *St Matthew's Passion*, a performance of which Mendelssohn himself conducted in 1829. There were also many other revivals. The past was very much still manifest, as all composers wrote in Classical forms, in particular the symphony, sonatas and the string quartet. The Classical system of harmony was still the basis of their music.

Key characteristics

Key genres
- There was a rich variety of types of pieces composed – from large-scale opera, and instrumental forms such as the symphony and concerto, to intimate drawing room piano pieces and songs.
- New genres were developed and established: the *lied* (song), the programme symphony, the symphonic poem and the concert overture. The enormous expansion in music written for piano led to a new form of piano piece – the character piece or miniature.
- The older forms including the symphony, concerto, sonatas and chamber music all continued but in modified form.

Romantic composers

Key Genres	Composers
Symphony	Schubert, Schumann, Mendelssohn, Berlioz, Bruckner, Brahms, Liszt, Tchaikovsky, Dvorak, Mahler
Symphonic Poem	Liszt, Berlioz, R. Strauss
Piano Music	Schubert, Schumann, Mendelssohn, Clara Wieck Schumann, Chopin, Liszt, Brahms
Concerto	Mendelssohn, Schumann, Chopin, Liszt, Brahms, Tchaikovsky, Dvorak, Rachmaninov
Chamber Music	Schubert, Schumann, Brahms
Lied	Schubert, Schumann, Brahms, Hugo Wolf
Choral	Berlioz, Verdi, Bruckner, Brahms, Mendelssohn, Liszt
Opera	Meyerbeer, Gounod, Rossini, Donizetti, Bellini, Verdi, Weber, Wagner, Bizet, Puccini, R. Strauss
Opéra Bouffe	Offenbach, Gilbert and Sullivan, J. Strauss
Concert Overture	Mendelssohn, Dvorak, Tchaikovsky, Rossini
Suites/Ballet	Mendelssohn, Bizet, Grieg, Tchaikovsky

Romantic Forms

Based on sonata form, the symphony, concerto, overture, chamber music and piano sonatas continued to expand from the Classical period throughout the Romantic period. The significant change was in the use and treatment of sonata form. The individual musical expression sought by the Romantic composers strained at the limitations of the structural balance and equilibrium of the Classical sonata form. The infrastructure of sonata form is built on the development of motifs, balanced statements and structured tonal relationships. The long lyrical melodies of the Romantic composers were not as conducive to motivic development as those of the Classical period. The chromatic harmony and wide-ranging modulations of the Romantic era pushed at the boundaries of sonata form, eventually irretrievably shattering the framework in the pursuit for increased emotional range. It became increasingly more difficult for the extended forms to hold together as a unified work. Gradually, large works came to be sectionalised, rather like episodes, each with a different character.

Having loosened the underpinning of the Classical sonata form, composers explored ways of holding whole sections or movements together by the recurrence of a particular motif or melody which reappeared in different transformations throughout the work, as a kind of 'hook'. This approach can be seen in Schubert's *Wanderer Fantasie*, Schumann's *Symphony No. 4* and Berlioz's *Symphonie Fantastique* with the *Idée Fixé*. It was Liszt, however, who coined the term thematic transformation and who is most remembered for establishing the method of unifying a work through the transformation of a theme. This is particularly evident in his symphonic poems.

Melody

Classical melodies were well balanced, closed rather than open and frequently built on scalic or arpeggio-like passages. In contrast, Romantic composers sought to write long expressive melodic lines, sometimes constructed from a series of short phrases, other times as a seamless flow. There was less emphasis on rhythmically energetic motivic themes, suitable for development. Key characteristics of a Romantic melody are wide leaps of 6ths, 7ths, diminished or augmented intervals for expressive purposes.

The range of melodies also increased in the Romantic age; phrases were not so regular and balanced; melody with accompaniment was the prevailing texture. The difficulty of using lyrical themes, in part or in whole, for motivic development – an integral part of sonata form structure – played a significant role·in loosening the form and in works becoming more sectionalised, each section based on a new lyrical theme. The nationalist movement introduced melodies that incorporated folk-like characteristics, or subtly infused melodies with a flavour reminiscent of their country.

Harmony

There were remarkable achievements in harmony techniques throughout the Romantic period. A key point was the change in approach and attitude to harmony. As a means of expression, it was the main preoccupation with composers in the nineteenth century, with frequent use of the chords as a means of expressive colour. The main changes to harmony are as follows:

i) Great development in chromatic harmonies, complex chords, freer use of non-harmonic tones, chromatic voice leading. Common chords used for colour and expressive effects include the augmented triad and augmented 6th and the Neapolitan 6th which was used both for harmonic colour and as a means of blurring the tonal 'home' key. The Romantic composers were fond of long delays in resolving dissonances to create heightened effects of yearning and longing, often adding 3rds on chords to create chords of the 9th, 11th and 13th; in chord progressions, resolutions are often enharmonic, delayed and even non-existent.

ii) Composers used dissonances so frequently that the dominant and diminished chords became almost consonances against more serious dissonant chords, thereby rising the 'dissonance threshold'.

iii) Some chords were almost over used for expressive purposes; the diminished 7th F♯-A-C-E♭ was a favourite chord used for expressive purposes to depict emotional tension or storms.

Tonality

One of the most crucial elements of Romantic music is the expansion of the tonal framework. In the Classical period, tonic, dominant and sub-dominant relationships assumed greatest importance. In the Romantic age, modulations to the mediant and sub-mediant assumed importance equal to the dominant and related key relationships. Sudden key changes and unusual shifts were common. The use of the minor key for whole works dramatically rose as this key allowed for greater expansion and use of chromatic harmonies. The interchange of harmonies and keys from major to minor and vice-versa was common. In the same ways that the circle of 5ths dominated Classical music, a kind of circle of 3rds developed in the Romantic age, influencing chords, key relationships and modulations. Distant modulations, tonal ambiguity, and a growing tendency to avoid distinct cadences were common. These key features all operated to extend and eventually to blur the outlines of tonality and the formal boundaries of the Classical structure.

Texture

Denser, weightier textures were common, with bold contrasts, exploring a wider range of pitch, dynamics and tone colours.

Rhythm

Freedom and flexibility broadly define the characteristics of Romantic rhythm. In general, there was less focus on this aspect, with rhythms tending to be less vital, and more on lyrical, expressive melodies. More frequently we see long sections, and even whole movements based on one unbroken rhythmic pattern; cross-rhythms – particularly twos against threes – and in piano music, irregular groupings of notes in the right hand against regular quaver beats in the left hand. As the nineteenth century progressed, changing metres, and the constant shifting of a steady pulse grew more frequent, intended to disguise expected pulse divisions and to blur the regularity of the barline.

Instrumentation

In the nineteenth century there was an enormous emphasis on broadening the range of instrumental colour and diversity. The orchestration of Berlioz initiated a new era. His *Treatise on Instrumentation* written in 1844 was the first ever textbook on this subject. New sonorities were discovered, new instruments were added to the orchestra and the older instruments were redesigned to be more full-sounding and more flexible. The orchestra nearly trebled in size, not for the purpose of expanding the volume but for enhancing the range of sonorities, to be used like a large artist's palette for broadening the range and mix of sounds. For example, the extended string sections with individual sections often divided to achieve richer sounds. The range of instruments used to play deeply expressive melodies broadened; in particular the cello was frequently used. In general, the variety of timbre required to perform works increased enormously. Orchestral players needed to adapt their tone colour to suit individual composers' style. A rich variety of timbre was needed for vocal works, which ranged from those in a light operatic style to the powerful and dramatic operas of Wagner. Technical virtuousity improved greatly during this period, to meet the demands of the music and of the mass public audience.

The symphony

The extraordinary achievements of Beethoven were like a lead weight on composers after him. The achievements of those who followed immediately after him were initially overlooked;

composers later in the nineteenth century tended to be compared to Beethoven to see how well they matched up. It is well known that Brahms was 'coming to terms with Beethoven' until he was in his forties, and only then did he write his first symphony.

Composers tended to take two routes after Beethoven – those that followed the more conservative, classically-based route included Schubert, Mendelssohn, Schumann, Brahms and Bruckner; and those who took a more radical route, notably Berlioz, Liszt and Wagner. The more conservative Romantics remained broadly faithful to the Classical conception of the symphony, retaining the four-movement plan and recognisable forms for their movements. The 'radicals' took the view that Beethoven was pushing forward the outer limits of instrumental music: for instance, in his *Pastoral Symphony No. 6* and *Choral Symphony No. 9*. In these works they considered Beethoven had sought far reaching sources for inspiration outside purely instrumental music.

Schubert (1797–1828)

Of the symphonies of Schubert, the *Unfinished Symphony in B minor* (1822) is a good example of a Classically-orientated symphony with Romantic characteristics. This symphony heralds the Romantic age in a number of ways: the opening theme played in the bass, the atmospheric quality of the opening, the second subject taking on the language of a Romantic song with piano accompaniment, the key change from the opening B minor to the second subject G major. The lyrical nature of the theme lends itself well to variation.

A typical feature of the Romantic sonata style is the sectional nature of the music. Schubert often uses a one-note link to connect one 'block' with another. The development is a good example of how Schubert, influenced by the motivic development of Beethoven, uses a motif from the introduction for the development. Thus, we see the same variety within unity as in Beethoven, combined with Mozart's

formal clarity and balance, and Schubert's own expressive warmth.

Mendelssohn (1810–1847)

Mendelssohn's *Italian Symphony* is another good example of a Classical instrumental symphony form with Romantic characteristics, notably greater lyricism and perhaps more use of orchestral tone-colour for its own sake.

Schumann (1810–1856)

Schumann is another Romantic composer whose roots lie in Classical conception. It took a long time before he felt ready to write his first symphony, and his *Op. 1 – 23* are all piano pieces. Of his four symphonies, Schumann sought new ways of unifying them, as in his cyclic treatment of *Symphony No. 4*. These symphonies are all four-movement works and show well nineteenth century modifications of Classical styles.

Brahms (1833–1897)

Brahms' symphonies contain many examples of Classical techniques of counterpoint and motivic development, while Romantic elements are found in his harmonic language and orchestral sonorities. Brahms' character is exemplified in his music – sober-minded, careful, disciplined, ordered. He wrote them when he was in his forties and his works do not display the fresh impetuousness of youth. He avoided the Romantic extremes of impulse and excessive emotionalism.

Bruckner (1824–1896)

In his symphonies, Bruckner took his point of departure from Beethoven's *Symphony No. 9* while embracing some of Wagner's innovations. These included his tonal and harmonic inventions, his large-scale structures, and his orchestral innovations, notably the extensive use of brass. Bruckner was very much an individualist.

Tchaikovsky (1840–1893)

Another composer who may be classed as a conservative Romantic is Tchaikovsky. He adhered to the Classical forms even though his music was in the Romantic style. However, the popularity of his works is clear and his symphonies remain a staple ingredient of the traditional orchestral concert programme. Tchaikovsky was a strong influence on many composers after him, notably Rachmaninov and Stravinsky, and also on twentieth century film music.

> ### Tchaikovsky
> Symphony No. 5, 2nd Movement

Tchaikovsky was a mature and successful composer when he wrote the fifth of his six symphonies in 1888. It was one of the works made possible for him to compose through the financial support he received from Nadezhela von Meck. This wealthy widow was passionate about his music, and sent him a monthly allowance for fifteen years, but only on the condition that they never met. This they never did, but wrote intimate letters to each other. This symphony, together with his fourth and sixth symphonies were immensely popular, and contributed greatly to the popularity of the genre in concert programmes. The more progressive composers of the time were convinced that the appeal of the symphony as a form had ended.

Analysis: 2nd movement

Listen to CD1, track 33.

Symphony No. 5, 2nd movement
Tchaikovsky

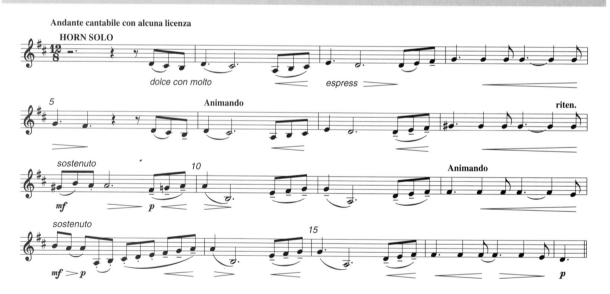

Melody

The melody of the second movement is a marvellous example of Tchaikovsky's characteristic melodic warmth. It is 26 bars long, and made up of short phrases that work together to create a beautiful *cantabile*, expressive melody. Notice how expressively the link is made to the repeat which is played by the cellos, and how, before repetition tarnishes its beauty, the full melody is interrupted and taken up by the violins. This builds up in ever-shortening phrases to the climax (bar 57) before dying down to begin the middle section of the movement. The melody has a remarkable shape. It is marked *dolce con molto*, and detailed throughout with tiny dynamic and articulation shadings. It begins almost song-like, with the strings introducing it with low chords. Over the years, this melody has been set to several sets of words to make it a popular song.

Harmony

The key of this movement is D major, in contrast with the rest of the symphony which is in E minor and of the end of the first movement. The harmonies accompanying the melody are diatonic and generally move at a pace of two chords per bar. In bars 19 and 23 the pace is quickened to four chords per bar which has the effect of moving the music on. Later in this passage the key changes to a bright F♯ major, the effect being one of release from the haunting, deep atmosphere of the opening section. As the music presses on, the harmonic scheme is elaborated with increasingly chromatic lines, using diatonic and chromatic harmonies, particularly diminished 7th and 9th, and chromatically-altered chords, but the predominant tonality remains D major.

Rhythm

Two distinct rhythms permeate the bars in the excerpt, and indeed the entire movement. One is the triplet figure, which plays an integral part of the main melody and is then used almost continuously from bar 24 as a throbbing accompaniment pattern. The other is the motif first heard at bar 24 which is, in fact, derived from the Romantic falling 7th leap heard in the melody.

Instrumentation

Much of the brilliance and power of Tchaikovsky's orchestral works is a result of his skill and method of orchestration. He was influenced by the orchestrations of Berlioz, with his emphasis on the pure colours of a single instrument and groups of similar instruments rather than a mix of instruments. There are, therefore, many beautiful and brilliant solos for individual instruments, such as in this work, with the opening melody played by solo horn, and then repeated by the sonorous, expressive cellos.

Another characteristic is Tchaikovsky's use of a large orchestra in a slow movement. The second movement is scored for three flutes, oboe, clarinet, bassoon, four horns, trumpets, three trombones, tuba, strings and percussion. The four horns combined play a prominent part in this section, giving a sombre, deep colouring to the music.

Further work and listening

- Listen to and study the rest of the second movement of Tchaikovsky's fifth symphony. How does the movement develop? Look closely at the way the melody is used to build tension and release points as the movement progresses.
- Try composing a similar melody of your own. It is not as easy as it sounds, to create a long, unified, *cantabile* melody with shape and direction.

Berlioz (1803–1869)

As we have seen, the 'radical' Romantics – Berlioz, Liszt and Wagner – took their point of departure from Beethoven. Berlioz was particularly influenced by Beethoven's *Pastoral Symphony* and took this as his starting point, expanding the framework of the Classical symphony to incorporate a story, or programme. This expansion can be clearly seen in his *Symphonie Fantastique*. This is also a good example of a symphonic work unified by a theme – in this case the *Idée Fixé*. It also shows Berlioz's extraordinary expansion of orchestral tone-colour.

Symphonic Poem

The most significant composer of programme music after Berlioz was Liszt. Liszt wrote 12 symphonic poems which in many ways sum up the character and spirit of Romantic movement in music. The works are continuous, unlike the traditional symphony four-movement separation, and held together by themes that are transformed, developed or varied in some way and which represent the application of the ideas of thematic variation, or *thematic transformation*. Other significant examples of the genre include the Bohemian composer Smetana's *Ma Vlast (My Country)*, based on episodes from Czech history, Dukas' *L'apprenti-sorcie* – a marvellous example of a narrative type symphonic poem and R. Strauss' *Don Juan, Till Eugenspiel, Also Sprach Zarathustra* and *Don Quixote* – all of which show Strauss' masterful techniques of transforming themes as well as brilliant orchestration.

Mahler (1860–1911)

Mahler was predominantly a composer of symphonies and songs. His symphony writing was mainly influenced by the dramatic choral writing in Beethoven's ninth symphony, the ideas and music of Wagner, and the lyrical song writing of Schubert, together with his own literary interest in poetry and philosophical ideas. His preoccupation with the soul and the nature of infinity resulted in his symphonies using enormous vocal and orchestral forces to depict his ideas. His *Symphony No.8* is known as 'the symphony of a thousand'. This is because of the enormous orchestral and vocal requirements of male, female and children's choirs, as well as special brass and conventional orchestras, demanding approximately 1000 people for a performance! Mahler was also capable of producing very light, delicate orchestral scoring, using the full palette of orchestral colour. However, it was his use of keys, key changes and tonal excursions into ever-increasing far ranges without returning to any tonal 'home'

key that marked the final disappearance of the boundaries of the Classical symphony.

The concert overture

The concert overture flourished in the Romantic era. Most are connected with a programme, or are descriptive in some way, usually in the character or mood of the subject. For example, the *Hebrides Overture* (1832) also known as *Fingal's Cave*, expresses how Mendelssohn felt when he visited the Outer Hebrides. Mendelssohn, like Beethoven, was more interested 'in the expression of feeling than painting'.

Rossini (1792–1868)

Opera in Italy at the time of Rossini was extremely popular. New works were continually in demand and composers and librettists often worked under great pressure to meet deadlines and to satisfy singers. Singers were often well aware of their 'celebrity' status and were not averse to altering composer's music if they felt it did not suit their particular style. Rossini is a significant figure in the development of opera. He continued the old traditions of *opera seria* in works such as *Otello* (1816) and *opera buffa*, as in *The Barber of Seville* (1816), but changed many old opera conventions. For example, he included more and longer ensembles in his works and brought the chorus into the centre of active opera participation. In his operas the accompanied recitative is more dramatic and the orchestra takes on a greater prominence.

Overture to The Barber of Seville
Rossini

Rossini
Overture to *The Barber of Seville*

Rossini's opera overtures are among the most exciting and thrilling works in this genre. The overture to his opera, *The Barber of Seville*, is often played as a concert opening, separate to the opera. In many ways it falls into the categories of both concert overture and opera.

Listen to CD1, track 34.

Form

The form of this overture is typical and consists of a slow introduction; a fast main section in shortened sonata form – the development section is replaced by a transition section which brings the music back to the tonic key; and a coda, at an even faster tempo.

Melody

Much of the overture is based on the melody heard in this excerpt which is played first by the clarinets. This catchy, spontaneous melody is characteristic of Rossini's style. Notice how the phrases are classically balanced, made up of short but lyrical two-bar motifs. The spacious scoring is very song-like, the string accompaniment to the melody playing a steady four crotchet beats per bar. The melody which begins at bar 201 is derived from the opening bar of the previous melody.

Harmony

The speed of this overture is fast, marked *Allegro vivace* and the general harmonic rhythm of the passage is therefore one harmony per four bars. Tonally, the music stays in the key of E major. The passage is based mainly on tonic and dominant 7th chords. However, chromatic appoggiaturas, as in bars 181 and 196 add touches of colour to the diatonic harmonic scheme.

Instrumentation

The overture is scored for piccolo, two flutes, two oboes, two clarinets, two bassoons, two horns, two trumpets, four trombones, strings and percussion. The brilliance of Rossini's orchestration techniques are clearly apparent here. The solo instruments stand out against contrasting instrumental colours, for example the bassoon solo which begins at bar 189. Notice characteristic points of musical wit such as the motifs from violins I at the end of the melody in bar 181. This has the effect of contrasting the instrumental colour and also adding excitement and thrill to the music. The technique is repeated in bar 185 but this time, in contrast, is played by the cellos. Typical of Rossini is the lively writing for strings, as, for example, from bar 200 to the end of the overture, and the prominence of the horns.

Rossini was famous for his continuous crescendos. Listen carefully to the way that the composer builds in the crescendo in the music which starts at bar 200 and ends on the final chord. This has been achieved by a gradual addition of instruments and an increase in the dynamic level. On their entry, the horns play a dotted rhythmic motif which signals the start of a new, highly charged energetic theme. This is subsequently whipped up by full woodwind and strings, the violins adding to the excitement by playing very rapid, short, ascending scalic bursts. The melody gradually rises throughout, reinforced by rapid bursts from the cellos and basses. In the final section, the tempo characteristically quickens, full brass enter and rapid runs from the lower strings work in contrary motion with exciting syncopated phrases from

the violins. The final passage is marked *fortissimo*, and heightened by percussive effects.

Further work and listening
- Listen to one or two other concert overtures by Rossini, or another composer. In what ways do the composers make these works exciting and attractive for concert audiences?

Opera

Opera became increasingly popular amongst the public audience during the nineteenth century. The popularity of the operas of Rossini, Donizetti and Verdi, and of French grand opera, particularly those of Meyerbeer, meant that Italian and French opera dominated the opera scene in the early nineteenth century.

Significant new developments took place in Germany: the introduction of the subject of myths and legends through the Romantic spirit, and the move towards greater continuity based on transformation of themes gradually broke down the traditional opera forms, culminating in the creation of a new genre by Wagner – the music drama.

In his music dramas the music is continuous throughout each act, with no divisions for recitatives, arias and so on. The music is held together by means of *leitmotifs*, musical themes of motifs, each of which is associated with a particular person, emotion or idea central to the drama. They change and develop as the ideas within the opera develop. *Leitmotifs* are usually first heard in the orchestra and used to connect ideas, to carry particular emotional connections and even to move the action on by recurring in particular circumstances.

Wagner's music dramas work on two levels, one telling the story and moving the action on through the songs, and the second on a deeper level, embodying the inner emotions of the human condition. It is in this way that they are masterworks of musical art. *Tristan and Isolde*, *Die Mastersingers von Nürnberg* and *Der Ring* des Nibelungen are great works of the genre, and in the entire history of opera. Wagner brought German opera to its consummation making him a figure of extreme importance. Nineteenth century German Romantic opera also owes much to Weber, whose opera *Der Freischutz* embodies the ideals of German Romanticism, a fact very much appreciated by Wagner.

Throughout the century, Italian and French opera continued to evolve, but in a different way from Wagner, achieving a new intensity and highly expressive style in the last operas of Verdi and in the *verismo* operas of Puccini – which dealt with the unpleasant realities of life, such as poverty, low social status and brutality, for example *La Bohème*. French *opéra comique* evolved into a mix of grand opera and through popular demand by the continuing rise of the *bourgeousie*, a lyric-sentimental style. The operas of Gounod and Bizet are characteristic of the style.

Nationalist composers also wrote operas, notably Mussorgsky and Smetena, their main operatic interest lying in depicting national themes.

In England, the operettas of Gilbert and Sullivan made Sullivan the most popular English composer of the time. In these operas Sullivan fused attractive tunes, choruses and brilliant orchestration with Gilbert's satire of grand opera and contemporary musical theatre, ballad and song trends.

W.S. Gilbert and A. Sullivan

'When the Foeman Bares His Steel' from *The Pirates of Penzance*

The Pirates of Penzance (1879) is one of the best known of Gilbert and Sullivan operettas; others include *H.M.S. Pinafore* (1878), *The*

Mikado (1885) and *The Yeoman of the Guard* (1888). The word operetta means a short, light opera, generally with spoken words and is often interpreted as 'musical comedy'. Gilbert and Sullivan operettas are as successful today as they were in the nineteenth century. This is partly due to the staging of the works throughout the twentieth century by the D'Oyly Carte Company, and partly because they are accessible for amateur theatrical productions.

One of the key features of this chorus from *The Pirates of Penzance*, and indeed of all of Gilbert and Sullivan operas, is the marvellous setting of English words to attractive, catchy, music, to present a light-hearted musical work. The wit, musical dialogue and parodies are well worth studying. Sullivan's style is based very much on the comic opera style of Mozart. The musical score contains many features of comic opera – spoken dialogue, recitative, aria, duets, ensembles, choruses, often where contrasting lines create a polyphonic texture.

Music and words

The chorus 'When the Foeman Bares His Steel' includes a male chorus, chorus of girls, three female soloists and orchestra. Briefly, in this chorus the local police force has been sent for to march against the pirates. The girls urge on the somewhat timid police into combat, if necessary, to die for the glory of defeating the pirates, as they would then be heroes.

The opening introduction below, with its dotted rhythms and march-like, military character sets the scene for the entry of the police. The dialogue between the sergeant and the chorus of police is typical of Sullivan – balanced, diatonic phrases which integrate musical wit with that of the words. The humour is further emphasised

by the orchestral steady 4/4 very static harmonies, almost as if the police are still marching but on the spot.

The key of the chorus is C major and the harmonies are straightforward tonic and dominant 7th chords. The modulation at the point where the orchestra takes over the melody adds a frisson to the music. Notice the effectiveness of the simple device of the melody played by the orchestra while the chorus maintain the strong dotted rhythm singing on one note, a line of 'tarantaras'. Notice also the trumpet fanfare at the words 'trumpets martial sound'. All these features are characteristic of true comic opera.

An example of Sullivan imitating the aria syle of opera can be seen in the solo sections for one of the girls, the first phrasze of which is given below.

The melody line here is very elaborate, involving almost *coloratura* characteristics – coloratura translates as 'coloured' music and means the decoration of a melody by runs, cadenzas and other devices. Following immediately after the light 'tarantara' section, the contrast of this almost 'over the top' melody, combined with equally exaggerated words, creates the kind of humour that makes these operettas so popular. The music also works; the melody here is accompanied by triplet accompaniment figures which give the effect of a sense of urgency, while creating contrasts from the previous dotted rhythms.

The full chorus, a short extract of which is given below, is a good example of Sullivan's art of contrasting different musical lines within a contrapuntally conceived texture. Note here that the texture, part writing and characteristics of lines are similar to that of a quartet ensemble. The soprano lines continue the elaborate aria-like lines, the chorus of girls maintains the harmonies in the middle of the texture and the bass, singing the police marching theme supports the harmonic structure, played by the orchestra. The rhythm is a strong feature, combining triplets with dotted rhythms, through which Sullivan builds up the climax of the chorus. In the final passage we hear choral techniques again based on the Mozart ensemble style, making for a very exciting ending.

Listen to CD1, track 35.

'When the Foeman Bares His Steel' from The Pirates of Penzance
Gilbert and Sullivan

The lied

A vast number of songs were written in the Romantic period. This can be loosely classified into three principal kinds: ● the *lied* ● the French *romance* ● French *mélodie*. The lied is by far the most important and popular and one of the few genuinely new genres in the Romantic era. Early lied composers include Reichardt and Zumsteeg, the latter most influencing Schubert. Beethoven is claimed to be the creator of the Romantic lied, but it was Schubert's setting, particularly of the poems of the poet Goethe, that first embodied the poet, text, scene and song, which characterises the finest nineteenth century *lieder*. Other notable composers of the genre include Schumann, Mendelssohnn, Brahms and Hugo Wolf.

Piano music

The development of piano music in the Romantic era can be attributed to the spirit of the times and the emphasis on the individual. It was also due to the reshaped, mechanically improved and enlarged piano to full concert grand form. As a solo instrument, the piano was ideal for the times as it suited both the intimate drawing room and the large concert hall. The rise in demand for music from the mass public led to an expansion of the genre to produce a new form, the miniature or character piece. The sonata continued in a much longer form, and was also modified in a variety of ways, to suit the Romantic character and musical spirit.

Concerto

The concerto maintained its popular position in concert programmes throughout the nineteenth century, but underwent several changes: the double exposition was collapsed into a single exposition, the soloist often entering immediately instead of after the orchestral exposition. In order to avoid meaningless and distracting virtuosic display from soloists, composers wrote out their own cadenzas. Composers experimented with the concerto form, and particularly with ways of linking together the three movements. Liszt, for example, wrote his second piano concerto as a single movement using his technique of thematic transformation.

As the orchestral forces of symphonies expanded, so, too, did those of the concerto. In particular, the expanded technical capacity of the instruments and the demands from soloists for ever more challenging works led to composers writing increasingly difficult solo parts. Dazzling and brilliant soloists such as Paganini and Liszt attracted a public adulation that can be compared to some pop celebrities today.

The concertos composed in the nineteenth century are numerous. As well the works of composers such as Liszt, Brahms and Tchaikovsky, the virtuoso violin concertos of Viotti, Spohr, Bruch and others were also extremely popular. Although concertos were written mainly for piano and violin, composers also wrote them for other instruments, notably the cello with its new technical and expressive capacity. Schumann, Dvorak and Saint-Saens each wrote a concerto for this instrument.

Liszt
Piano Concerto No.1 in E♭

Stimulated by the amazing technique of Paganini and by the spectacle of his playing, Liszt was determined to achieve similar miracles with the piano. He therefore pushed the technique of the instrument to its furthest limits, both in his own playing and in his composition.

He was also, however, influenced by the lyrical melodic qualities of Chopin, his *rubato* playing style and harmonic innovations.

Liszt also created contrasting dialogues between piano and orchestra; as an intimate duet with first clarinet, then violin, then cello, showing the expressive warmth and the capacity of the piano for Romantic *cantabile* melodies; and later in combative mood, pitched against full orchestral forces.

Dvorak
Cello Concerto in B minor Op. 104

Although written during the last year of his second visit to America, Dvorak's *Cello Concerto in B minor* displays none of the 'New World' characteristics of his other works composed at this time. Instead it is full of characteristic Slavonic flavour. The first movement follows the general design of the Classical sonata-form concerto, with a long opening exposition for orchestra and a second exposition for the soloist's restatement of the main themes. What is remarkable about this concerto is the marvellous writing for the solo cello and the way that it is virtuosic – not as meaningless display but as a fully integrated part of the whole concerto.

Further work and listening

- Listen to the other movements from these two concertos by Liszt and Dvorak, noting the relationship between the soloist and orchestra
- Try composing a piece for your own instrument and small orchestra, bearing in mind the ways to achieve a successful balance.

Sacred music

An important characteristic of the Romantic movement was its interest in music of the past. Several composers, including Gounod, Liszt and Bruckner revived the sixteenth century form of the mass, but composed theirs in nineteenth century Romantic style, using full vocal and orchestral forces. Inspired by Handel, Mendelssohn composed his oratorio *Elijah* and based it on the Handel model of recitatives and arias, choruses and orchestra.

The requiem mass increased enormously in size. Requiem masses were written for special occasions, bearing no relation to church music. The requiem masses of Berlioz and Verdi are both magnificent, lengthy works which use large and powerful choral and orchestral forces. In contrast to these colossal dramatic works, Fauré's *Requiem*, which is also an important sacred work, is short, quiet, and contemplative, with subtle and complex harmonies characteristic of his style.

Further work and listening

- Listen to a symphony by a Classical composer and one by a 'conservative' Romantic composer such as Schubert, Schumann or Brahms. Comment on the differences between the two works.

- Listen to and study the structure of Liszt's symphonic poem *Les Préludes*. Why did Liszt 'invent' thematic transformation?

- Listen to some German *lieder*. Study the structure of the songs and the ways in which the vocal line and the piano accompaniment convey the meaning of the text.

- Make up two short programmes of Romantic piano pieces, one for the public concert hall and one for the salon, to illustrate the range of types of pieces and styles for the particular venues. What pieces would you include in each? How would you make the programmes interesting?

- Listen to a piece or programme music. How does the composer convey the emotion and meaning of the programme in the music?

- Listen to a part of the whole of an opera. Is it necessary to know the plot in detail to fully appreciate the opera, or is the music alone enough?

- Of the pieces that you have heard, which do you consider to be most characteristic of the Romantic style? Listen to your choices again and describe the features that led you to choose particular works.

- Try composing a piece in Romantic style. Consider the stylistic characteristics that you would include in your piece.

Breaking with tradition

Since the Baroque period, when the major/minor key system evolved out of Medieval and Renaissance modality, composers had used the relationship between keys – most notably the tonic and dominant keys – as the foundations for their musical structures. The major forms of the Baroque and Classical periods – the binary forms of the dance suite, ritornello, rondo and, most importantly of all, sonata form – were built on this tonic/dominant relationship.

Form and tonality

In the Romantic period, the sonata form and its related structures were still important and were used copiously by every major composer. However, other developments in Romantic music and artistic matters in general began to undermine the importance of tonality as a means of musical structure and expression. The Industrial Revolution had led to the development of wind and brass instruments that were capable of playing completely chromatic lines. The development of programme music and the preference of Romantic composers to write personal, expressive music meant that they used increasingly chromatic music with a wide range of dynamics and colourful instrumentation in their compositions. The operas of Wagner brought this Romantic movement to a height, and Wagner's work was a catalyst for many of the musical developments that were to take place in the early twentieth century. Wagner's musical language was continued and developed in different ways by the Austrian composers Hugo Wolf and Gustav Mahler, and the German composer Richard Strauss. Mahler and Strauss composed large, expansive orchestral works and took different but equally innovative approaches to orchestration. Mahler, in particular, is noted for his sparing and selective use of instrumental timbres and his work paved the way for the *Klangfarbenmelodie* style of Schoenberg, Berg and Webern that we will explore later.

A time of change

At a time when, following the rise of chromaticism in the late nineteenth century, composers were beginning to question the role of tonal structures in music, European society in general was also undergoing a period of immense unrest when old orders were being questioned and challenged. Movements that led to the outbreak of the World War I, the rise of Communism in Russia, and the overthrow of the monarchy and/or the aristocracy in a number of European countries meant that, in the early years of the century, Europe was a volatile region. In many ways, this was an ideal environment for the development of new, exciting ideas in the arts and it is not surprising that so many innovative movements in music, dance, drama, and the visual arts emerged at this time. Added to this was the development of recording technology which, as we shall also see with the development of popular musical styles, did much to spread and cross-fertilise these new ideas.

New methods of organisation

As tonality, as a means of musical structure, disintegrated, composers searched for a new way of building compositions. Some composers developed new scales and/or tonal relationships. Others moved the emphasis to other elements of music, such as rhythm. Some composers went back to the past to before the chromatic excesses of Romanticism and re-examined Classical structures, the use of modes, or folk music.

The study of twentieth century music should rightly start with three composers who studied and grew up with the Wagnerian chromatic style, but whose geographical roots – and consequential exposure to two traditions in the arts – led them to develop very different but equally influential schools of composition. Those composers are Debussy, Schoenberg and Stravinsky.

Impressionism

During the second half of the nineteenth century, a group of French artists – including Monet, Manet and Pissarro – developed a distinctive style of painting which became known as impressionist. In their work, the artists created images that set out to capture the mood and ambience of their subject or scene, rather than creating a hard, graphic illustration. Their painting techniques included using broad brush strokes, with washes of colours which merged together rather than abutted each other. For these artists, colour and light became more important than the defined form and shape of their subjects. Their aim was to depict the mood or 'impression' rather than giving a graphic illustration of what they saw.

Claude Debussy (1862–1918)

The French composer Claude Debussy was well versed in all the arts, including painting and literature, and he knew the works of the impressionist painters well. Studying in Paris and Rome in the 1870s and 1880s, he was well aware of the expressive, chromatic Wagnerian style. As his own personal compositional style developed, Debussy took this chromaticism and applied it to an approach to orchestral writing that has also been called 'impressionist' (although Debussy himself did not like that label for his music!).

The first, and best known of Debussy's orchestral works in the impressionist style is *Prelude á L'Aprés-Midi d'un Faune* which, rather than giving a graphic account of a series of events, paints an atmospheric picture of a warm, hazy, sleepy afternoon in a forest. In a similar vein are Debussy's orchestral works *La Mer* and the three *Nocturnes* (including one movement called *Nuages*). Debussy was also a prolific composer of piano music, including the *Images*.

Features of Debussy's style

In order to achieve his Impressionist musical style, Debussy used a number of compositional devices. These include:

- chromatic melodies, often moving by step, to give melodic lines a blurred image
- similarly, chromatic chords used to give a blurred or colourful effect
- added chords (9ths, 11ths, 13ths), often written in parallel movement
- subtle syncopations and use of complex rhythms and cross rhythms to blur the metrical line of the music
- sensitive exploitation of instrument timbres – either by selection of register (high/low strings, high/low woodwind, etc), by choice of playing techniques (tremolo strings, muted horns, etc.), or by use of exotic and/or delicate instrumental sounds (harp, celeste, antique (Chinese) cymbals). In some of his later work, Debussy explored exotic scales and timbres from other cultures, such as the Indonesian Gamelan
- use of non-diatonic scales to blur the sense of the tonic/dominant, and thus further obscure form and line in the music. Debussy also employed modes in place of major/minor scales in some of his compositions, and he sometimes used the textures of Medieval/Renaissance vocal music – that is, organum and polyphony. Debussy also used the whole-tone scale shown below.

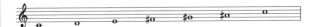

Note that the 'tonic' and the middle notes of the scale are a tritone apart, which is one reason why the whole-tone scale detracts from the sense of tonic/dominant in a piece of music.

Debussy's approach to composition was influential in the development of much twentieth century music and, as we shall see, a variety of composers took on elements of his style.

Atonality and serialism – Arnold Schoenberg (1874–1951)

The Austrian composer Arnold Schoenberg was born in 1874 and, although he did not study music on a formal, full-time basis, grew up at a time and in a place where Wagner's music would have been a great influence. Schoenberg's early work, such as the string sextet *Verklärte Nacht* (1899) and the orchestral tone-poem *Pelléas und Mélisande* (1903) is clearly rooted in the late Romantic programmatic, chromatic tradition. During the first decade of the new century, Schoenberg's works became increasingly chromatic to the point that the short (30 minute) music-drama piece *Erwartung* (1909) was completely atonal – that is, it had no sense of key whatsoever and, as such, was also completely unstructured. That the music-drama is written for a female singer who spends the entire half-hour on a guilt and angst-laden journey of anger through a forest searching for her missing lover, only to find his dead body at the very end of her journey, gives an indication of the musical torment and instability that is within Schoenberg's score.

Expressionism

This period of Schoenberg's compositional career is often referred to as his 'expressionist' period where, for the composer, the expression of emotion and state of mind was of complete importance over any form or structure in the music. 'Expressionist' was a term that was also applied to the visual arts, to the work of painters such as Kandinsky, Klee and Munch (whose painting *The Scream* is possibly the most well-known expressionist painting, with an obvious link to Schoenberg's *Erwartung*). Like Debussy, Schoenberg was extremely interested in the visual arts, and was himself an able painter.

The early work of Stravinsky (1882–1971)

At around the same time that Schoenberg was composing his expressionist works in Vienna, and Debussy his late-impressionist works in Paris, Igor Stravinsky was working in St Petersburg on the three great ballet scores of *The Firebird*, *Petrouchka* and *The Rite of Spring*. As Schoenberg's style was influenced by Wagner and expressionism, and Debussy's style grew from Wagner and impressionism,

Stravinsky's early style owed much to the great Russian composers that preceded him, especially Rimsky-Korsakov, and to Russian folk culture. His orchestral writing is, in many ways, an extension of Rimsky-Korsakov's work with large and colourful selections of instruments in all sections. It is also worth noting that in this early work, Stravinsky does not only write full-blooded orchestrations (we know that he admired Debussy's work), there are also moments of selective and delicate orchestration to be found. Like Debussy, he explored new combinations of instruments and unusual performance techniques.

Igor Stravinsky

Polyrhythm and polytonality

Like Schoenberg and Debussy, Stravinsky worked at a time when the long held dominance of the tonic/dominant structures in music was coming to an end. Stravinsky's response was to create an equally individual solution through a number of compositional techniques which, at face value, might seem rather primitive but which, in total, create some incredibly complex musical textures.

Rhythmically, Stravinsky took an extremely flexible approach to both metre and accent. Often, in his contrapuntal textures, a number of different metres and/or accented rhythms are playing at once – what is referred to as a 'polyrhythm'. Another favourite Stravinskian rhythmic (and melodic) device is the *ostinato*. Similarly, Stravinsky sometimes has two simultaneous keys playing – giving a jarring bitonal effect which is often added to through use of extremely dissonant harmonies. Add these to his off-beat, off-metre rhythms and the effect is electric.

Stravinsky (1882–1971)
The Rite of Spring

Listen to the two extracts from *The Rite of Spring* that can be found on CD1, tracks 45 and 46. The first, Extract A, comes from the very start of the work. The second, Extract B, is from the very end.

Texture and rhythm

- Clearly, the two extracts are at opposite extremes in terms of texture – the first is constructed from a number of individual lines, the second is homophonic. However, both are extremely flexible in their approach to rhythm. In the first extract, the note durations are extremely varied and precise, with the same melodic motif being presented in an ever-varying rhythm form.
- Look at the opening six-note bassoon phrase and then see how it is repeated with rhythmic variation in the next two bars. The metre of these opening bars changes constantly, and the phrase structure of the melodic line goes across the bar lines.
- In each instrumental line the rhythm

patterns and phrasing is different, giving a truly polyrhythmic effect to the whole orchestral sound.

- There are metre changes in the second extract, too, although here the changes are not so extensive. What makes the tempo jump about so much here is, again, the cross-bar phrasing and the fact that, whilst the texture is homophonic, there are a number of groups of instruments playing different blocks of rhythm against each other with parallel harmonies.
- Stravinsky places dynamic accents sometimes on, sometimes off 'the beat' to give the overall rhythm an extra kick. Stravinsky's use of silence should not be overlooked – in both extracts, the careful placing of general silences are very effective in terms of the overall rhythm and sound of the music.

Orchestration

- Together, the two extracts give a good representation of Stravinsky's approach to orchestration. The first extract shows his careful and subtle combination of instrumental timbres for colour – for example, the high, reedy bassoon solo, the dark cor anglais, and the piercing clarinet in D. The second extract shows Stravinsky using the full orchestra, together with his punchy rhythms, in a show of brute force.
- Note how both extracts are built around ostinato figures and how, when individual lines are taken unharmonised, how simple many of Stravinsky's melodic figures are. It is only when all of the elements are combined that the distinctive Stravinsky sound is heard.

Extract A

The Rite of Spring (Opening)
Stravinsky

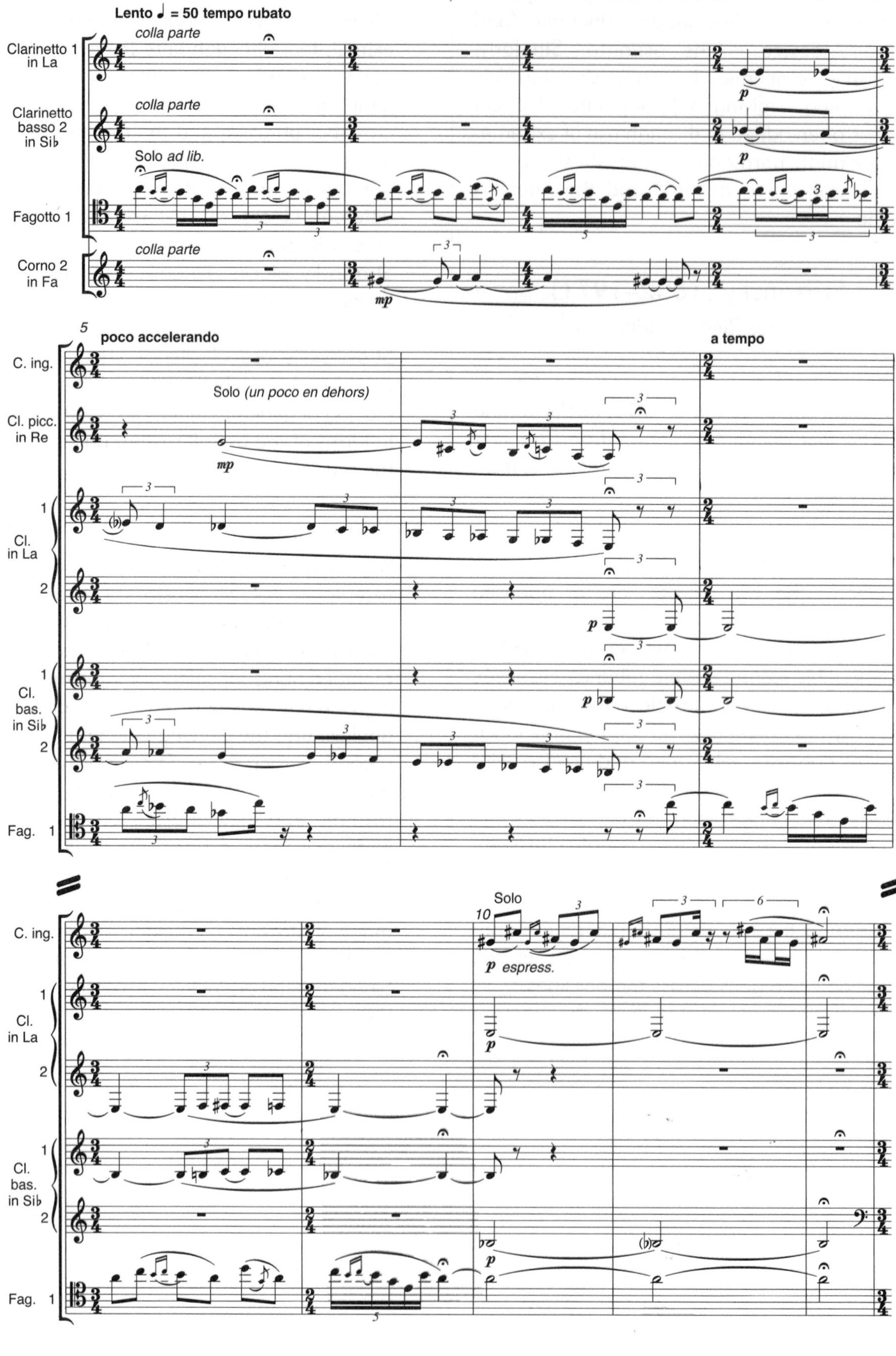

Extract B

The Rite of Spring (Ending)
Stravinsky

Inventing new languages, reinventing old ones

Schoenberg and serialism

Totally free expression, with no form or tonal boundaries was all well and good but the movement was clearly limited. As he worked through his expressionist period, Schoenberg realised that music needed a new means of defining form and structure which would also embrace the atonally chromatic musical language. The solution came in his serial composition techniques, which he first used in the *Five Pieces for Piano Op. 23*, the *Serenade Op. 24*, and the *Suite for Piano Op. 25*.

The principles of serial composition

In the chromatic spectrum, there are a total of twelve different pitches:

Schoenberg's theory of serial (or twelve tone) composition requires the composer to invent a series, or 'tone row'. The series is a melodic line that includes all twelve pitches in an order determined by the composer, but without repeating any of the pitches before the other eleven have been sounded.

For example, the series that Schoenberg used as the basis of the third of his Op. 48 songs is:

As you can see, each pitch in the semitonal spectrum has only been used once. This is called the 'prime' series.

Once the tone row has been formed, as shown above, it is then possible to derive three further variations of the series, namely:

The 'retrograde', which is simply the original row played backwards, starting with the last note and ending with the first. The retrograde of the Op. 48 No. 3 tone row is:

(Note that in serial music, enharmonic notation is frequently used – B♭ = A♯, etc. and that in the tone row or its variants notes can be transposed by an octave.)

The 'inversion', which is produced by reversing the direction of the intervals in the original tone row, so that an ascending minor 3rd becomes a descending minor 3rd, and so on. In the course of the twelve notes, each pitch is still only heard once. The inversion of the Op. 48 No. 3 tone row is:

Lastly, there is the 'retrograde inversion', which is the inversion played backwards! The retrograde inversion of the Op. 48 No. 3 tone row is:

So, the composer of serial music has four basic melodic lines to work with – the prime (P) version of the tone row, its inversion (I), its retrograde (R) and the retrograde inversion (RI). But he can go further – in the same way that tonal music can modulate to other keys, each version of the tone row can be played starting on each of the twelve notes of the chromatic spectrum. Thus, the original tone row, in its prime version starting on C♯.

can also be transposed to start on D. It is still the same tone row, with the same intervallic patterns; it is only the starting note that is different.

This version of the tone row is called 'prime 1' (P1), played one semitone higher than the original prime version of the tone row. Taking this process to its full conclusion, and applying it to the prime, retrograde, inversion and retrograde inversion of the tone row, you then have a possible forty-eight versions of the tone row to work with in a composition. In addition to the linear melodies created by these forty-eight rows, the composer is able to create chords from the tone row by combining adjacent notes to form chords – notes 1–4 of the row forming a chord, notes 5–8, and so on.

All of this might seem incredibly mathematical, but in reality the application of the *Twelve Tone Theory* by Schoenberg and his pupils Alban Berg and Anton Webern produced some haunting and extremely expressive music. Berg, in particular, took a lyrical approach to serial composition and many of his tone rows are constructed in a way that includes tonal triads. Schoenberg explored the *klangfarbenmelodie* technique, where individual notes of the tone row are assigned to different instrumental timbres, creating a kaleidoscope of sound (rather than the row being played in its entirety by one instrument).

The analysis of a movement from Schoenberg's *Piano Suite, Op. 25* that follows is intended to show the serial composition theory in musical practice.

Arnold Schoenberg (1874–1951)
'Trio' from Suite für Klavier Op. 25

Listen to the recording of this piece, which is on CD1, track 47.

About this piece

Schoenberg composed his *Piano Suite Op. 25* in 1924, and it was first published the following year. It is a noteworthy work for two reasons. Firstly, it is a good example of an early twentieth century composer using forms from the past to shape and structure his own, original compositions – what is known as 'neo-classicism' (see page 104) although Schoenberg is using the *Baroque* dance suite as his model! Secondly, and most significantly for the development of twentieth century musical styles, the suite is one of the first compositions in which Schoenberg employed the serial (twelve tone) approach to composition. The example used here is probably the most straightforward and easiest to understand of all Schoenberg's serial compositions and is thus an excellent starting point for your further study of serial music.

Form

The extract given here is the trio section from a longer minuet and trio movement. In the Baroque/Classical tradition, the movement runs in a 'minuet-trio-minuet' *da capo* form. Furthermore, both the minuet and trio are in the conventional binary form.

Melodic and harmonic construction

The trio is constructed using a tone row heard in the left-hand line of bars 1–2 :

As we shall see, Schoenberg stretches the intervals of the series to create a very characterful melody. However, with the series written down in close formation, as it is here, we can see that the tone row has been carefully constructed using a three-note step-wise motif (notes 1–3), the interval of a perfect 4th (notes 4–5 and 6–7), the interval of a tritone (notes 3–4 and 7–8), and two semitonal shifts (notes 9–10 and 11–12). So, in its basic form, the tone row has

its own distinctive character. When Schoenberg announces the series for the first time in the trio, he adds even more character by expanding or inverting some of the intervals and giving the row a quirky rhythm which is enhanced by carefully placed articulation and dynamics.

(If you are going to perform this piece yourself, you might think about how you get the crescendo through the first note that you have to play, leading in to the *sf* on the second beat!)

In the second bar, the right hand enters with an inverted, transposed version of the tone row:

Note that the inverted version of the tone row is transposed – rather than starting on the original note (E), it starts on B♭ – that is, six semitones up from E. If the original tone row is called the prime version (P0), then this new version is the inverted version starting six semitones higher than the original prime version (or I6). You will not have failed to notice that the interval between E and B♭ – the starting notes for these two versions of the tone row – is a tritone which, you will remember, is one of the key intervals within the original tone row.

Having finished playing the original tone row through once, in bar 3 the left hand plays the inverted version of the tone row, exactly imitating the line started by the right hand in bar 2. This time, however, this inversion starts on an F♭

(or, in other words, E), so the version of the tone row played by the left hand in bars 3 and 4 is the original prime inversion. Then, from bar 4, the right hand plays the prime version of the tone row, but this time starting on a B♭, or version P6.

All this in the space of four or five bars! Work through the first half of the trio, and annotate your score. Using coloured highlighters will help (provided this is your own, personal copy of the book!). Play through the piece, at an even speed – although this analysis may seem incredibly dry and mathematical, the piece really is very effective as a musical composition.

To clarify matters even more, here is a graphic illustration of those first five bars:

Bar	1	2	3	4	5
Right hand		Inverted version of tone row, starting six semitones higher on B♭ (I6)		Original version of tone row, starting six semitones higher on B♭ (P6)	
Left hand	Original version of tone row, starting on E (P0)		Inverted version of tone row, starting on F♭ (E) (I0)		(Repeat of bar 1)

'Trio' from Suite für Klavier Op. 25
Schoenberg

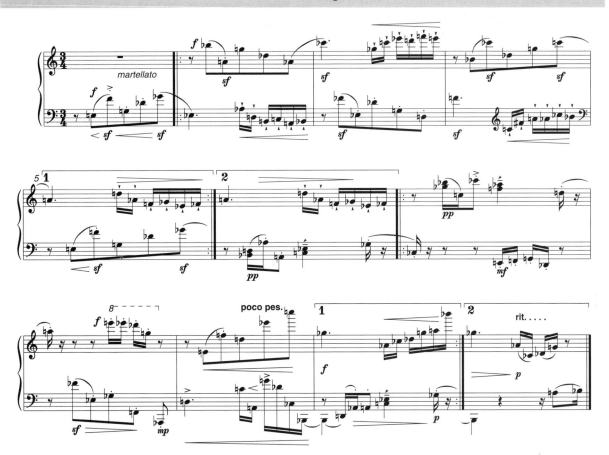

Further work and listening

- Look at the second half of Schoenberg's 'Trio'. You will notice that the texture thickens to include three part chords at some points. Using the tone row analysis that is given here for the first half of the piece as your model, make your own analysis of the second half of the trio.

- To increase your understanding of this piece, try performing it, or using it as a sequencing exercise. If you choose to use it as a sequenced arrangement, experiment with different timbres for the various entries/versions of the tone row. You could even try applying the principle of *Klangfarbenmelodie* by allocating individual notes from the tone row to different timbres.

- Refer back to and think about the way in which Baroque and Classical composers used binary form in their dance movements. In particular, consider the way that the binary form was structured using the polarities of the tonic and dominant keys. These keys are very closely related to each other. Schoenberg, too, has structured his binary form movement using two tonal 'centres' – but these two centres are a tritone apart. What does this say about Schoenberg's approach to tonality?

- Refer back to the analysis of Bach's G *minor Fugue*, and in particular consider the way in which Bach manipulated his thematic material. What similarities can you see between the compositional techniques of Bach and Schoenberg?

Neo-classicism

In many ways, the time of World War I was a turning point for Western art music. As we have seen, the old concepts of a tonic/dominant based tonality that had governed musical style and form for three hundred years had disintegrated. The social order of Europe was disintegrating, too, with monarchies being toppled and old orders of opulence and grandeur being dismantled.

In music, as in society, a new order was needed. Schoenberg's answer was in the development of the serial school of composition, which looked forward to a completely new way of organising musical sounds. Stravinsky and others, in contrast, looked to the past and developed a new compositional technique which became known as 'neo-classicism', where composers revisited forms and structures from previous eras – the Renaissance and Baroque, as well as the Classical period – and used them as frameworks onto which they grafted elements of twentieth century musical style.

Stravinsky's neo-classical period

Stravinsky is often cited as being the originator of the neo-classical movement. In truth, a number of composers began working in this style in the opening two decades of the century. As early as 1901, Debussy composed a sarabande for piano, using the form of the dance suite movement as a framework for his own, impressionist compositional style. In 1917 Stravinsky's young compatriot Prokofiev composed his classical symphony – see analysis below – but it was Stravinsky's ballet music for *Pulcinella* which really gave birth to the wider neo-classical movement.

Stravinsky's music for this new ballet – which, remember, came after the excesses of the three great orchestral ballet scores – was modelled on melodies thought to be by Pergolesi, who lived a short life between 1710 and 1736. The 'Pergolesi' melodies are certainly traceable in Stravinsky's score; the orchestra is small and chamber-like and much different from the gargantuan forces required for *The Rite of Spring*. However, all other aspects of the work are, without doubt, from the early twentieth century. The orchestration is full of carefully chosen effect and instrumental timbres, with solo double bass melodies, rasping trombone solos and challenging wind ensemble writing. Stravinsky's liking for rhythmic displacement and cross-phrasing is there too, as are bitonal moments and harmonic twists. This is certainly not pastiche composition or simply arrangement – this is the work of a twentieth century composer creatively using material from the past and fashioning it into something new and of the age.

Paul Hindemith (1895–1963)

Throughout the 1920s and 1930s, a number of composers used the music of the past as a framework for the musical language of the present, and it is interesting to note that some composers mirrored the national styles of the former periods in their neo-classical compositions. The German composer Hindemith – who was a music theorist and noted viola player, as well as a composer – wrote sonatas for almost every orchestral instrument and had a particular interest in the textural forms of the Baroque, including fugue. In England, Vaughan Williams looked back to the polyphony of the English church music composers such as William Byrd, as well as taking inspiration from aspects of English folk music.

Prokofiev (1891–1953)
Symphony No. 1, 3rd movement

A recording of this piece is on CD1, track 48.

About this piece

Prokofiev's *Symphony No. 1* was composed in 1917, about two years before Stravinsky composed *Pulcinella* and, as such, is an early and in some ways quite simple example of neo-classicism. In Prokofiev's own words, the symphony is written in a style that Haydn might have composed in had he been alive in the early twentieth century.

Form and structure

The form of the whole symphony is the standard Classical pattern of four movements. The movement shown here is the 3rd movement. However, unlike most of Mozart and Haydn's symphonic 3rd movements, it is not a minuet and trio – instead, the dance style chosen is a gavotte (which, perhaps, makes this style neo-Baroque). There is the usual 'trio' section, but again a baroque dance style is chosen – this time the musette. So, then, the form of this movement is gavotte–musette–gavotte (rather than minuet–trio–minuet).

Instrumentation

The orchestration is for the standard Classical orchestra – two of each woodwind, trumpets, horns, timpani and strings.

Melody, harmony and tonality

It is the melodic, harmonic and tonal techniques employed by Prokofiev that identify this extract as being from the early twentieth century, rather than from an earlier period. After the four-note anacrusis – a figuration that could have been taken straight out of Mozart operatic aria – the first four full bars of the piece present the following decidedly un-Classical features:

- the angular melody, containing three consecutive octave leaps – see the Violin I part
- the parallel 5ths in the flute parts
- The parallel modal harmonies in bars 1 and 2. With an harmonic rhythm of two harmonies per bar (on beats 1 and 3), the harmonies are D major – C major – B major. Interestingly, whilst this presents a downwardly shifting harmonic scheme, the way in which the chords are inverted presents an upwardly shifting bass line:

Chord of D in root position   Chord of C in first inversion   Chord of B in second inversion

- In bars 3 and 4 the melody suggests that, instead of the expected Baroque/Classical move to chord V or the dominant key at the double bar, we are to have a perfect cadence in the relative key of B. However, Prokofiev twists the cadence to give an unexpected interrupted cadence.

Another unexpected and more sophisticated tonal twist comes at the end of bar 10. The chord that we hear on the fourth crotchet of that bar seems to be chord V7 in D major and, indeed that is how the chord is written. However, with the enharmonic changing of the G into an F##, the chord becomes a German 6th chord (a version of IVb) in C# major. This enables a modulation to C# major, and the first chord of bar 11 is chord Ic in this new key.

V7 in D   IVb German in C#

It is only at the end of the gavotte that we get the definite (and rather ironic) perfect cadence back in D major.

The musette has the typical tonic/dominant drone that we associate with the Baroque dance. However, you will be able to hear the parallel modal harmonic shifts from the gavotte (albeit in the new key, G major).

Further work and listening

- Go back to the Baroque section of this book and re-examine *Les Moissonneurs* by Couperin. In what ways is it similar and in what ways is it different to this twentieth century gavotte?
- Compare and contrast Prokofiev's early neo-classicism with neo-classical works by Stravinsky and Hindemith.

Symphony No. 1, 3rd movement
Prokofiev

Politics and music in the soviet union

Prokofiev's *Symphony No. 1* was composed in 1917, around the time of the Bolshevik revolution in what is now the Soviet Union. The revolution brought with it significant implications for music. As with every aspect of life, the Soviet authorities had an official policy on the composition of music. This policy, together with the formation of the 'Association of Proletarian Musicians' led to significant restrictions being placed upon composers and performers. Fundamentally, the aim of the Soviets was to rid Russian music of what they considered to be the excessive, decadent influences of the West – in other words, the excessive chromaticism and atonality prevalent in European music at the time were inappropriate and not to be used. For the Soviets, music was to be for the people, which meant clearly defined forms, with clearly defined and accessible melodies and harmonies. Furthermore, any programmes used in musical works should reflect the magnificence and benevolence of the State, or the struggle of the Soviet people against oppression.

Dmitri Shostakovich (1906–1975)

For many composers, such a regime would have resulted in their writing bland, formulaic and conformist music. However, the greatest of the composers to emerge from the Soviet Union after the 1917 revolution, Dmitri Shostakovich, took on this challenge and produced music that, whilst being firmly rooted in the forms and conventions of the major/minor tonal system, uses often highly chromatic and sometimes dissonant harmonies, angular melodies with sudden modulations, and highly colourful orchestrations.

Nationalism and folk music

Jean Sibelius (1865–1957)

Not surprisingly in a half-century that saw two major world wars, many composers took an interest in protecting and promoting the culture and heritage of their homeland. For some composers, such as Jean Sibelius (Finland), this nationalism took the form of using national legends or themes to inspire programmatic orchestral works, by the choice of nationalistic poetry to set for songs, or by the arrangement of traditional folk melodies for voice with art music accompaniments. Sibelius' music is often described as reflecting the wide, open but sometimes rather dark landscapes of his homeland and, although this is not something that Sibelius purposefully set out to do, his orchestration techniques and extremely economical use of motifs over broad symphonic and orchestral canvasses do give that impression. The same could be said of English composers such as Elgar and Walton, whose orchestral music in particular seems to capture perfectly the pride, confidence and yet solid reserve of the English in the first half of the century.

This sometimes rather stirring form of nationalism, whilst producing some popular and enduring music, was firmly rooted in the traditions and styles of Romantic music and was not as innovative as other musical developments of the time. (Elgar's first symphony dates from within two years of Schoenberg's *Erwartung*!) However, in Eastern Europe and in England two groups of musicians took a rather different approach to their national musical heritage and used it to produce music that, whilst reflecting the past, was very much part of twentieth century innovation.

The early impact of technology

As Western art music and tonality had developed, from the Renaissance through to the Romantic periods, the folk music of Europe had been maintained through the oral tradition and through performance. However, at the start of the twentieth century, it became clear that many of these folk traditions were in danger of being marginalized or even extinguished. The Industrial Revolution, followed by technological innovations such as Edison's phonograph (1878) – which allowed for the mass reproduction of musical performances – meant that, in

113

cultural terms, the world was getting smaller. During the course of the twentieth century, this would lead to an incredible amount of cross-fertilisation of musical styles, as we shall see, but at the start of the century it seemed that the new technology and society could spell the end for some aspects of folk cultures.

Bela Bartók (1881–1945)

Aware of this change in society, the young composer Bela Bartók set out in the early years of the century to 'collect' folk songs and dances from the regions of his native Hungary and from neighbouring Romania. This he did with his colleague Kodaly, by transcribing and notating the music and (ironically) by recording some of the music on an Edison phonograph! Thus they were able to preserve the music of the past. What Bartók then did was to assimilate aspects of this folk music style into his own compositions. He did not merely arrange the tunes – he took essential elements of the music and manipulated them within his own unique twentieth century style, which was also influenced by his studies and knowledge of, amongst others, Debussy.

Bela Bartók

The characteristics of Eastern European folk music

Before looking at a work by Bartók, it is worth highlighting the key characteristics of Eastern European folk music, as found by Bartók and Kodaly in Hungary and Romania. These include:

- rhythms with strongly accented dactylic patterns – that is, long–short–short (or crotchet–quaver–quaver). Interestingly, this matches naturally occurring patterns in the Hungarian language, where every word is stressed on the first syllable.
- the frequent use of the scotch-snap rhythm
- the use of drones and pedal basses, often in 4ths or 5ths, and the use of rhythmic and melodic ostinato patterns
- melodies constructed from a variety of modes, including the extreme Lochrian mode (B–B). Pentatonic melodies are common too – not just using the most familiar pentatonic scale (C–D–E–G–A), but different pentatonic scales constructed from various combinations of intervals
- cross phrasing and a flexible approach to metre
- a variety of instrumental timbres including the fiddle (often played with double stopping), and the dulcimer or cembalon.

Folk music from Hungary

Listen to the two short extracts of Hungarian folk music on CD2, track 1, and trace the musical features outlined above as you listen. The instrumental piece is called *Rózsa Sándor szereti a táncot*, and the song is entitled *Párhuzam*.

Bartók (1881–1945)
Dance Suite

A recording of this piece is on CD2, track 2.

About this piece

Bartók composed his orchestral *Dance Suite* in 1923 (just a year before Schoenberg's *Piano*

Suite!) The suite is in six movements; the extract featured here is from the end of the 1st movement and the beginning of the 2nd movement.

Follow through the score as you listen and look for the following devices that Bartók has taken from the style of Hungarian folk music:,

Violin melody at bar 6–23 :	*Melody in the transposed Aeolian mode*
Celli, violas and horns in bars 6–25 :	*Pedal notes*
Clarinet in bar 23 :	*Scotch-snap rhythm*
Strings from bar 26 :	*Dactylic rhythms*
Strings from bar 26 :	*Ostinato figuration*
Woodwind from bar 28 :	*Cross rhythms*
Whole orchestra from bar 40 onwards :	*Changes of metre*

Further work and listening

- We have seen the influence of Hungarian folk music styles on Bartók's music. Which aspects of the music identify him as being a twentieth century composer?

- Compare and contrast the musical styles shown by the works by Schoenberg, Prokofiev, Debussy, Stravinsky and Bartók featured in this book. How are the five styles different? Do the styles have anything in common?

Dance Suite
Bartók

A new direction

Before 1945, Western art music had seen the development of a number of diverse schools and styles of composition, generally (but not exclusively) centred around individual composers, geographical areas, or both – impressionism, serialism, neo-classicism, nationalism, and works influenced by folk music were distinct compositional styles. Developments after 1945 were to see a new generation of composers take elements from all these traditions, from the popular and art music styles that had developed in America during the first half of the century, and from the rapidly developing possibilities of electronic music, blending them into their own unique and diverse musical styles.

Anton Webern (1883-1943) – pointing the way

The serial compositional technique developed by Schoenberg in Vienna was used and developed further by his great pupils and disciples Alban Berg and Anton Webern, who brought new perspectives to twelve tone music. Berg took a more lyrical approach to the style, whilst Webern extended and concentrated the *Klangfarbenmelodie* techniques of Schoenberg to produce highly economic, pithy compositions that are often described as pointillist in style. After Webern's death in 1945, other composers continued the serial tradition, including Stravinsky in his third period of compositional style.

Webern's approach to constructing tone rows was somewhat different to Berg. Whereas Berg preferred a lyrical, melodic style of composition, Webern's tone rows and his textures are characterised by a strident, angular style. Webern was also interested in the possibilities of symmetrical relationships within the tone row, as we shall see. It is these aspects of Webern's style that were to have an enormous influence on the style and direction of music composed post-1945.

Anton Webern

Webern (1883–1945)
Symphony Op. 21

A recording of this piece is on CD2, track 3.

About this piece

Webern's *Symphony Op. 21* dates from 1928, and is generally recognised as being the first of his 'final period' works. This extract is from the start of the 1st movement of the symphony.

Orchestration

Webern's *Symphony Op. 21* is scored for clarinet, bass clarinet, two horns, two harps, violins, violas and cellos.

Tone row organisation

This movement is built on the following tone row:

On close inspection, we can see that the row is constructed in a four dimensional symmetrical pattern.

- Firstly, the interval between the 1st and 12th, 2nd and 11th, etc. notes of the row is always a tritone;

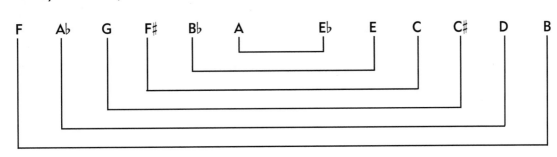

- Secondly, there is a symmetrical pattern of semitones within the tone row:

- Thirdly, the second half of the tone row (notes 7–12) is the retrograde of the first half (notes 1–6), transposed by a tritone;

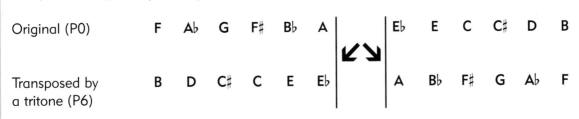

In other words, versions P0 (the original version of the tone row) and R6 (the retrograde of the original tone row, transposed by a tritone) are one and the same – they are palindromic.

- The fourth symmetrical aspect of the tone row can be seen when placing version P0 (the original tone row) next to version I9 (the inverted version of the tone row transposed up nine semitones):

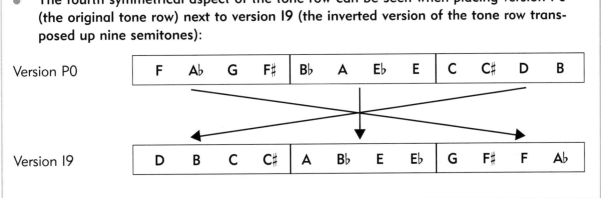

A complex texture

This gives you some idea of the complex detail that Webern undertook in his compositional process. Now, study the score of bars 1–24 of this 1st movement and trace these various versions of the tone row through the music. Start with the harp in bar 2 and follow version P0 through the strings. You will notice that, in the spirit of *klangfarbenmelodie*, the notes of the tone row are tossed between instruments.

You will also notice that there are two canons taking place – between the two French horns and the clarinet/bass clarinet. The canons are not simple, of course, but involve transposed and inverted versions of the original tone row.

Further work and listening

- Compare and contrast the texture and approach to serial composition of this movement and the extract from Schoenberg's *Piano Suite*, analysed on pages 101–2.
- The movement from which this extract is taken is in sonata form. What are the similarities and differences between Webern's definition of sonata form – as demonstrated here – and the sonata form of the Classical Viennese composers such as Mozart and Haydn?
- Webern uses a Classical form (sonata form) to structure this work, and Schoenberg's Op. 25 suite uses Baroque dance forms, but neither work is truly neo-classical. Why not?

Symphony Op. 21
Webern

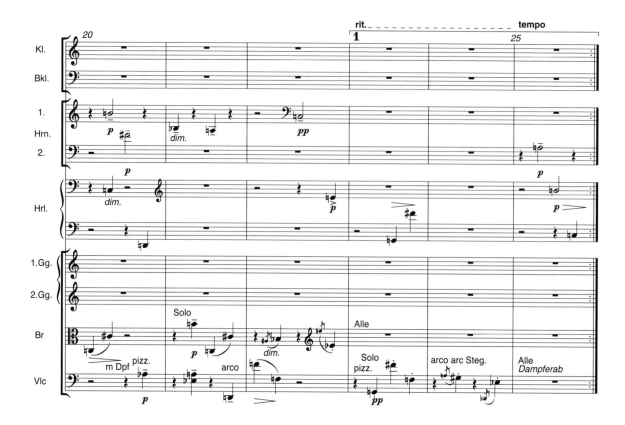

Oliver Messiaen (1908–92)

The French composer Oliver Messiaen's musical language is derived from a number of varied sources, including Greek metrical rhythms, Hindu traditional music, the serialism of Schoenberg, the impressionist language of Debussy, and birdsong. In the same way that Bartók travelled around Hungary 'collecting' folk music, Messiaen visited all of the French provinces, noting down and recording different birdsongs. Messiaen's work and life deeply influenced by the spirit of Catholicism, in which he had a deep belief, and his view that birds, as God's creatures, carry a divine message, played heavily on his work.

Following on from his interest in Schoenberg's serial techniques, Messiaen developed his own 'mode de valeurs et d'intensities', where not only pitch but dynamics, rhythm and articulation were subject to cyclic organisation. Messiaen first used this technique in his 1949 piano piece of the same name.

Boulez (b. 1925) and Stockhausen (b. 1928)

Messiaen's two greatest pupils, Pierre Boulez and Karlheinz Stockhausen, took influences from all these post-Schoenberg composers as they developed their own compositional style.

Interestingly, Boulez – who was born three years before Stockhausen – was a mathematics student before he started serious musical study. Since 1945, Boulez has been prolific as both composer and conductor in Europe and America. He has held principle conductor positions with the BBC Symphony and New York Philharmonic Orchestras, amongst others.

Like all composers, Boulez's style follows from those who went before him. There are four main musical influences on Boulez's methods of composition:

Schoenberg	The serial (twelve tone) method of composition
Webern	The pointillist, angular approach to musical texture

Messiaen	The 'mode de valeurs et d'intensities', an early form of total serialism
Debussy	The impressionist style, particularly with regard to colour and rhythm.

Like all great composers, Boulez's achievement is that he took on these musical influences and moulded them into his own, unique compositional style that took all of the techniques even further.

Pierre Boulez

Total serialism

Taking his lead from Messiaen, Boulez developed a system where the tone row principle of serialism was applied to duration, tone colour (timbre), dynamics and tempo as well as to pitch. What this means, of course, is that nothing is left to chance, every single musical event is pre-determined. Added to this, Boulez – as a conductor – writes meticulous instructions for his performers, meaning that the composer has complete, rigorous control over both the score and the performance.

Boulez (b. 1925)
Structures

About this piece

Boulez composed two sets of Structures for piano duet – the first in 1951–2, and the second between 1956 and 1961. This piece is an example of Boulez's experiments in total serialism.

Serial organisation

In this work, Boulez employs the following serial techniques:

Pitch	The standard twelve note tone row technique is used
Duration	A twelve-duration row is used, featuring 12 values from a demisemiquaver to a dotted crotchet
Dynamic	A twelve-dynamic row is used, featuring twelve values from *pppp* to *ffff*
Articulation	A ten-articulation row is used, featuring ten values from *staccatisimo* to *legato*

Style

Even in this short extract, you will be able to see the complexity and precision that this style of composition causes. You should also be able to see and hear the influence of Webern's pointillist style of composition.

Further work and listening

- How desirable do you consider it to be for the composer to have total control over every aspect of the music, including the performance? If the composer is to have this total control, then is there any purpose in giving live performances of the music?
- Listen to other compositions by Boulez from the 1950's, such as *Le Marteau Sans Maitre*.

Structures
Boulez

More new directions

With Boulez and Stockhausen having worked through 'total' serialist composition techniques (embracing absolute organisational control over pitch, duration, dynamics, timbre and texture) it might have been difficult to see the future direction of art music. In addition, one could have taken the view that composers were now taking so much control over performers – through their meticulously written scores – that the central and musically essential role of performance interpretation had been sacrificed in the cause of control and accuracy. Western art music had reached an impasse. In the second half of the twentieth century, composers were to explore a number of different paths, including aleatoric or indeterminate music, electronic music, minimalism, and music that parodied and integrated music from the past.

Electronic music

The development of the magnetic tape recorder in the 1940s was the catalyst for the birth of the *Musique Concrete* movement. Before then, the use of electronic sound sources in art music had been limited as the time and labour involved in

setting up and then playing electronic instruments was considerable – and then those instruments were only capable of playing very limited timbres, albeit quite effectively. Magnetic tape made it possible for composers to record, multi-layer, process, reverse and generally be creative with electronic sound sources. Furthermore, in the isolation of the studio, they could work in their own time without the need for performers.

Before long electronic composition studios were established in Europe, by Pierre Schaeffer and Pierre Henry at Radio France in Paris (where both Boulez and Stockhausen came into contact with electronic music) and by Herbert Eimert at North-West German Radio in Cologne.

Working in the Cologne studio in the 1950s, Stockhausen developed, first, techniques in *Musique Concrete*, where all of the music was recorded, processed and performed electronically, and, later, works which brought together pre-recorded electronic elements with lines that were to be performed live, by instrumentalists or singers.

Stockhausen (b. 1928)

Kontakte

Listen to the extract which is on CD2, track 4.

About this piece

Kontakte was composed from 1958–1960. It is composed for electronic tape, which is manifest through four channels played through four loudspeakers – managed in performance by a 'sound-projectionist' – and piano/percussion parts for two live performers. (Clearly, this is a work to be heard 'live', since the spatial separation of the four electronic channels is an essential part of the piece. Our recording is in stereo!)

The meaning of *Kontakte*

The 'contact' in this work is between pre-recorded electronic sounds and live acoustic sounds. Stockhausen chose percussion instruments because, like electronic sound sources, they can produce both determinate pitches and untuned 'noise' better than any other instrument family, and they also have a great range of tone-colours.

Form

Kontakte is in what Stockhausen calls 'moment' form. You will see from the score that the music is divided not into bars, but into 'moments' and 'events' of specific duration. For example, the section between 1B and 1C takes place from 15.7 seconds to 39.3 seconds into the piece. This is one 'event' in the first 'moment' of the piece, which lasts from the start of section 1A to the start of section 2A (or the beginning until 2 minutes and 10 seconds into the piece).

Notation

As you can see from the score, Stockhausen uses a combination of graphic and conventional stave notations. With electronic music, there is so much information that can be recorded in a score and commentary. In addition to the 'event' notation that Stockhausen provides in the score, he also gives 63 pages of commentary about the electronic settings and compositional procedures. If you are planning to submit an electronic composition for your AS or A level coursework, take note!

Further work and listening

- Stravinsky famously once said 'what interests me most about electronic music is the notation, the score'. Do you agree with Stravinsky? When you studied the extract from *Kontakte* were you more interested in the score or by what you heard? When making an assessment of the effectiveness and quality of an electronic musical composition, should we assess the sound or the score?
- What is the purpose of a written score? Has that purpose changed in the course of music history between 1500 and 2000?
- If music is a language, what message is *Kontakte* conveying?

Kontakte
Stockhausen

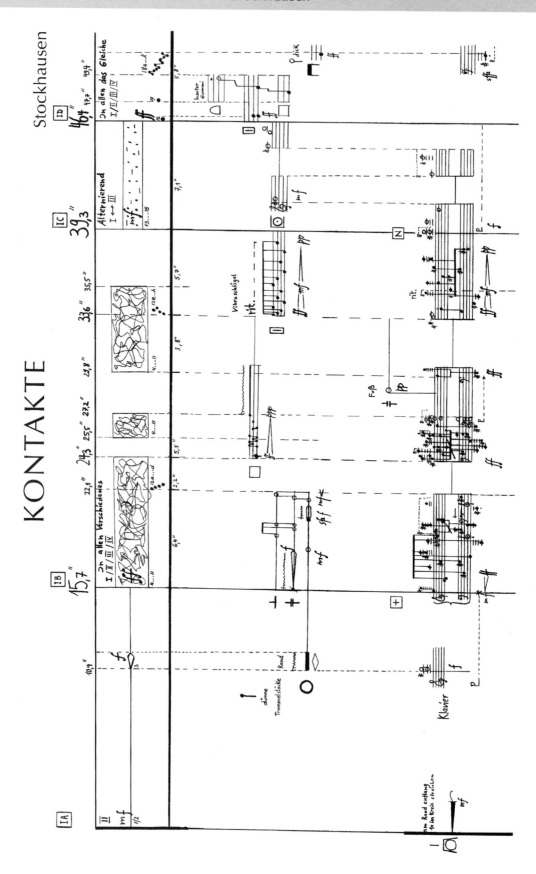

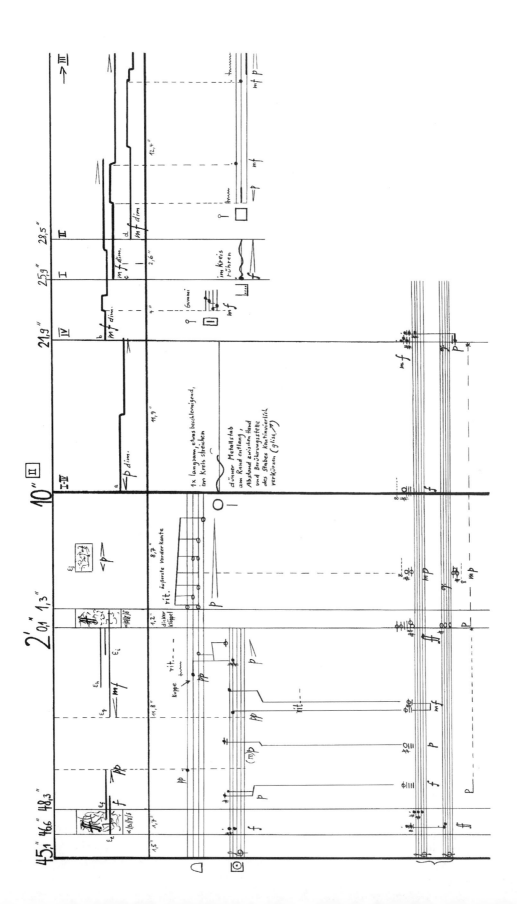

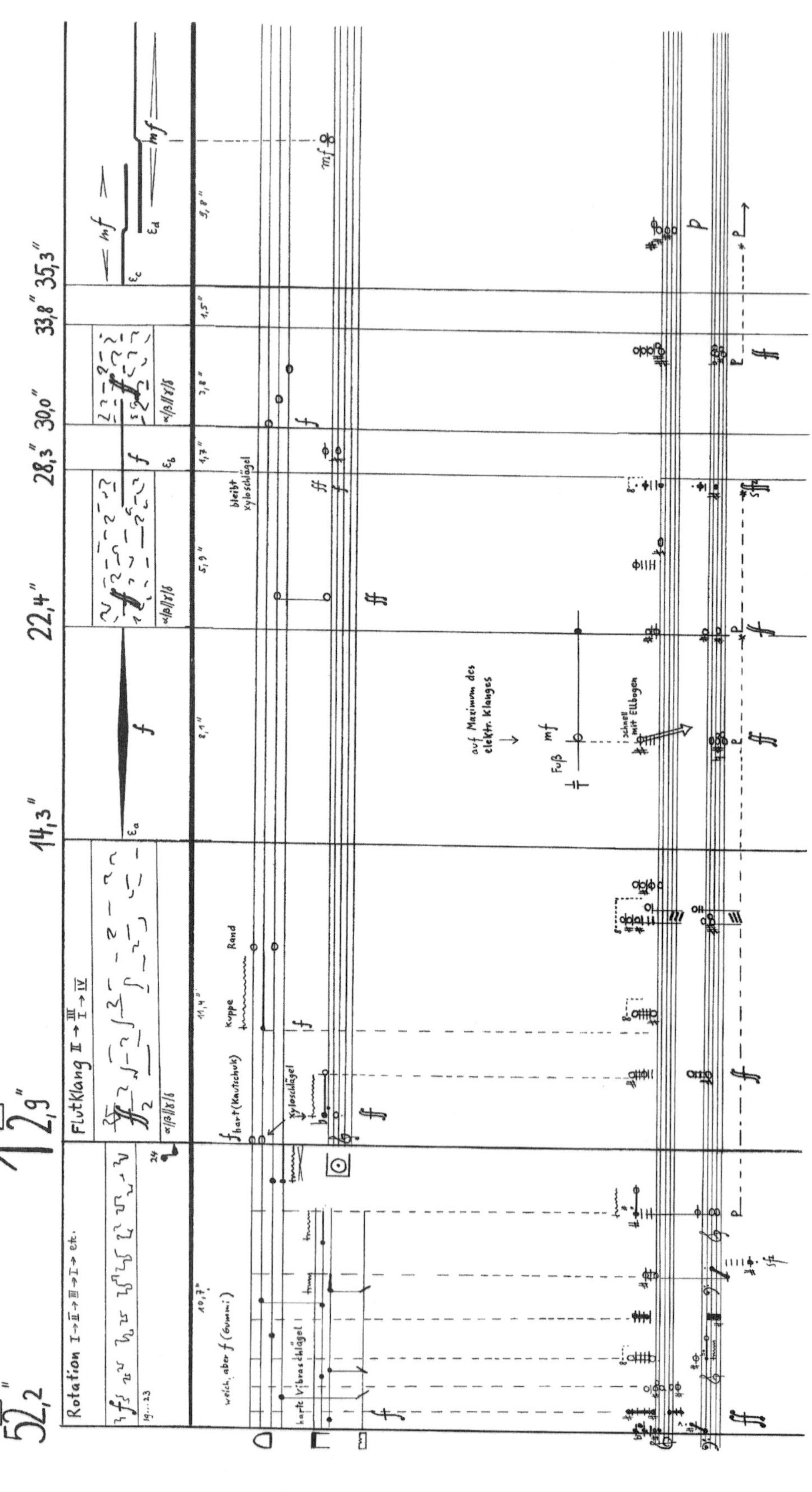
IE
52,2"
IF
1'2,9"
14,3"
22,4"
28,3"
30,0"
33,8"
35,3"
Rotation I→II→III→I→ etc.
Flutklang
weich, aber f (Gummi)
harte Vibraschlägel
hart (Kautschuk)
Xyloschlägel
Kuppe
Rand
bleibt Xyloschlägel
auf Maximum des elektr. Klanges
Fuß
schnell mit Ellbogen

Aleatoricism and the absurd

The antithesis of total serial music – aleatorical or 'chance' music, where outcomes are not pre-determined by the composer but, rather, are dependent on choices made by the performer or by the unique circumstances of each performance – was one route explored by some composers in the United States and Europe.

Famous for 'four minutes and thirty-three seconds'

One of the first composers to work in this aleatoric or indeterminate style was the American John Cage. His most famous work is 4'33" (1952), a composition for piano in three movements. The score for the three movements is basically:

I

T a c e t

II

T a c e t

III

T a c e t

The whole point of 4'33" is that the performance is a reverse of normal convention – the performer is the audience and the audience is the performer. What the audience does during the performance is entirely a matter of chance and, even if the audience remains absolutely silent during all three movements, there will always be some sound – the hum of the lights, passing traffic, etc. Why not try a performance of 4'33" in assembly – having first talked it through with your headteacher or head of year, of course!

4'33" is reactionary – the title alone, giving an absolutely precise requirement for the duration of the performance, is a sardonic comment which may have been directed at the total serialists. It is absurdist, too, in the same way that Samuel Beckett's play Waiting for Godot (1953) comments on the absurdity of life and the human condition.

The prepared piano

Another of Cage's experimentations was with the prepared piano, where he aimed to extend the timbral range of the piano by inserting various objects between the strings, attaching them to the hammers, or requiring the pianist to climb inside the piano and strike or pluck the keys in unconventional ways. Works of this kind include Amores I which is for piano prepared with nine screws, two nuts and three strips of rubber inserted between particular strings. You are advised not to try this at home!

Stockhausen experimented with aleatoric techniques, too. His Klavierstück XI (1956) is made up of nineteen small fragments of music written on a single sheet of paper, in no particular order. The performer may choose to play the fragments in any order. Dynamic and tempo markings are given at the end of each fragment; these markings tell the performer how the next fragment should be played. The piece is brought to an end when a fragment has been played for a third time; it does not matter if some fragments have not been played at all.

Stockhausen suggested that Klavierstück XI should be played at least twice during a concert programme (presumably, to make the point that it is an aleatoric work).

Performance and technique

The response of Luciano Berio – who himself also composed 'totally' serial and electronic music, founding the Milan electronic music studio with Bruno Maderna in 1955 – was in his series of ten sequenzas for solo, unaccompanied instruments (including voice), composed between 1958 and 1985. In the sequenzas, Berio set out to compose pieces that would stretch performers' techniques to the extreme – as, indeed, composers have done throughout every musical era. He also wanted to do what, for solo woodwind and brass instruments, appears the impossible; to compose solo, unaccompanied music that wasn't limited by monophony – in other words, write a form of polyphonic music for these solo instruments to play.

Gesture

Another interest of Berio, when composing the sequenzas, was *gesture* – that is, the dramatic impact of a musical performance in both the way the performance looks and sounds. In fact, dramatic gesture is a common thread that runs through most of Berio's works, including *Circles*, a setting of texts by e.e.cummings, and *Recital*, a piece of music theatre which tells the story of a concert singer going through a mental breakdown.

Berio (b. 1925)
Sequenza I for Solo Flute

Listen to the extract from this piece which is on CD2, track 5.

About this piece

This is the first of Berio's ten sequenzas, and was composed in 1958. Other sequenzas in the series include works for female voice (III), viola (VI) and clarinet (IX).

The organisation of the flute sequenza is based on three levels of density (high/medium/low), applied to four dimensions (tempo, dynamic, pitch and morphology – i.e. the way the flute produces sounds). At any one time at least two of these dimensions are at their maximum level. Silence is also used by Berio as an important structural and expressive device.

The score

One glance at the score of this extract – which is the end of the piece – will tell you that, like Stockhausen in *Kontakte*, Berio has used a seemingly unconventional approach to notation.

Firstly, there is no clef, either at the start of the piece or on any of the staves. One assumes that, being the flute (with a natural register extending no lower than middle C) that the clef is going to be the treble clef. (Interestingly, the practice of not writing a clef is that of popular music styles where 'lead sheet' notation has a clef on the first stave only, if at all, on the same presumption that if a part is headed up 'clarinet', it will be in treble clef.)

There is no time signature, nor are there any bar lines. However, Berio does give clear guidelines about tempo and duration in his preface to *Sequenza I*. He suggests that:

- notes that are grouped together ♩♩ should be given the same duration
- the notes written in small-head notation should be played as quickly as possible
- notes with the pause mark above them ⌐⌐ may be held as long as desired by the performer
- tempo changes are marked by the sign **60 M.M.** , which appears above two marks on the stave. This indicates that sixty of these sections should be played in one minute – i.e. each section between the marks | | lasts for one second. Look closely at the score and you will see these marks in the place of bar lines. This technique is called **proportional notation**. The duration of notes that stand independently ♪ are determined by the articulation mark given (or not) to that note, by the number of those notes within the section and by the speed of the section. It therefore follows that in terms of duration, not all quavers are equal, and that consequently there is no maintenance of pulse throughout the piece.

Flute techniques

There are a number of demanding flute performance techniques demanded by Berio in this piece. They are demanding in themselves and because they are required in quick succession. The techniques include:

- flutter-tonguing and normal tongued/slurred notes intermingled
- angular melodic lines across the high and low registers of the flute
- wide-ranging dynamics in all registers, with rapid changes of dynamic
- Harmonics (indicated by the sign ° above the note)

- a continuous trill played percussively and *crescendo* on the keys whilst the blown tone fades away (*con le chiavi – on the keys*)
- single percussive notes on the keys (indicated by the sign $^+$ above or below the note)
- rapidly repeated double-tongued notes (indicated by the sign `····` above the note.

Further work and listening

- How would you go about learning this music? How important would it be for you to undertake technical studies and exercises? How would you annotate your score to help you in your performance?

- How successful do you think Berio is in creating moments of 'non-monophonic' music for solo flute?
- Listen to unaccompanied flute pieces by earlier twentieth century composers, such as Debussy's *Syrinx* and Varese's *Density 21.5*. Compare and contrast the way in which these earlier composers and Berio write for the flute.
- Compare and contrast this piece by Berio with the totally serial, totally controlled compositional style of Boulez as shown in *Structures*. Which style is easiest to perform?

Sequenza I for Solo Flute
Berio

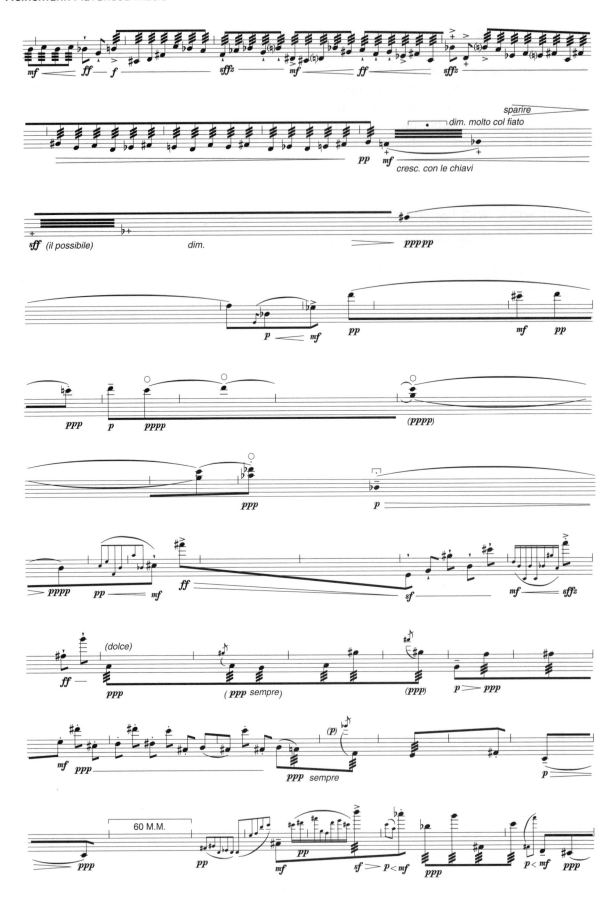

Minimalism

In many ways, minimalism is a compositional style that has brought together not only a number of post-war art music movements, but also the worlds of art, popular and world musics. The idea of systematic repetition and organisation was fundamental to the serial composers, tape loop and multi-tracking techniques that were developed in the electronic music studios and the riff-based textures of popular and jazz styles all have echoes in minimalist music. Non-western musical styles that are also built on repetitive techniques, such as the Indonesian Gamelan and West African drumming, draw a parallel with minimalism too.

The first two recognised minimalist composers are the Americans La Monte Young and Terry Riley, both born in 1935. Young studied for a while with Stockhausen, and some of his early works have a Cage-ian absurdity to them. An early piece has the performance instruction 'draw a straight line and follow it'. In his minimalist compositions, Young based much of his music around drones and plainsong-like chants, with the music taking a static approach to repetition. This approach has also been taken by the Estonian composer Arvo Pärt.

In contrast, the minimalist works of Terry Riley take a constantly evolving approach, where a short motif is constantly repeated with, occasionally, a small change being applied to the motif or the musical texture to bring about development in the music. Steve Reich (b.1936) who, with Philip Glass (b.1937) did much to establish the reputation and commercial success of the Minimalist school of composers described this technique as 'gradual changes in time'.

Terry Riley
In C

About this piece

In C is one of the first minimalist compositions to gain widespread recognition and, in many ways, it is the work that defined the minimalist style.

Performance instructions

In C is notated on a single sheet of score, as fifty-three short cells to be repeated as required/desired by the performers but played consecutively – i.e. each performer must start with the first cell, then move on to the second, and so on. All of the cells are written at pitch, so any instruments not in C must transpose their music. It is acceptable to play the cells up an octave, although Riley discourages playing down an octave unless this is done by several performers. Concerning dynamics, Terry Riley asks for all 'exits and entries' to be as inconspicuous as possible.

The decision to move from one figure to the next is up to the individual musician, though the players are advised to stay within four or five cells of each other. It ends when all the players have reached and abandoned cell 53. To synchronize the performers, Riley asks that a pulse is kept on the two top C's of the piano repeated in quavers for the entire duration of the performance. The composer suggests that this simple pulse 'is traditionally played by a beautiful girl'. We leave it to today's generation of performers to decide whether this particular instruction is either appropriate or necessary to the success of the performance!

In C is designed to be played in all manner of venues and with all sorts of performers, amateur or professional. Any instrumentalists can participate, and it is acceptable for any instrument to be amplified if necessary and appropriate. Riley suggests that the performers sit as close to each other as possible, in the round, with the 'pulse player' sitting in the middle.

We encourage you to try – although you should bear in mind Terry Riley's comment, in his introduction to the work, that if the figures are repeated often enough a performance could last for a day, a month, or a year – perhaps with a cell for each week of the year so that a performer would start playing on the first week of one year and finish on the first week of the next year. That's an entire AS or A2 music course!

In C
Terry Riley

British music post-1945

With the exception of Henry Purcell, Sir Arthur Sullivan and a handful of Renaissance composers, almost all of the pre-1900 'art' music we have examined is by non-British composers. This is not to suggest that there were no British composers of note or importance in the Classical or Romantic periods.

However, it is true to say that the twentieth century saw a remarkable renaissance in British composition – not just the art of composition, but also in the moulding of a cosmopolitan but distinctly British school of composers.

We have already discussed the contribution to the national style of Vaughan Williams and Elgar. William Walton – who made a rapid rise to fame in his early 20s – in many ways took on Elgar's mantle as **the** national composer, writing symphonies and concertos, the magnificent oratorio *Belshazzer's Feast*, as well as a large amount of film music and music for great national ceremonial occasions.

Benjamin Britten (1913–76)

The most important twentieth century British composer is considered by many people to be Benjamin Britten. Like so many great musicians, Britten was equally active and adept as a composer, performer and conductor. Like Purcell before him, Britten had a great gift for word setting and, in particular, for capturing the nuance, expression and accent of English texts through his settings in operatic works such as *Peter Grimes* and *Billy Budd*, his arrangements of British folk songs and his church music.

In a similar vein to Purcell, Britten is a master word-painter – not just the literal meaning of the words that he sets, but the general mood and emotion of the text as a whole. Important to this aspect of his compositional style is Britten's own moods, personality and beliefs. He was a committed Christian and pacifist, and he was openly homosexual. These elements, together with the moral and political atmosphere of the times, created particular tensions and sufferings in Britten's life and works.

Michael Tippett (b. 1905)

Although older than both Walton and Britten, Tippett's development as a composer took much longer. Like Britten, Tippett was also a pacifist and one of his best-known works, *A Child of our Time* is overtly anti-war and integrates the music of American spirituals into the score. Tippett also composed operas with English texts – writing his own libretti – together with song cycles, choral and symphonic music.

British music today

Peter Maxwell Davies and Harrison Birtwistle were both born in 1934 and studied together at what is now the Royal Northern College of Music in Manchester and form (with Alexander Goehr, born in 1932) what is known as the 'Manchester School' of composers. Maxwell Davies and Birtwistle are very different in style and approach, but equally important in their influence. Peter Maxwell Davies is somewhat of an eclectic composer, and has integrated references to music from the Renaissance through to modern pop and jazz styles in his music. Throughout his composing career, Birtwistle has been fascinated by time, pulse, and formal organisation in works such as *Refrains and Choruses*, *Verses*, *Meridian* and *Ring a Dumb Carillon*. Both composers have written extensively for music-theatre, their best known works in this genre being *Eight Songs For A Mad King* (Maxwell Davies) and *Punch and Judy* (Birtwistle).

The younger generation of British composers includes the Scot James MacMillan – whose eclecticism is very much in the tradition of Maxwell Davies; George Benjamin – whose influences include Messiaen and Boulez, both of whom he studied under; and Thomas Ades.

Integration, parody and fusion

In the first two decades of the twentieth century, some composers looked back to the musical styles of the past as a way of finding a way forward from the excessive chromaticism and atonality of the day. As well as the overtly neo-classical composers, atonalists and serialists such as Berg (most famously in his *Violin Concerto*) quoted from music of the past. At the end of the twentieth century, some composers once again turned to music of the past as the avant-garde and experimental schools of composition threatened to isolate contemporary art music from its past and traditions.

Some composers, such as Luciano Berio – who, like Bach before him, and his contemporary, Stockhausen, has embraced a wide variety of musical styles and genres in his career – made reverential references to works by Mahler, Debussy, Monteverdi and Stockhausen (amongst others) in his highly original *Sinfonia* of 1968. Other composers such as John Taverner have taken the structures and textures of the past – in Taverner's case, the polyphonic textures of the Renaissance and Baroque – and moulded them into his own distinctly twentieth century style.

At the start of the twenty-first century, a paradox seems to be taking place in both 'art' music and popular musical styles. On the one hand, there has never been so much, and so varied an amount of music available as there is today. This is almost entirely due to the technological advances that have given us digital recording, the Internet, multi-channel broadcasting and fast, inexpensive world travel. And yet, stylistically, music today is becoming increasingly more difficult to categorise as different strands, styles and traditions cross-fertilise with each other.

Over a hundred years after the birth of modern popular and jazz musical styles, many people still divide music into two distinct categories. They think of it as 'classical' (by which they mean all art music styles, not just music from what we call the Classical period) and 'popular'. Quite apart from the absurdity that this suggests (much classical music is popular, and many pop songs are now 'classics'), as students of music we recognise that all music – whatever the style or cultural heritage – comes from the common elements of pitch, tempo, rhythm, dynamic, texture, timbre and harmony. What distinguishes one style of music from another is the way in which composers select, use and combine these elements. When we analyse music from any style, this is what we are looking at. When we learn to compose and perform in these styles, we learn how to control and manipulate these elements in a way that imitates or is influenced by the methods of the original composers. This has been the case in the 'art music' sections of this book, and it will remain so in this section on pop, rock and jazz styles.

The twentieth century

The twentieth century was a unique period in the history of western music in that, alongside 'art' music, a second strand of musical culture was developed – popular music, rock and jazz. Fundamental to the story of popular music is the development of recording and broadcasting. It is also impossible to separate the composition of popular music from the performance of it. Whilst popular music composers may notate frameworks for their compositions, these frameworks will always be developed and adapted in rehearsal, in performance or in the recording studio. Consequently, when we analyse a work in a pop, rock or jazz style, it is important for us to combine theoretical analysis (using a score) with aural analysis (using a recording). What is essential to the understanding of the way in which popular music has evolved over the past 100 years is a realisation that recordings and technologies have enabled the cross-fertilisation and fusion of musical styles. They have also brought these musical styles to every corner of the globe. At the start of the twenty-first century, popular music is an incredibly complex web of cross-influences and mixed cultures. World music is fast becoming a similarly complex world-wide network.

The background to the blues

Central to the development of popular and jazz music in the twentieth century was the harmonic structure known as the twelve-bar blues. This grew out of the music of the former African slaves merged with western harmonic structures. The first half of the twentieth century saw the blues evolve through to bebop and the foundations of modern jazz. In the second half of the century, the blues spawned the birth of rock and roll and the hybrid of popular musical styles that we have today. Before we examine the early blues styles, however, it is worth considering the musical influences that led to the creation of pop and jazz styles.

Adzido
'Ndenduele' and 'Jarawa'

Listen CD 2, track 24. You will hear two pieces of music segued together. The first is called 'Ndenduele' and is a chant from Zambia. The second is 'Jarawa', a chant from Nigeria. Both pieces give a good idea of the musical heritage that the music of the former African slaves brought to the blues, jazz and popular music.

Listen particularly for:
- the call-and-response patterns in the vocal music
- the pitch shapes of the vocal lines, which are coloured by a greater flexibility and expressiveness than would be used for performing western art music
- the heavy rhythmic beat and repetitive drum rhythmic patterns.

Further work and listening

- As you work through the analyses and different styles of popular music and jazz in this book, keep coming back to these chants. Trace the heritage that African music has given to other musical styles.

During the eighteenth and nineteenth centuries, black slaves – formerly from West African countries such as Ghana – became increasingly involved in the life of the United States although, segregation and unequal rights continued well after the abolition of slavery in all States (in 1865). One important aspect of this involvement was the conversion to Christianity of many black people, even though they were forced to worship separately from the white people. On joining organised churches – including the Baptist and Methodist sects – the former Africans were introduced to the western tradition of hymn and psalm singing. More importantly, they were introduced to western concepts of melody and harmony. The music for these Christian songs was often simple, in line with the pure and simple life endorsed by the churches; for example, the Shaker hymn 'Tis a Gift to be Simple' is better known by us today as 'Lord of the Dance'.

Traditional, words by John Newton
Amazing Grace

Amazing Grace is one of the best-known of the American chapel hymns, and is thought to date from the start of the nineteenth century. Although there are a number of printed versions of the hymn from as early as 1835, it is likely that most congregations would have learnt the hymn aurally. It would then have been passed to other churches and generations orally. There is no doubt that the new black congregations with limited or no verbal literacy, let alone musical literacy, would have learnt the hymns in this way.

Amazing Grace
Traditional, words by John Newton

This is indeed a simple and direct hymn. Musically, what is of most interest (in the context of the development of popular musical styles) is the harmony. Only chords I, IV and V are used. Whilst it is possible that there may have been more sophisticated harmonisations, in country churches it is equally likely that such a basic harmonisation would have been employed.

As they learnt and joined in with these hymns, the former African slaves brought aspects of their own innate musical heritage to the performances. Most notably, the call-and-response vocal pattern became a feature in worship songs, as it had been in the songs that the slaves had sung as they were working their long hours on the plantations. These hymns became known as 'spirituals'. When the strong African-influenced rhythms were imposed on to the hymns and spirituals, and improvised clapping became a feature of the songs, the 'gospel' style was born.

Further work and listening

- Choose one or two nineteenth century hymns. Re-harmonise them, using only chords I, IV and V.
- Try making a more complex harmonisation of 'Amazing Grace'.
- Try making your own arrangement of 'Amazing Grace' – if not in gospel style, then with a distinctive rhythm pattern.

The Blues

The musical form that we now recognise as 'the blues' formed the backbone of so much of our popular musical culture during the twentieth century. As we have seen, it evolved from a number of musical traditions practised by the former African slaves in the United States in the second half of the nineteenth century. Most of these originated in the African musical roots of the former slaves – call-and-response patterns; strong rhythmic patterns with a heavy beat, and a distinctly non-western approach to vocal melody and intonation, with frequent bending of notes.

The early blues singers incorporated this African method of singing flexible, pitch-bent notes. The notes that were 'bent' – for expressive reasons, reflecting the emotion and meaning of the words being sung – were focused on the 3rd, 5th and 7th degrees of the scale that were sometimes sung approximately a semitone flat.

As we will hear in the musical examples that follow, the pitching of these notes was never as precise as the transcribed Western notation might suggest!

In the early blues songs, these elements came together, joining with other influences such as western primary chord patterns, learnt from singing simple hymns in church (see page 142). As with most musical structures, the blues developed orally and aurally rather than invented theoretically. The 'standard' twelve-bar blues chord pattern that evolved at the start of the century was (in C Major):

(Line 1)	C	C	C	C
(Line 2)	F	F	C	C
(Line 3)	G	F	C	C

This simple harmonic structure was at the heart of many diverse developments in popular music during the twentieth century. At the outset of the era, however, two main styles grew out of the blues. These were the more formal New Orleans jazz style in the southern States, and the rather more relaxed 'city blues' movement around northern cities such as Chicago.

Anon
Mean Old Bed Bug Blues

Listen to CD2, track 25. This is a very early recording of a blues song by Bessie Smith. She sings alone, accompanied by a guitar and a piano and, although the quality of the recording is poor, we can clearly hear the origins of the musical style.

Listen particularly for:
- the call-and-response provided here by the singer (call) and the instruments (response)
- the extremely flexible and equally bold vocal performance, with plenty of pitch-bending
- the strong and constant beat provided by the vamp of the piano left hand
- the simple harmonic structure using chords I, IV and V.

Bessie Smith

Further work and listening
- Listen to songs by other early blues singers such as Ma Rainey, Leadbelly, and Ida Cox. What do we mean when we refer to their songs as 'raw blues'?

W. C. Handy
St Louis Blues

Listen to the recording of this song on CD2, track 26. Follow this simple vocal score as you listen.

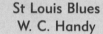

About this song and the arrangement

W.C. Handy was one of the first musicians to formalise blues songs by writing out parts and making arrangements of traditional songs, and writing new blues songs of his own. As a result of his work, the blues became extremely popular and widely known. 'St Louis Blues' dates from 1914. The performance featured on the CD, which dates from 1941, is played by the standard New Orleans/Dixieland jazz band. The band's instruments divide into two sections – the 'front-line' instruments (in this case, trumpet, trombone and clarinet) which provide melody and melodic improvisation, and the 'rhythm-harmony' section (in this case drums and double bass) which provide the harmonic structure and the beat.

Melody

'St Louis Blues' is fundamentally a pentatonic tune. The use of the pitch-bent blues notes is clear to see on the score. However, the score doesn't give a completely accurate representation of the vocal melody. Putting down a blues melody – or, indeed, a melody in most forms of pop and jazz – is not easy to do accurately. The flexibility and subtlety with which singers deliver their tunes – melodically and rhythmically – almost militates against regular notation. You will see this if you try to make a totally accurate score of the vocal performance on the CD!

Harmony

Follow through the score, tracking the twelve-bar blues chord sequence. As you can see, there is a slight variation in this plan for the first verse of 'St Louis Blues' – but this is not unusual, since the twelve-bar blues was and never has been a fixed form. It is typical of New Orleans jazz to make variations to the chord sequence and, for that matter, the melody. Try to find two identical recorded versions of 'St Louis Blues'!

Even within this song, the twelve-bar blues pattern isn't standardised. Notice how the third verse of 'St Louis Blues' deviates in two ways. First, the structure is not twelve bars – it's sixteen. Second, the tonality changes to the tonic minor of C minor. Of course, this has been alluded to previously through the blues notes in the vocal melody, but this is the first time that the harmony has taken a minor flavour.

The chord sequence for this third verse is:

(Line 1)	Cm	Cm	G	G
(Line 2)	G	G	Cm	Cm
(Line 3)	Cm	Cm	G	G
(Line 4)	G	G	Cm	Cm

Rhythm

The bass drum provides a strong beat, four to a bar. Here, the bass drum is played with a pedal as part of a kit, but in marching bands the bass drum would have been worn to the chest and beaten with a stick. The double bass reinforces this heavy on-beat bass line, as an early type of walking bass. On top of this, the cymbal and snare drum provide a basic dotted-quaver-semi-quaver pattern with fills. This rhythm can also

be heard in the vocal line, and is typical of trad. jazz.

Improvisation

In trad. jazz, improvisation is mainly confined to the front-line instruments, most usually the clarinet, but also the trumpet and the trombone. There is often a feeling of 'collective improvisation' by the front-line instruments, perhaps based on short motifs or riffs. This improvisation sometimes weaves its way around the vocal line, but more often comes as a quasi-improvised fill at the end of vocal phrases.

Further work and listening
- Listen to some early, raw blues by artists like Bessie Smith, Jelly Roll Morton and Ma Rainey.
- Compare and contrast the Chicago style of jazz and blues with the New Orleans style. In particular, listen to music by Louis Armstrong, King Oliver, Kid Ory and Bix Beiderbecke.
- Listen to 'St Louis Blues' once more, and then listen to later manifestations of the twelve-bar blues form – try Glenn Miller's 'In the Mood', 'Hound Dog' by Elvis Presley, and 'Can't Buy Me Love' by The Beatles. The twelve-bar blues is simple, both structurally and harmonically. Why has it held so much appeal for pop and jazz composers over the past 100 years, and why has it worked in such a wide variety of musical styles?

Ragtime, boogie-woogie and the city blues guitarists

Both ragtime and boogie-woogie are early jazz piano styles, and their names are derived from their rhythmic characteristics.

Ragtime

Ragtime is the earliest of the two forms, dating from the late nineteenth Century. The two hands play distinct but interlocking parts. In typical ragtime pieces, the *left hand* plays a steady, regular pulse, providing a strong harmonic basis. Commonly, the bass note (most often the root of the chord) is played on the beat with the rest of the chord coming on the following half-beat in piano 'vamp' style. This rhythmic style derives from the military-style marching bands that were so popular in the United States in the nineteenth century. Again, this is an example of white people's music being adopted and adapted by black musicians to form a new, exciting musical style.

Chords in ragtime are, like the twelve-bar blues, more often than not primary chords. However, it is not uncommon to find the use of more complex harmonies such as secondary and diminished 7ths. The *right hand*, in contrast, plays a syncopated (ragged) rhythm unharmonised (or in octaves) with copious use of runs and arpeggios. The overall 'ragtime' feel to the music is enhanced by the interaction of the syncopated right hand and the on-beat left hand.

Scott Joplin

Ragtime became very popular in the United States and in Europe through the mass publication of works by composers such as Scott Joplin and James Scott. In addition, the development of the coin-operated mechanical piano and pianola rolls meant that rags were played in bars and clubs too small to host a band or live pianist – an early example of media promotion of popular music.

Boogie-woogie

Whilst ragtime developed at around the same time as the blues, the boogie-woogie piano style developed out of the blues in the northern and western cities of the United States such as Chicago, as part of the 'city blues' movement. The standard or varied twelve-bar blues chord structure is the usual harmonic foundation for a boogie piece, with the bass line (left hand) playing the characteristic boogie-woogie rhythm. Over the top of this, the right hand plays a variety of patterns. These include fast tremolo octaves of thick chords or thick chords played in cross-rhythms (often crotchet triplets against a dotted-quaver-semiquaver bass). Boogie-woogie is often highly chromatic, with a blues 3rd played against the natural 3rd a favourite device.

The city blues

Ragtime and boogie-woogie were 'house and bar' styles – that is, they were played in bar-houses or private residences as entertainment, when a full swing band would have been too costly or too loud. The city blues pianists were joined by other musicians, particularly guitarists who came to the northern cities like Chicago from the country. These guitarists, such as Muddy Waters, B.B. King and Howlin' Wolf, played their own part in the development of blues by using the guitar as an instrument of total accompaniment. With them, the guitar provided strong rhythm and beat, harmonic structure and an intricate melodic foil to the vocal line, with the use of guitar riffs, fill-ins or 'licks'. The advent of the amplified electric guitar in the 1940s brought a new dimension, with the possibility of a new range of sonorities and effects. It was these musicians who laid the foundation for the rhythm 'n' blues bands of the 1960s, such as The Rolling Stones, and for the great electric guitarists such as Eric Clapton, Jimmy Page and Jimi Hendrix.

Jazz

Swing

Early jazz was performed by small groups, and much of it was improvised around standard patterns. By the 1930s, when the United States was starting to come out of the Great Depression, jazz was becoming more popular. As more dance halls opened, demand for big, upbeat, rhythmic jazz increased. The result was the swing bands containing twelve or more players. Inevitably, because of the numbers involved, the music had to be 'arranged' (that is, written down) and this, in turn, meant that the musicians who played swing had to have a certain degree of music literacy. Classically-trained musicians like Benny Goodman and other white bandleaders such as Glenn Miller formed dance bands that achieved immense popularity with their tightly disciplined sound. The music was, to a certain extent, commercialised – records sold extremely well in America and Europe – but it still retained many of the music features of earlier jazz styles. Perhaps what made swing most popular was that it was extremely suitable for dancing to, so that non-musicians could participate.

If you listen to early examples of swing-band music, you can hear the dotted quaver-semiquaver rhythmic units so typical of New Orleans blues (see 'St Louis Blues' on page 144) and boogie-woogie bass lines. This rhythmic style was relaxed in the swing period to become the 'swung triplet' bass that is now familiar as the swing style. Another characteristic swing bass line is the 'walking bass', where the bass moves at a steady pace, to the beat, whilst moving in even steps along the notes of a scale or an arpeggio figure.

Generally, in swing there is a much tighter feel to the music, with the instrumental groups (brass, saxophones) playing homophonically as sections. It is in swing music that we first hear brass sections playing 'stab' chords. Swing composers continued using the twelve-bar blues chord pattern as the foundation for compositional structures, but often with the basic chords enhanced diatonically to include added 7ths, 9ths, 11ths and even 13ths. The 12-bar structure was expanded to 16 and then 32 bars, to make what we now call 'standard' form – see the analysis of 'All the Things You Are' on page 148. Swing also included the use of riffs throughout the musical texture.

Jazz standards

As jazz became more sophisticated and formalised, and composers and bandleaders became more skilled in notation and musical arranging, it was almost inevitable that the raw structure of the twelve-bar blues would develop, both in terms of length and harmonic repertoire. What evolved was the form which is now known as 'popular song form 'or simply 'standard' form.

Standard form is usually thirty-two bars long, with these bars being divided into four equal phrases of eight bars each. The first phrase is usually repeated as the second phrase and again (with a little variation) as the fourth phrase. The third phrase is generally a contrasting theme. The form, therefore, can be expressed as AABA. Although it is not strictly in the middle of the form, the third phrase (B) is also known as the 'middle eight'. It is not difficult to see a resemblance between this form and the classic blues form (AAB). The differences are that in the blues, each phrase lasts for four bars, and in the blues there is generally not a fourth phrase – although, of course, we have seen an exception to this rule in 'St Louis Blues'.

The expansion of form meant that the harmonic repertoire used in standard form had to be expanded too. The primary chords – I, IV and V – remained fundamental to the harmonic strength of the standard, but other harmonies were used too. As in swing, added chords were used freely to add spice and depth to the harmony with 7ths, 9ths and 13ths being particular favourites. Often, these chords were organised in patterns, such as the chain of 7ths that is analysed in 'All the Things You Are'. The chain of 7ths was often used in combination with a circle of 5ths, as illustrated in the same example.

Composers also took advantage of the expanded form to try modulations – not just to closely-related keys but also, through enharmonic changes and chromatic shifts, to more distant keys.

Melodically, standards make much use of repetition – either exact, in sequence, in variation or even in inversion. Again, 'All the Things You Are' is a classic of its kind.

Although the example analysed here is from the late 1930s, the 'Golden Age' of jazz standards, it is interesting to see how the same basic structure, harmonic patterns and melodic shapes have endured. They are still being used today, particularly by composers for the stage and screen.

Jerome Kern and Oscar Hammerstein II
All the Things You Are

The 'lead sheet' score for this song – vocal line and chords – is given on the next page. Try singing through the song before you read the analysis. You could even try to realise the chords on keyboard or guitar. When you've analysed the song, you could try making an arrangement from the lead sheet for a small jazz group!

'All the Things You Are' dates from 1939. The composer, Jerome Kern, and the lyricist, Oscar Hammerstein II, collaborated on a number of musical theatre projects, including the very successful show *Showboat*, and many standards.

Form
The song follows the standard AABA form. The first three phrases are the usual eight bars in length, with the final phrase extended to twelve bars long.

Melody
Like all good popular melodies, the tune of 'All the Things You Are' is meticulously crafted using just a few musical ideas. The central intervallic motif in the A theme is the fourth; the other main melodic germ is the monotonal repeated idea in bar 3. These ideas join together and are repeated in sequence throughout the song. Sequence is used in the middle eight, too, although the melody is more angular (in contrast), featuring intervals of the 6th and 7th.

Tonality and harmony
The tonic key of this song is A♭ major. However, it is not until the end of the final phrase that listeners feel that they have 'arrived' in this tonic key. For the majority of the song, the tonality is constantly shifting. The opening five bars are firmly in A♭, but because of the use of the circle of 5ths and the chain of 7ths – where the 3rd of a chord is held over to become the 7th of the next – and because we do not hear Chord I until bar 4, there is no firm sense of the tonic key. Then, at the end of bar 5, there is a chromatic shift from D♭ to D minor, prefacing a firm modulation to C major. This is a tertiary harmonic shift from the tonic key of A♭.

The second phrase is an exact sequential repetition of the first phrase, but a 4th lower. The chord sequence starts with the chord of C minor which means that the second phrase is in the dominant key of E♭ major. Note the way that Kern moves from C major at the end of the first phrase to C minor at the start of the second phrase.

The chromatic tertiary modulation at the end of the second phrase leaves us in the key of G major, ready for the middle eight which again uses the circle of 5ths and chain of 7ths, another semitonal shift (from G to F♯m), and another circle of 5ths, and leaves us on the chord of C – with a sharpened 5th – at the end of the third phrase. Conveniently (!) this is the dominant chord for F minor which, as we know, is the opening chord of the first phrase. In the final phrase, Kern extends his chain of 7ths/circle of 5ths to the chord of G♭ before bringing us back to the tonic of A♭ through a B diminished chord – the only diminished chord in a complex harmonic structure, which makes it all the more effective.

Note the alternative harmonies suggested when the A theme is repeated. Of course, it would be usual for jazz musicians to play harmonic variations on such repeats. In much the same way, J.S. Bach offered alternative harmonisations of repeated phrases within chorales, or even alternative harmonisations of complete chorales!

What is most remarkable about the melodies and harmonies of this song is the way in which Kern unashamedly uses clichés and formulae but at the same time produces a song of such natural elegance and smooth movement. It's little wonder that this, and other similar songs, have been covered and adapted by so many jazz musicians.

The arrangement

The score provided here is in the form of a 'lead sheet' containing the melody and chords only. This is a conventional way of presenting stan- dards for performance, allowing jazz musicians to make their own arrangements and build their own improvisations around the basic melody and harmony.

Further work and listening

- Listen to other standards from the 1930s and 40s. Try 'Ain't Misbehavin' by Fats Waller or another Jerome Kern composition, 'Smoke Gets In Your Eyes'.
- Listen out for later songs in standard form – try 'Yesterday' by Lennon and McCartney, 'Music To Watch Girls By' as sung by Andy Williams, and 'Will You Still Love Me Tomorrow' sung by The Shirelles or by Carole King.
- What is it that makes standard form feel so balanced to the ear? Think carefully about matters such as phrase lengths, harmonic structure and strength, and harmonic devices such as sequence.

All the Things You Are
Jerome Kern and Oscar Hammerstein II

Bebop

By the time of World War II, swing jazz was losing its allure for a growing number of musicians. The necessarily formulaic nature of the music inevitably lead to predictability and clichéd writing in harmonic and rhythmic patterns. Most importantly, the rigid nature of the arrangements meant that opportunities for improvisation were limited. More often than not, quasi-improvisatory passages were written out by the composer, rather than being worked out by the performer from the composer's guide. Listen to two different recordings of Glenn Miller's 'In The Mood' and you'll understand what the musicians felt.

The response to this was a new, experimental period in jazz performance and composition which became known as 'bebop'. The movement started in New York, specifically at a night club called 'Minton's', where small groups of musicians met with the freedom to experiment and play as they wanted, without the restrictions of notation or the commercial pressures that were imposed on them by swing. Of course, these musicians (such as John 'Dizzy' Gillespie and Charlie 'Bird' Parker) had their roots in the blues, boogie-woogie and swing. So when they improvised and experimented at Minton's they started with standard jazz forms and, indeed, tunes. Many of the greatest bebop numbers are, in fact, based on jazz standards. However, what the bebop musicians did with these tunes was far from standard and far removed from the conventions of swing.

Melodically, bebop musicians embellished their tunes with copious use of passing notes – accented, unaccented, chromatic, harmonically essential or unessential. Harmonically, triads were added to at will – not just diatonically with added 7ths, 9ths and the like as in swing, but also chromatically. Augmented and diminished chords were common, with the tritone a favourite interval harmonically and melodically.

Temporally and rhythmically, bebop generally has a fast and often furious feel to it. However, this is not to say that bebop rhythms are heavy and rigid – far from it. The set patterns of swing, in terms of four-square beats to a bar and constant swing quaver rhythms are gone and replaced by lighter and always more complex rhythmic counterpoints, often arranged in irregular length phrases. The bass line plays an important part in creating this feel, characteristically taking a quick-moving and agile line. The drummer places much emphasis not upon a heavy bass drum beat, but upon light bright ride or hi-hat right hand cymbal rhythms, and more complex left hand work on the snare and toms. The pianist, rather than simply providing a rhythmic-chord support, takes on a more melodic role, with the new electric guitar taking on more of the harmonic support.

Bebop was more than just a reaction to swing. The innovations forged by Gillespie, Parker and their contemporaries paved the way for cool jazz, fusion and free jazz. What it is most important to remember is that this music was composed through performance, experimentation and improvisation and that bebop restored the spontaneity to jazz that many thought was being lost through the formality of swing.

Cool jazz

The intense, frenetic, 'anything goes' sound of bebop was itself, in time, bound to be reacted against. For all the restrictions of swing, the earlier big band style was commercially successful and the written arrangements made performance (and repeat performances) accessible. Not least, there was a feeling that jazz should sometimes be more reflective in composition, performance and audition.

In 1949, the trumpeter Miles Davis produced an album called 'The Birth of The Cool' featuring a new style of playing and jazz composing which itself became known as 'The Cool'. After bebop, it might be easy to regard cool jazz as a retrograde development. Certainly, there was a return to strong melodies and harmonies, to a strong square rhythmic basis provided by the drums and bass. However, cool jazz went far beyond the formalities of swing and itself brought innovation.

Cool jazz was attractive to a wide audience, and brought musicians from a variety of backgrounds to jazz composition and performance. Composers and performers with a formal, academic training, like Dave Brubeck of 'Take Five' fame, merged art music metres, rhythms and structures with jazz techniques. Five, seven and eleven beats to a bar were experimented with. The use of modes, in combination with or replacing diatonic scales, was of interest to musicians such as Gerry Mulligan. Many composers, like Antonio Carlos Jobim, drew on the rhythms of Latin American dances such as the rhumba and tango and blended them into jazz structures. This paved the way for other types of jazz-fusion in the 60s and 70s. New instruments

were introduced into the jazz combo, as much for the new sound colours that they offered as for giving more musicians the opportunity to participate in jazz performance.

Antonio Carlos Jobim and Newton Mendonça
Samba de Una Nota So

Listen to CD2, track 27. Cool Jazz doesn't come any cooler than this piece! As we will see, the title of this piece is deceptive – it's more than just 'samba' and it certainly isn't monotonous. The piece follows a simple structure, with a sixteen-bar verse and a contrasting middle eight. But what exactly is it that makes the piece sound so cool and laid back? Analysis of the individual music components of the song reveals more than the title might suggest.

Samba de Una Nota So
Antonio Carlos Jobim and Newton Mendonça

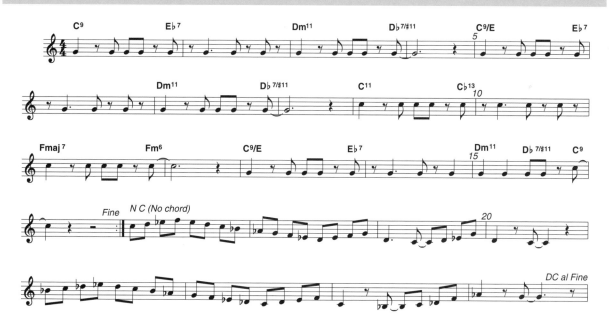

Melody

The main sixteen-bar verse of this piece (bars 1–16 on your score) is divided into four equal, square four-bar phrases which form the structure AABA with the 'melody' shown on the score. This melody is, in fact, merely formed from the uppermost note of the guitar chords

which are far more interesting. The tonal centre of the piece is C major; the A phrases feature the dominant note (G) – the 'So' in the title – and the B phrase features the tonic note. Not quite a one-note melody but pretty monotonous in pitch at least. Is monotony cool, in an almost arrogant way?

What is more interesting, in terms of melodic shape, is Stan Getz's tenor saxophone solo that comes in at bar 17. What makes this sound really cool is the way in which he doesn't conform to the bossa nova rhythm that permeates all of the other instrumental parts. The first, long sustained note followed by a florid descent through the instrument's range is made to sound even more laid back because of Getz's soft, breathy tone – an effect that can be obtained by blowing softly on to a fairly hard reed. Here is an example of instrumental performance technique contributing to a compositional style. Compare this style with the hard, manic playing of the bebop saxophonists.

Rhythm

Western music theory books tend to categorise Latin American dances by giving them definitive rhythmic identities. The rise of electronic keyboards with preset rhythms has also helped to perpetuate a somewhat stereotypical view. The reality is that in Brazil 'samba' is a generic term for a versatile and ever-varying rhythmic style. The bossa nova, which is the rhythmic style of this song, was a new ('nova'!) rhythmic style developed by Jobim in the 1950s, and is part of the samba stylistic tradition. The recording on CD2, track 27, uses a typical Latin percussion section, embracing a variety of contrasting timbres which help to pick out the complex rhythmic strands. Listen particularly for the cool quaver shaker pattern, and the rimmy snare drum clicks.

This score is of a typical bossa nova rhythmic pattern:

Instrumentation

The guitar in the excerpt, played by Charlie Byrd, carries the main melody and harmony in the main verse. The way in which this guitar part is played figures largely in creating the tight, rhythmic feel. Not surprisingly, the Latin/Latin-jazz guitar style has a close affiliation with the 'rascuedo' techniques of Spanish flamenco, where the fingers are thrown downwards onto the strings from an initially clenched hand, followed by the palm coming down on to the strings to give a short dampening effect. Compare this with the similarly tight guitar 'shank' style of reggae guitarists.

Harmony

Generally, the harmonies change at a rate of one new harmony per bar – not really frenetic. Where the overall movement of the music is faster – in the middle eight – the instruments play in unison, unharmonised. Close examination of the chord sequence reveals not just a colourful selection of harmonies, contrasting with the slightly less than colourful melodic line. When viewed as a continuum, the chords reveal a chromatically descending bass line, travelling from E to C in semitone steps. Internally, the chord sequence contains other stepwise chromatic lines. How smooth can you get?!

The middle eight

As we have already seen, the middle eight is contrasted to the main sixteen-bar verse of this piece by being an unharmonised, unison melody. This section is also contrasted by the use of the transposed Aeolian mode, in a four-bar sequential passage.

Further work and listening

- Listen to other pieces by Jobim, especially some of his songs. Try 'Wave', 'Desafinado' and the very well known 'The Girl from Ipanema'. Can you trace the stylistic features that you have identified in 'Samba de Una Nota So' in these songs?
- Listen to other examples of cool jazz by Dave Brubeck, Miles Davis and Gerry Mulligan. Play some of their tunes and harmonies. What is it about the music that makes it 'cool'?
- Research the musical backgrounds of these composers, including Jobim. What personal qualities and experiences did they bring to jazz composition and performance?

Rock 'n' roll in the 1950s

Bill Haley and The Comets' 1954 hit 'Rock Around the Clock', is generally acknowledged to be the first great rock 'n' roll record. The origins of rock 'n' roll are diverse and, indeed, the way in which it has spawned so many different musical styles is what makes it so important.

Rock 'n' roll is strongly rooted in the twelve-bar blues, with the standard three-line format using chords I-IV-V. This form evolved through the first half of the twentieth century, through boogie-woogie, swing and bebop (see pages 143–50), and had developed into sixteen- and thirty-two-bar structures used in jazz standards. It was also adopted by the white folk (or 'country') musicians, particularly around the Southern states of America. The raw music that these musicians produced in the 1930s and 40s, combining traditional hillbilly tunes with influences of the blues' chord patterns, and sometimes the rhythms of boogie-woogie became known as the 'country blues' or 'Rhythm 'n' Blues'. Many features of these country R'n'B songs are identical to features of the early rock 'n' roll numbers:

- use of the twelve-bar blues (or adapted twelve-bar blues) chord structure
- a strong bass line, much like the 'walking' bass lines of swing but played with a more percussive attack
- a rigid, four-square drum rhythm with what came to be known as the rock 'n' roll 'backbeat' – a heavy accent on beats two and four – and the use of the dotted 'boogie-woogie' rhythm
- vocal arrangements that experimented with 'call-and-response' patterns, although with less accented rhythms.

What turned the relatively low-key rhythm 'n' blues movement into the high profile, commercially successful rock 'n' roll was a series of cultural and economic circumstances which followed the end of the World War II.

- Developments in jazz (see the section on bebop on page 150) were making this style of popular music less accessible to the public. Swing had been extremely popular, not least because it was good dance music with mass appeal.
- America was becoming more affluent after the War, and teenagers were starting to demand more freedom from their parents. Sexual mores started to become more liberal, too. Rock 'n' roll gave an expressive outlet for both of these changes in society, as, indeed, it has done ever since!
- The development of the electric guitar brought more power, more volume, and a more strident timbre that fitted perfectly with the more strident lyrics.
- Sadly, the fact that the early rock 'n' roll songs were performed by white musicians gave the music commercial validity at a time when there was still much racial prejudice in the United States.

Try listening to 'Sh-boom' by the Crew Cuts, a typical R'n'B song which entered the charts just two months before 'Rock Around the Clock' and you'll hear the musical similarities and the cultural differences between the two styles.

Of course, the rhythm 'n' blues and country and western musical styles have endured and developed to this day, but there can be no denying that the white rock 'n' roll explosion of the mid-1950s was the most significant commercial event in the history of popular music. Later in the decade, black musicians, such as Chuck Berry, made an impact on the rock scene, but the man who brought both all of these musical influences together in his performances was Elvis Presley. Elvis was a performer, not a composer and many of his recordings were cover versions of older songs.

Elvis brought together all kinds of musical influences in his performances

Jerry Leiber and Mike Stoller
Hound Dog

Listen to this song performed by Elvis Presley on CD2, track 28.

<pre>
              C   C   C   C
   You ain't nothing but a hound dog,   crying all the time.

              F7   F7   C   C
   You ain't nothing but a hound dog,   crying all the time.

    G7   F7   C   C
Well, you ain't never caught a rabbit and you ain't no friend of mine.

              C   C   C   C
   Well they said you was high classed,   but that was just a lie.

              F7   F7   C   C
   Well they said you was high classed,   but that was just a lie.

    G7   F7   C
Well, you ain't never caught a rabbit and you ain't no friend of mine.
</pre>

Jerry Leiber and Mike Stoller, the composers of this song, have an impressive portfolio of songs that includes 'Jailhouse Rock' and 'Treat Me Nice', both of which were also recorded by Presley. They also wrote the soul classic 'Stand By Me', and the Elkie Brookes hit single 'Pearl's a Singer'. 'Hound Dog' dates from 1953 when it was first recorded by the country blues singer, 'Big Mama' Thornton. Elvis Presley recorded this version of the song in 1956.

Melody

The melody is neither particularly adventurous in pitch range (it spans the minor 6th between G and E♭) nor in melodic shape. The use of the E♭ (the 7th over chord IV) gives a bluesy feel to the music. However, the most distinctive feature of the melody is the way that Elvis Presley performs it. His southern drawl, slight *portamento* between notes, and the bluesy E♭s – not to mention the implied meaning of the lyrics – give more than a hint of sexual suggestion. In 1956, this caused outrage, especially when accompanied by his hip-grinding television performances!

Tonality and harmony

This recording is in the key of C major. Each verse, and the instrumental break, is organised into the classic twelve-bar blues structure with chords IV and V having added 7ths.

The arrangement

Elvis Presley is accompanied by the typical country blues band – a sparse combination of guitar, bass and drums. From 1954, Elvis' guitarist was Scotty Moore. Because he was the sole guitarist, Moore developed a mixed style of playing that amalgamated elements of the rhythm and lead guitar functions. You can hear this style clearly in this recording. Although he is playing on his favoured Gibson Les Paul hollowbody electric guitar, Moore's solo style has a flavour of the steel slide guitar used in country and western music. The slides in the guitar part are, perhaps, a mirror of Elvis's vocal style.

Note the backing singers in the instrumental break, providing a harmonic wash to the lyric 'ooh' – a flavour of the 'doowop' groups, perhaps.

Rhythm

The minimal drumkit plays the four-square backbeat typical of early rock 'n' roll.

Further work and listening

- Scotty Moore chose the Gibson Les Paul hollowbody electric guitar because of that instrument's unique timbre, as well as for ease of playing. How important is choice of instrument for composers and performers? In your answer, refer to your own compositions and experiences as a performer.
- Is Elvis Presley's delivery of this song as exciting and alluring today as it was in 1956? Give reasons for your opinion.

Gospel meets rhythm 'n' blues: sweet soul music

Earlier, we discovered how the music of the former African slaves had brought about a new type of church music which came to be known as 'gospel'. This music has remained popular to the present day, but towards the end of the 1940s a number of gospel singers began to experiment by combining the vocal styles of their sacred songs with the rhythmic and harmonic styles of secular styles such as swing and rhythm 'n' blues. Think back to what was said about popular music being a complicated web of influences and cross-influences. Both gospel and the rhythm 'n' blues styles evolved out of the 'call-and-response' and American church music traditions, but they had developed in different directions. Now they were turning in to each other to create another musical style!

The new style became known as 'soul', a blend of gospel vocal harmonies and jazz/blues rhythms and accompaniments. Like the rock 'n' roll songs that were popular at the same time and many rhythm 'n' blues numbers, the early soul lyrics had a high degree of sexual connotation which matched the slick, smooth, bluesy vocal style of the soul singers. Ben E. King (who was also lead singer of The Drifters), Ray Charles and 'The Godfather of Soul', James Brown, all made their names during the first decade of soul music, the 1950s. At the same time, all-male soul vocal harmony groups became popular, with a distinctive close-harmony style and an equally distinctive use of onomatopoeic lyrics which prompted the name 'doo-wop'.

In the 1960s, like all strands of popular music, soul became much more commercialised. In soul, more than in any other style of popular music at the time, the roles of the producer and the songwriter were arguably more important than that of the performers. The three great musical strands of 1960s' soul music were created not by the performers, but by the producers, composers and arrangers. They are:
- Phil Spector's 'wall of sound'
- Tamla Motown
- Atlantic Soul.

The wall of sound

Phil Spector produced a stream of quite different singers and groups in the late 1950s and early 1960s, including the black all-girl group The Ronettes, the white male duo The Righteous Brothers, and Ike and Tina Turner. The vocal styles of all these singers was firmly in the soul tradition, but what made the Phil Spector sound most distinctive was his 'wall of sound'. As arranger, Spector favoured the use of a large orchestral sound including cascading strings, punchy brass and timpani to punctuate cadences in addition to the standard rock band line-up of guitars, drums and keyboards. Furthermore, he used (the then new) multitrack recording techniques to expand the orchestral sound, making a small ensemble sound like a symphony orchestra. Combined with the soul and doo-wop vocal styles and the use of a heavily accented backbeat rhythm, this made for a distinctive sound. This Spector orchestral

sound was much imitated throughout all styles of popular music in the 1960s. It was Phil Spector who produced The Beatles' final album, *Let It Be*, in 1969. Listen to the title track and 'The Long and Winding Road' from that album and you'll hear the unmistakable 'wall of sound'.

Driving music from Motor City

Berry Gordy was the man behind the Tamla Motown record label. Unlike Phil Spector, Gordy produced only black artists. Like Spector, Gordy realised the commercial importance of developing a 'house' style for all of his records and consequently he employed a team of composers (Smokey Robinson, Marvin Gaye, Lamont Dozier and the Holland Brothers) and a group of studio musicians who would provide the songs for all the artists on the Motown label. All the 1960s Motown singers have their own distinctive vocal styles, but the instrumental arrangements and production of their songs are all unmistakably Motown. Listen to Motown songs and notice the characteristic dotted crotchet-quaver bass rhythms, the use of chord III with a sharpened 3rd as a secondary dominant in major key songs, the orchestral arrangements with high horns and scalic strings and, of course, the drum backbeat. You will also hear a great deal of repetition in the vocal lines of Motown. It was Berry Gordy who first exploited the idea of a 'hook' in popular music – the use of a catchy vocal line that, if repeated frequently at key points in the song, would 'hook' the listener who would then go and buy the record!

Stax of Soul

The third strand of 1960s soul music developed simultaneously at the Atlantic and Stax record labels. In contrast to the highly commercial, produced sound of Motown and Spector, the Atlantic/Stax soul sound was tied more closely to the roots of soul in gospel music. The vocal style of the Atlantic songs was very much in the call-and-response tradition, with a solo singer and harmony backing group. The instrumental accompaniments were generally simpler than the other Soul sounds, often featuring just a standard rock band with brass ('horns') and/or saxophones. Aretha Franklin's 'Respect' is an excellent example of the Atlantic soul style. Compare and contrast the song and the performance with songs in the Spector and Motown styles.

Gary Jackson, Carl Smith and Raynard Miner
(Your Love Keeps Lifting Me) Higher and Higher

Listen to CD2, track 29, performed by Jackie Wilson.

D   Em/D   D
Your love lifted me higher   than I've ever been lifted before.

Em/D   D
So keep it up,   quench my desire,   and I'll be at your side forevermore.

Em/D
You know your love (Your love keeps lifting me; your) keeps on lifting (love keeps lifting me),

D
Higher (lifting me) higher and higher (higher and higher, higher)

Em/D
I said, your love (your love keeps lifting me; your) keeps on   (love keeps lifting me,)

D
Lifting me (lifting me) higher and higher (higher and higher, higher).

About this song

Jackie Wilson started his career as a lead singer with a number of Detroit-based groups before working as a solo singer from 1957. Although he was not part of the Motown group of singers, his music bears resemblance to the Motown style of soul, particularly in the rhythm sections. 'Higher and Higher' dates from 1969.

Melody and vocals

The call-and-response vocal patterns of gospel are more than evident in this song. The bvox (backing vocals) singers not merely echo the lead singer, but make their own unique close-harmony contribution to the texture. Interestingly, it is one of the bvox phrases – 'Your love keeps lifting me' – that has become the memorable hook of the song.

The solo melodic phrases are short, mainly only one bar long, out of necessity, to allow for the bvox interjections. Jackie Wilson's vocal range is not extensive in this song, covering just a 7th in span.

Harmony and tonality

This song is in the key of D major, and it does not modulate away from this key at any point. In fact, the song only uses two chords – chord I (D) and II (Em). This is unusual in that the second of these chords is not a primary chord. In the vast majority of popular music, where only a limited number of harmonies are used (q.v. twelve-bar blues), these are primary chords (I, IV and V). Normally – whether in popular or art music styles – this might lead to a weak sense of harmony through the use of 'parallel' chords. What the composers do here is to bind the two harmonies together by using a constant bass tonic pedal throughout the song.

The arrangement

This song is scored for the standard rock band of drums, rhythm guitar and bass guitar.

However, the arrangement is not as opulent as those produced by the Spector and Motown organisations. Although there is a string section, it is not particularly full in sound, nor are there other orchestral sounds. There is, however, a horn section, so characteristic of 1960s' soul. Note the way that the horns play homophonically to give a kick to the each vocal phrase.

Rhythm

The strong backbeat rhythm, so typical of soul, is clearly heard in this song. Entwined in this simple basic rhythm is a variety of more complex rhythmic riffs including the bvox, funky bass guitar, and horns. The bass guitar riff, centred around the tonic pedal of course, is the most memorable. It also picks out the skeleton of the alternating I/II harmonies.

Further work and listening

- Compare and contrast 'Higher and Higher' with other soul songs from the period, such as Aretha Franklin's version of 'Respect'.
- 'Higher and Higher' only uses two chords. The bass line plays a constant tonic pedal throughout the song. It contains only a limited number of short melodic ideas. What, then, has made this song a classic of its type and given it such enduring appeal?

The British beat and The Beatles

It is widely accepted that The Beatles were the most original and the most influential British musicians of the 1960s. The group's musical life spanned almost the entire decade, and through their work one can trace the changing musical styles of the times. The fact that they constantly developed their musical style is an indication of their greatness, and is a major reason for their having lasting appeal. They also wrote memorable music with strong harmonies, catchy melodies and powerful arrangements.

Influences on The Beatles

To say that The Beatles were original is not to imply that they were without influences. Today, when we are able to access almost every style of music from every corner of the globe at the flick of a switch, it is perhaps difficult to appreciate the more complex ways in which musical influences were spread, even forty years ago. Like the Britpop bands that took their lead from their forebears, The Beatles started life as a skiffle group, imitating the music of Lonnie Donegan who himself had brought this homemade form of American country blues to Britain – complete with tea-chest double bass and washboard! The original group was called The Quarrymen and, significantly, it was John Lennon who was the original member of the group and it was he who invited Paul McCartney to join the group.

The Beatles

A complementary partnership

Most of The Beatles' songs are credited as joint compositions by John Lennon and Paul McCartney. As with many popular music compositions, there was a great deal of collaboration between the two, in writing and working through the songs in performance. However, Lennon and McCartney brought their own perspectives and personalities to The Beatles' songs, and with most of the numbers there is a Lennon or McCartney influence.

Lennon brought the rock 'n' roll songs of Chuck Berry and Elvis Presley to the group. This resulted in their use of the classic twelve-bar blues structure in their songs ('Can't Buy Me Love') and the imitation of the high octave-leap falsetto of Chuck Berry ('She Loves You'). To this they added the 'beat' – a strong emphasis on every beat of a four-four bar, as opposed to the stress on beats two and four of American rock 'n' roll. This became known as the 'Mersey Beat'. The Beatles took the close vocal harmonies of the black doo-wop singers and added a distinctly British accent and, importantly on a commercial level, a youthful smile.

Paul McCartney's musical strength lay in the ability to write strong melodies and harmonic progressions. McCartney's influence on The Beatles' songs showed through the composition of mainstream ballads in 'standard' song form ('Yesterday'). Also with the help of producer George Martin, The Beatles used art music style accompaniments for their songs, such as the string quartet in 'Eleanor Rigby' and 'Yesterday', and the Baroque piccolo trumpet and quasi-recitative vocal writing in 'All You Need is Love'. It is interesting to note that in recent years Paul McCartney has collaborated extensively with art music musicians on large-scale orchestral and choral works.

A developing style

In the mid-60s, when psychedelia was in full swing, The Beatles developed their straightforward, direct songwiriting approach by experimenting with changing metres ('Lucy In The Sky With Diamonds'), experimenting with new recording techniques, and introducing non-western musical elements such as the sitar into their songs. They acknowledged their musical heritage by writing songs which clearly acknowledged the past without being pastiche copies. In many ways The Beatles were a catalyst for British pop music. Like other catalysts in the history of popular and art music, they were important because they assimilated and summarised all that had gone before them, and forged new musical and commercial traditions that continue to influence musicians some forty years after the band first worked together.

The modern sound of 60s Britain

The Rolling Stones

At around the same time that The Beatles emerged from Liverpool with their distinctive British beat sound, the London-based Rolling Stones were producing an equally distinctive but quite different sound. Whereas The Beatles were influenced in their early days by the rock 'n' roll sound of Chuck Berry and the 'clean' vocal harmonies of the doo-wop groups, The Stones took their lead from the rhythm 'n' blues musicians and particularly the city blues guitarists like Muddy Waters and Howlin' Wolf. Vocally and instrumentally, The Stones' early recordings have an earthy, raw feel to them. Mick Jagger's sometimes aggressive yet sometimes soulful voice gave no doubt as to the emotion of the songs, and guitarists Keith Richard and Brian Jones brought a new, heavier style to guitar playing.

The sound – and the image – that The Stones produced certainly had an impact, and was again as contrast to the clean-cut music (and image) projected by The Beatles' early work. In many ways, The Stones shocked the mid-60s public in a way that the Punk bands would shock the public some fifteen years later.

The Rolling Stones took the lead in the British rhythm 'n' blues revival of the early 1960s, and their success was built on by groups such as The Yardbirds, The Animals and Cream. These groups, in turn, produced a succession of great British blues guitarists, such as Jimmy Page, Eric Clapton and Mick Taylor.

The Who

A third style of British rock music emerged in the mid-60s with the Mods. Like so much popular music, Mod music was linked to developments in teenage clothing fashion. Fashionable clothes and dancing were very much the vogue with the Mods as were energy-boosting drugs. The greatest 'Mod' band is generally acknowledged to be The Who, fronted by Pete Townshend. Whilst their music had much energy and was beloved by the Mods – a fact that undoubtedly helped the band's commercial success – their music was in fact from the same traditions as The Stones. As with The Stones' guitarists, Pete Townshend introduced a range of new lead and rhythm techniques which laid the foundation for the heavy rock bands of the 1970s.

All Day and All of the Night
Ray Davies

Listen to CD2, track 30.

About this song and The Kinks

The Kinks, fronted by singer Ray Davies, were a London band that emerged around the same time as The Rolling Stones. Their music had elements in common with both The Stones (a heavy guitar riff based sound) and The Beatles (a popular melodic style and a willingness to experiment). 'All Day and All of the Night' was the Kinks' second hit single, reaching number 2 in the UK charts in late 1964.

Tonality, harmony, melody and riffs

This song has a key signature that suggests G minor. However, from the very first bar, we can hear that both the melodic and harmonic styles have very strong modal overtones, with heavy emphasis placed on the naturalised leading note (F and, of course, the first chord played by the guitars is G major). In aural effect, the opening melodic section of the song (introduction and up to bar 8 on the score) is in the transposed Aeolian mode. Of course, the flattened 3rd and 7th used in the song are derived from the rhythm 'n' blues heritage of The Kinks.

You will immediately have observed that the opening of the song is rather minimalistic in that the guitar riff that opens the song is an exact repetition of the vocal line. The vocal line itself only uses a limited range of notes (three pitches, spanning the interval of a 4th) and this melody is harmonised with parallel harmonies – they move in parallel with the melody with the root of each chord being derived from the pitch of the melody line. This is all extremely effective and makes the song memorable, but if continued for a great length of time could make the song tedious.

In order to move the song forward, from bar 9 on the score onwards, the composer effects two modulations which give the song added direction and momentum. Firstly, the music moves to B♭ (the relative major key of G <u>minor</u>). Then, almost immediately, the music modulates to the dominant key of D. Note that the chord played before we hit D – A, which is chord V in D minor – contains the sharpened leading note, C#. This is the first time that we have heard a melodically sharpened leading note in this song as, up to now, we have always heard the modal/bluesy flattened leading note. (You may also hear a flattened leading note being played simultaneously in the guitar riff – a type of 'false relation'!)

At the same time, in the four-bar section from bars 9-12 on the score, the harmonies are no longer parallel with the melody, again giving more momentum to the music. You will also notice that throughout the whole of the song, the guitar riff – using the distinctive rhythm and melody derived from the sung line – is played throughout as a constant reference through the tonal changes.

Further work and listening

- Listen to the cover version of 'All Day and All of the Night' performed by the Stranglers in 1988. Which version do you prefer, and why?
- What is it about 'All Day and All of the Night' that has made it a classic song of the 1960's? Which elements of the musical style make it so memorable and well-liked?

Guitar greats of the 60s and 70s

Pete Townshend

The songs of The Rolling Stones and The Who were strongly rooted in the rhythm 'n' blues and soul traditions, with a distinctive and almost anarchic use of the electric guitar effects that were introduced in the mid 1960s. Like Keith Richard, The Who's Pete Townshend experimented with alternative guitar tunings, and made much use of distortion and feedback effects. Townshend's guitar lines were more than just effect, though. It is widely acknowledged that he helped lay the musical foundations for a whole generation of rock, heavy metal and punk guitarists. Townshend is responsible for promoting three guitar-based harmonic devices, all of which have a sound theoretical basis – although it is probable that Townshend favoured them because they gave him the sound that he wanted!

- The guitarist made great use of the pedal note – usually the tonic – over which he would play a chord sequence featuring chords I, IV and V.
- He also made extensive use of the 'sus' chord, where an essential note from one chord is held over into the next chord where it is not an essential part of the chord. In western art music, we know this as a suspension, of course! Townshend's favourite sus chords are the sus4 and the sus2, which might otherwise be known as a 4–3 suspension and a 9–8 suspension.
- Finally, Townshend is probably best known as the originator of the guitar 'power' chord – where a major chord is played with the 3rd missing but the root and the 5th doubled. Combined with the use of feedback and distortion, a fast, extrovert right hand strumming technique, and the full range of right hand techniques such as hammer-ons and pull-offs, this made for an aggressive, bare, distinctive and highly influential sound.

Jimi Hendrix

As flamboyant and innovative as Townshend was, even he was overshadowed by the work of the American guitarist, Jimi Hendrix. It is important to remember that Hendrix's musical roots were firmly in the rhythm 'n' blues tradition and in his early years he worked closely with the likes of B.B. King. However, what stands Hendrix apart from all other guitarists is that he took this tradition and applied it (with incredible energy and creativity) to the new guitar technology and the psychedelic music movement of the mid-to-late 1960s. There are so many innovations and techniques that Hendrix introduced into the guitar performance repertoire, some being:

- the use of almost every part of the guitar to produce sound – not just the strings, but the body, the neck, the head; and the use of unconventional methods of playing the strings themselves, including with his teeth and tongue and tapping the strings with his hands
- the copious use of a whole range of effects individually and in combination, including the fuzz-box, the wah-wah pedal and the tremolo arm (or the 'whammy' bar)
- the combination of rhythm and lead guitar styles, so that melodies and harmonies combine and interweave.

Hendrix's stage performance was notoriously flamboyant and did much to create his reputation, as did his death at the age of 28. His musical influence has been immense and, together with the techniques developed by the likes of Pete Townshend, led the way for the heavy metal and heavy rock bands of the next generation.

Heavy rock, heavy metal and grunge

Throughout the late 60s and 70s, the heavy rock styles founded by Pete Townshend and Jimi Hendrix, and the blues guitar style promoted by performers like Eric Clapton, were explored by a plethora of bands such as Led Zeppelin, the Australian AC/DC, Black Sabbath, Deep Purple, Iron Maiden and Nazareth. Their music, whilst being based in the rock, rhythm 'n' blues traditions, had a harder edge to it that led to the adoption of the label 'metal'. Their songs were substantial, in length, texture and lyrical content – this was serious rock music. Bands such as Bon Jovi and Guns'N'Roses continued the metal tradition in the 1980s. Whilst metal has

always enjoyed a large and devoted audience, these 80s groups brought much commercial success to the genre as well as spawning a faster, more frenetic cousin, 'thrash' metal.

In the late 1980s, a new variety of heavy metal emerged in the United States. 'Grunge' was unmistakably related to metal, with heavy overdriven guitar-riff based songs. The guitar styles of the grunge bands, such as Nirvana, were directly descended from the guitar styles of Townshend and Hendrix. The riffs and vocal lines were often made up of only a few pitches, in a minimalistic sort of way. Grunge had other influences too, including the punk vocal styles that were to colour the Britpop sound later in the decade.

Folk rock and protest songs

The ballad – a simple, reflective song used to tell a story – has always been a popular form in folk music. In the mid-twentieth century, American folk singers performed songs of social conscience, particularly when times were hard for many Americans, especially families living in the more rural parts of the United States. In the early 1960s, when it became clear that the brave new world promised after the horrors of World War II was not materialising and the world seemed to be heading for political and environmental disaster, a new breed of folk singers began producing contemporary 'protest' songs.

Pete Seeger and Bob Dylan, in particular, built on the traditions of previous folk musicians, such as Woody Guthrie, and added elements of contemporary popular musical styles. Their songs were simple in form, usually strophic with a repeated chorus, uncomplicated in harmony (centring around chords I, IV and V), and often simple in melody with pentatonic or restricted range tunes. Later in the 1960s, Bob Dylan's musical style became heavier as he began composing and performing in heavier rock styles, but his songs still retained elements of the folk-song style.

Music to turn and blow your mind

In the nineteenth century, Berlioz's *Symphonie Fantastique* told the story, through music, of a young artist who experienced a series of dreams and nightmares as a consequence of taking opium. Today, we are concerned with the associations that the drug Ecstasy has with dance music. In the 1960s, the drug was LSD. LSD is extremely powerful and can induce vivid hallucinations and radically alter the drug-taker's sensual perspective. Musicians who took the drug wanted to imitate these sensations in their compositions, and the result was psychedelic music.

Using contemporary recording and electronic amplification techniques, composers created what was at the time extremely weird and confusing music. Original recordings are played backwards (sometimes with unusual reverb effects applied) and guitar effects pedals are used copiously. Composers experimented with changing metres, unusual chord progressions (sometimes including chromatic harmonies), and new, synthesised electronic timbres. Today, with our advanced technology, it is perhaps difficult to appreciate the creativity of this music, or indeed the impact that the music had at the time. As the Psychedelic movement grew, so did the interest of popular musicians in spiritual matters.

The peace movements that developed in reaction to the Cold War and the Vietnam War found a natural home in the psychedelic pop music of the day, in the culture of drug-taking and in the communal rock festivals of the late 1960s. The particular interest in spiritual matters led to a number of influential musicians becoming involved in Buddhism and other world faiths. This involvement in turn had an impact on popular musical styles.

Music from India

George Harrison's studies with the sitar maestro Ravi Shankar in 1966, The Beatles' study tour of India in 1968 and the subsequent integration of elements of Indian classical music styles into the songs of The Beatles and The Rolling Stones (amongst others), brought non-western world musical styles into the popular western public arena for the first time. Although music has a unique place in Indian culture and, clearly, the musical accent is different from that of the west, the elements and structures of both styles are parallelled to a great degree.

- **Raga** – this is the Indian musical scale, from which melodies are drawn. Unlike western scales, there is no consistent intervallic formula for the construction of ragas. Rather, each raga has its own pattern which is linked to the mood of the music, or the time of day at which it should be performed. The number of notes in a raga can vary, but five-note ragas are common, giving a pentatonic flavour to the music. With stringed instruments such as the sitar favoured, together with an elastic and highly melismatic style of vocalising known as khyal, the melody of Indian music has a flexible approach to intonation, with much pitch-bending and subtle inflections.
- **Tala** – this is a rhythmic cycle (like an ostinato) which is constantly repeated but which also constantly develops throughout a piece of music. The tala is most likely to be played on tabla (a pair of drums tuned to different pitches) and the dhol (a drum at bass pitch).
- **Drone** – harmony in Indian music is based around the drone which, in turn, is usually formed from the two main notes of the raga. These notes are called the 'vadi' and the 'samvadi'. In western music we know these as the tonic and dominant.

It is not difficult to see parallels between western popular musical styles and classical Indian music. It is therefore not surprising that Indian-based melodies and rhythms should sit so comfortably in western popular music songs.

A rather neat reversal of this process has been the development in India and in Indian communities abroad of 'banghra'. This fuses elements of contemporary western dance and techno music with the traditional Indian musical styles.

Reggae

In the same way that the country and hillbilly music of middle America had been fertilised with the blues to produce rock 'n' roll in the 1950s, the mid-1960s saw American rock and blues mixing with the traditional folk and dance styles of the Caribbean to produce ska, rock steady and, in time, reggae.

As in early 1960s Britain, American rock records became well known in Jamaica through the import of records and radio broadcasts. The result was that a new style of music developed which amalgamated American rock with the rhythms and fast-moving harmonic rhythms of Jamaican folk dance and song. As this music was enthusiastically developed by young people, it inevitably took on a fast tempo and the dance that grew out of the music – the skank – gave rise to the music being named ska. When the tempo of the music slowed down, the music became known as rock steady and, eventually, reggae. Theories abound as to the meaning of the word reggae, but it is generally accepted that the word is derived from the Jamaican patois, or slang-accent, of the 1960s. Musically, the most appropriate explanation is that 'reggae' is patois for 'regular', referring to the infinitely repeated rhythmic and bass patterns that make up the musical texture.

Stars of reggae

Inevitably, though it started as a 'roots' form of music, reggae quickly gained commercial success through the promotion of artists such as Jimmy Cliff, Desmond Dacres (better known as Desmond Dekker) and Bob Marley. Since the 1970s, reggae has also influenced the musical styles of white European musicians such as The Police and Madness.

The musical characteristics of reggae

Ska, rock steady and reggae all share common musical characteristics. The most easily recognisable of these are:

- a heavy, repetitive chord rhythm. Short, sharp chords are played on the off-half-beats (1 **&** 2 **&** 3 **&** 4 **&**), usually on the guitar or organ. When the guitar is used for these chords, a downwards 'chop' stroke is always used and then immediately dampened by the left hand. Often, to make the stroke cleaner, only the top four strings of the guitar are used. This style of guitar-playing is sometimes known as the reggae 'shank' style

- tri-functional bass lines. Reggae bass lines provide a strong harmonic bass – the harmonies of reggae are mostly in root position. The harmonic function of the bass line is also emphasised by the fact that the bass often plays arpeggio figures which reflect the prevailing harmony. These bass lines often take on an almost melodic quality, providing a kind of counterpoint against the (often more static) vocal melody. Finally, reggae bass lines have a very strong rhythmic shape with use of syncopations (contrasting with the straighter almost constrained drum rhythms) and are frequently phrased across bar lines

- reggae hi-hat cymbal lines are most commonly in the form of continuous quavers, with occasional semiquaver fills at the end of phrases. (Compare this with the continuous semiquaver hi-hat parts in disco – see page 165.)

- in reggae, the snare and bass drums commonly play what is known as a 'one-drop' rhythm – in accented unison on the second and fourth beats of the bar, but with much less or nothing on the first and third beats. Again, compare this with other styles of pop music, where the backbeat snare on the second and fourth beats reacts against the bass drum on the first and third beats of the bar.

Put all of these rhythms together, and a unique rhythmic texture is created:

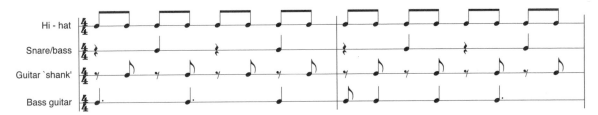

These reggae patterns combine to produce what is sometimes an almost hypnotic, trance-like effect. As with the dance-music genre 'trance' in the 1990s (see page 172), one has to consider the connection between reggae music and the culture of drug-taking that is sometimes associated with it. Reggae is also linked to the Rastafarian religious sect where cannabis is sacramentally smoked. Indeed, there are overt references to this in a number of reggae songs.

Rude boys

Much of reggae's early success in Jamaica can be attributed to the disc jockeys who played and promoted the new musical style amongst the 'rude boys' – young men who were frequently involved in street violence and other criminal activities. It was these same DJs who developed an off-shoot of reggae that, in turn, has had a great influence on the development of other popular musical styles. During their performances, the DJs would often talk and even sometimes recite poetry in rhythm with a reggae record as a backtrack. This practice became known as 'dubbing' or 'toasting'. In time, the B sides of singles would simply take the form of the A side with the vocals removed, to enable the DJ to dub freely. Some twenty years later, in the late 1980s, this practice was to develop in the United States as rap (see page 168) and the role of the DJ as a creative force would also develop.

1970s disco, 1980s house

From the birth of rock 'n' roll in the 1950s, we have seen that commercialism – the need and/or desire to sell records – has influenced the development of musical style. The output of Tamla Motown and the Phil Spector artists in the 1960s (see page 156) proved that 'formulaic' music, composed in a 'house' style, was commercially saleable and profitable. The development in the early 1970s of modern American dance halls equipped with vast banks of lights, powerful sound systems and, most importantly, large open dance floors almost went hand in hand with the emergence of a new musical style – Disco. Its roots were in Motown and Atlantic soul.

The musical characteristics of disco

Not surprisingly, as it is fundamentally a dance style, the central, most important musical element of disco is rhythm. Like swing in the 1930s, disco is built around a constantly repeating rhythmic motif. Note particularly that:

- the rhythmic motif is heavily based on semiquaver patterns, which contribute to the overall speed and movement of the musical style
- this semiquaver drive is invariably given to a tight hi-hat cymbal, closed on the beats of a four-four bar, but left open for the space in between the beats
- in addition, the semiquaver-based riffs are sometimes played by the rhythm guitar with swift, clean up- and down-strokes and played through the distinctive wah-wah pedal
- because of the velocity of the strokes,

Saturday Night Fever

disco guitar chords are often confined to the four upper strings (making less distance for the stroke). This results in a bright, clean tone

- disco bass plays a slower, but similarly repeating rhythmic pattern which emphasises the first and third beats of the bar, with the snare emphasising beats two and four.

Whilst disco was born and sold as an American product, European disco music – Europop – also enjoyed success, although it tended to be even more formulaic than the American original. Language was another problem – the rhyme and accent of American English was an integral part of the disco vocal style (as it was to be ten years later with rap). Other languages, or translated lyrics, sometimes stifled the musical style and nearly always limited the commercial possibilities of the recordings.

Disco, as a mass market commercial genre, continued in popularity into the 1980s. A new, harder-edged disco sound developed, known as 'Chicago House' (after the Chicago Warehouse, a gay dance club where it was first played). In Europe, the new 'house' music was promoted in the Mediterranean holiday resorts, notably Ibiza. There it became known as 'acid house'. This was not, as you might think, because of the music's associations with drugs, but because this new brand of disco music used synthesised sampling as an integral part of the musical texture. 'Acid burning' was an American phrase for 'sampling'. Much of the acid house music – disco played on synthesisers and drum machines with integrated samples – was produced by European groups such as Technotronic (from Germany) and Black Box (from Italy).

Fusion and funk

In many ways, jazz has always been a fusion of musical traditions. However, the term 'fusion' is given to a form of jazz that developed through the cool jazz period – when, as we have seen on pages 150–3, jazz musicians such as Stan Getz integrated other musical traditions into the musical texture. What makes fusion so distinctive is the way that the instrumentation, harmonic resource and melodic lines of jazz are blended with the rhythms of other popular musical styles such as rhythm 'n' blues and rock 'n' roll. In the 1970s, this blending of styles extended to disco to create the musical style known as funk.

The word funk is a rather unsavoury American slang word. Funk is certainly not unpleasant in the same way, but it is possible that the term refers to the 'dirty' bass line that characterises the style. Funk is much more complicated rhythmically than disco, it features more substantial uses of horn sections (with improvisations or quasi-improvisatory passages), the use of complex bass and keyboard riffs, and intense vocal harmonies. Popular funk bands include Earth, Wind and Fire, Weather Report, and the British groups Shakatak and The Average White Band.

Glam and glitter

The British 'glam rock' bands of the early 1970s were initially a reaction to the serious direction that heavy rock and heavy metal were taking, both musically (with album tracks extending to ten minutes or more) and in terms of image (male, aggressive, and with a distinctive predominance of dark colour and feeling). Glam groups all had their roots firmly in rock 'n' roll and you can clearly hear the rhythms and harmonic structures of the blues in their songs. But the groups also brought a sense of fun to their songs, together with a somewhat outrageous approach to their stage acts and costumes.

After the initial commercial success in the early 1970s, glam rock developed in a number of different directions. Some groups, such as Mud, The Sweet and Slade did not progress beyond the original glam rock style and, to this day, continue to give nostalgic if anachronistic concerts of their songs. Other artists developed their compositions and performances in keeping with other developments in popular music, whilst maintaining their stylistic heritage of glam rock. The group Queen, and the singer-songwriters David Bowie and Elton John are all examples of artists whose music is substantial in content, stylistically evolving and developing through the years but whose performance skills are clearly influenced by their having worked through the glam rock period.

Punk rock

When the boutique owner, Malcolm McLaren, imported the punk look into Britain and created the band The Sex Pistols, he broke the mould of British rock music. For the first time, a new popular music style and fashion was deliberately and commercially promoted, rather than evolving naturally out of musical traditions.

We have seen how the music of The Beatles grew out of the American rock 'n' roll, British skiffle and music hall traditions; we have seen how Atlantic soul had its roots in gospel; and we have seen how heavy metal grew out of rhythm 'n' blues and the innovative 60s guitarists. Initially, punk rock was not about musical heritage or, indeed, any heritage at all. It was a commercial fashion movement, designed to shock the establishment, give a front for the rebellious young to vent their 'anger' about the 'boredom' that was their lives, and provide an ironic antidote to the glit-

tery world of glam rock. This it did through the outrageous (and often obscene) behaviour of the punk artists, the ripped clothing, the extreme hairstyles and, of most concern to us, the raw and sometimes barbaric music.

The Sex Pistols were created by Malcolm McLaren for their image, not for their musical abilities. Legend has it that Johnny Rotten (real name John Lydon!), the lead singer of The Pistols, auditioned for the band by doing an act whilst miming to a recording. (It's ironic to note that, today, many of the 'clean-cut' bands also mime in performance in order to present a more commercially attractive sound and image, but that's another story!)

The musical characteristics of punk rock

The sound of punk rock is distinctive and contains the following features:

- a vocal style which is almost half-spoken, half-sung
- a limited melodic range – sometimes the melodies encompass only a 3rd or 4th and move mainly by step
- restricted chord patterns, with frequent use of parallel chords (involving minimal left hand guitar movement)
- much use of repeated riff ideas, particularly in the bass lines and, again, encompassing a limited pitch range and moving by step.

After the initial punk explosion, some groups adopted elements of the punk style – usually the instrumental textures and the vocal styles – and integrated these with a more skilful and structured approach in their compositions and performances. The messages of these groups' songs was usually a little more considered too, taking the form of a 'protest song' for the 70s, in the tradition of Bob Dylan. These bands were sometimes known as 'new wave' and, perhaps not unsurprisingly, it was these groups, like The Stranglers and Paul Weller's The Jam, who maintained their musical development throughout and beyond the punk era.

Having said all this, punk rock did leave a musical legacy of sorts which has had a degree of influence on subsequent musicians. In the early 80s, the 'new romantic' movement combined a kitsch visual image derived from glam rock with a sanitised musical variation of punk. In the 90s, the punky vocal style of Johnny Rotten and his colleagues can be heard in bands like Nirvana and Oasis, as we will see on pages 169–72.

The 1980s and new technology

We have already seen how, in the early 1980s, new innovations in synthesised and sampled music transformed disco into acid house music. The 1980s was certainly the decade of the synthesiser, with a whole range of musicians incorporating the new technologies into their work across a diverse range of styles. At one extreme, groups such as Erasure, Kraftwerk and The Human League abandoned acoustic or 'live performed' instruments in favour of pre-sequenced synthesised timbres and tracks.

MIDI

MIDI – Musical Instrument Digital Interface – is a method of linking, communicating between, synchronising and recording electronic musical devices. It was introduced in 1983, with the first commercial MIDI sequencing package available in the following year. Since then, MIDI sequencers have developed into sophisticated tools for manipulating every aspect of music performance, including every subtlety of tempo, dynamic, pitch and articulation. Today's MIDI sequencers are highly complex but in pre-MIDI or the early days of MIDI, the sequenced music often had a mechanical feel to it with the use of rigid quantisation and prominent use of controllers such as pitch bend. When General MIDI was agreed as the industry standard in 1991 the music became more sophisticated and musically crafted. The mechanical nature of the early sequenced artists was matched by the early 1980s dance crazes such as robotics and breakdancing.

MIDI triggered a number of other developments in music performing and recording. The sampler – where an extract of music, instrumental sound or spoken voice can be recorded and stored digitally and then replayed when triggered by a MIDI message – has caused a great deal of controversy in the music business. As with early MIDI sequences, early samples used in songs tended to be either less sophisticated, over-used, or simply pasted on to the musical fabric as an effect. Nowadays, with advances in sample editing and much more sophisticated MIDI sequence programmes, samples are totally integrated into musical textures.

MIDI can also be used to synchronise other electronic media, including lighting and video, so that music, lights and pictures can work in tandem. SMPTE is a time code which can be laid down as part of musical sequences, on video tapes and in computerised light sequences. It enables composers to match events in their compositions to exact images in a filmed or animated sequence. Clearly, this is of great help not only to composers of incidental film music, but also to the producers of the pop video. The first great pop video was Queen's 'Bohemian Rhapsody' in pre-MIDI 1975. By the 1980s, however, the production of a video to accompany a pop single release became almost obligatory.

Rap and hip hop

We have already seen how the reggae DJs 'toasted' over their records, in a recitative-like fashion (see page 165). In the late 1970s, DJs in American city dance houses developed this tradition by 'rapping' over disco records. Two factors contributed to the development of rap into a powerful, distinctive musical phenomenon. Firstly, rap wasn't simply a musical style, it was an attitude, a culture. Originally, the culture was somewhat aggressive and racially divisive; rap was black music and was promoted as such by groups like Niggaz With Attitude. However, as ever, the influence of rap eventually spread and white rappers such as Vanilla Ice enjoyed considerable success in the early 1990s.

The other significant factor in the development of rap – and in the development of later dance music – were the techniques and skills acquired by the DJs such as 'scratching', manually moving vinyl records on the turntable to create distinctive timbral effects; and segueing, where a stream of dance numbers with a similar bpm (beats per minute, or speed) could be joined together by combining them with a unifying beat provided by an electronic drum machine.

Rap in turn gave rise to the wider culture of hip hop, which embraced the rap musical style (including scratching), dance crazes such as breakdancing and moonwalking, the visual pop-art graffiti (or vandalism, depending on your point of view), and a certain amount of violent behaviour. Hip hop was an urban culture and was at its height in New York, with the subway the focus for the graffiti and 'steaming' (mugging of subway passengers).

Thankfully, most of the unsavoury influences of rap and hip hop have abated, while many of the musical influences play heavily on the dance music of today.

Britpop

One of the most fascinating aspects of popular music in the 1990s was the resurgence of interest in 'easy listening' music, alongside the rise of modern techno-dance styles. Sales of re-

mastered recordings (on CD) by artists such as Andy Williams and Frank Sinatra – complete with their lush, singing strings and punchy brass chord accompaniments – have rocketed. British groups from the 1960s, such as The Kinks, The Rolling Stones and The Beatles have all found a new generation of audiences and have themselves influenced a new generation of British bands such as Blur and Oasis. The Britpop groups have been compared and contrasted with their 1960s forebears, with good reason. Their music marked a return to the classic vocals-guitar-bass guitar-drum line up. Through the use of clear, uncomplicated harmonies and rhythms, tuneful melodies and catchy choruses, their songs have immediate appeal.

Arguably the most successful of these Britpop groups is Oasis. Much has been made of the similarities between Oasis and The Beatles, and the Gallagher brothers make no secret of their admiration for the songs of Lennon and McCartney. There is, without doubt, a close link between the musical styles of the two bands. But are Noel Gallagher's songs a mere imitation or pastiche of The Beatles' style? Or should we acknowledge that, whilst the songs of The Beatles (and those composed by John Lennon, in particular) are an important part of Gallagher's 'cultural baggage', they are no more than an influence on a uniquely personal compositional style?

Don't Look Back in Anger
Noel Gallagher

Slip in - side __ the eye of your mind, _____ don't you know you might _ find _____ a bet-ter place to play_

_____ You said __ that you __ ne - ver been_____ but all the things that you've seen_

_____ slow-ly fade a - way. So I start a re-vo-lu-tion from my bed, 'cause you

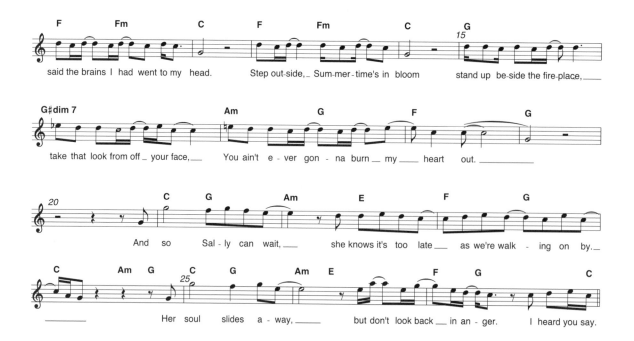

Instrumentation

The instrumental line-up for this song is two electric guitars, one bass guitar, drums and vocalist – a standard rock band line-up. Also heard are synthesised strings, piano and organ. Both guitars have melodic and harmonic roles to play, providing rhythm chords and fills at the end of phrases. One guitar has a lead (melodic) break after the second chorus. The bass provides a simple, straight quaver, mainly root bassline. The drums provide a standard eight-beat (quaver) rock drum pattern, with frequent semiquaver fills. The piano is only heard in the introduction. Thereafter, the organ and the strings provide a sustained harmonic pad, with no melodic interest.

Harmony

The general harmonic rhythm of the song is two harmonies per bar. The main exception to this pattern comes just before the chorus (bars 19–20) where the harmonic rhythm slows down to one harmony per bar. Tonally, the music stays in the key of C major for the whole of this song. However, three of the chords used are diatonically alien to C major. The first is the chord of E, which we hear for the first time in bar 6. This major version of chord III serves as a secondary

dominant to chord VI (the relative minor), which precedes it. The second alien chord is the minor version of chord IV (Fm), which we hear directly after the (usual) major version of chord IV in bar 13. There is no doubt that this harmonic progression is a favourite device of Lennon/McCartney in The Beatles' songs. Finally, in bar 20 a diminished 7th chord on G♯ is used. This chord actually serves the same function as the major III chord that we heard in bar 6 – as VII7 of A minor (chord VI in C major). It is also a substitute secondary dominant chord.

Musical influences

There are some obvious, almost 'direct' references to Lennon/McCartney songs in 'Don't Look Back in Anger'. The opening piano introduction is clearly related to the opening of John Lennon's 'Imagine'. The use of the major/minor versions of chord IV is a favourite Lennon/McCartney device. (Find an example from one of your own favourite Beatles' songs!) The use of the major III chord in a major key song is another device used by Lennon and McCartney; for example, in 'All You Need Is Love'. However, these harmonies are not exclusive to Beatles' songs. This altered chord III is a device favoured by the Motown house composers, amongst others, and it is not inconceivable that these could have influenced

Oasis

Lennon and McCartney. The most that we can say here is that all composers of popular music use a common musical and stylistic language, and that in all probability, Noel Gallagher has learnt the language through his knowledge of the songs of Lennon and McCartney.

Looking beyond 'Don't Look Back in Anger', Noel Gallagher has written modal melodies; for example, 'Morning Glory' is in the transposed Aeolian mode (E-E, with F♯). 'Wonderwall' and 'Roll With It' also have modal melodies. The Beatles also used exactly the same transposed mode as 'Morning Glory' for 'Eleanor Rigby', but there the similarity ends. (Compare the use of strings in 'Eleanor Rigby' and 'Yesterday' with the string pad used in 'Don't Look Back in Anger'.) In any case, modal melodies are commonplace in all styles of rock and pop. 'Satisfaction' by The Rolling Stones uses the same transposed Aeolian mode as Oasis in 'Morning Glory'.

Melodically, Noel Gallagher's songs favour the repetition – either exactly or in sequence – of short one- or two-bar phrases. This is in the style of punk rock songs from the 1970s, as are aspects of the vocal delivery which is tinged with the almost sneering tone of John Lydon (aka Johnny Rotten) and, perhaps, Mick Jagger before him. Compare and contrast the vocal styles of Gallagher and Jagger. Sometimes, one can clearly hear the anthemic, lyrical style of The Beatles. The chorus of 'Don't Look Back In Anger' is a great example of this. However, the Oasis vocal style obviously has several influences.

Pastiche or influence?

The question of influences, of course, is not just about Noel Gallagher and The Beatles. The same sort of question could be asked about the string quartets written by Mozart after he had discovered similar works by Haydn. All composers have 'cultural baggage' and formative musical experiences that go with them and shape their creativity. Often, composers will make reference to the musical style of others by way of a tribute. This was certainly the case with Mozart in K387, for example, and it could well be the case with Noel Gallagher in the introduction to 'Don't Look Back in Anger'.

If you are a composer yourself, you will certainly have your own influences. Learning to compose is all about acquiring and learning to use musical vocabulary, and this is done through playing and listening to the music of others. What is important in developing a compositional style is how you make the acquired language your own, with your own individual accent or fingerprint.

The compositional style of Noel Gallagher is certainly founded on a musical language inherited through John Lennon and others. There may even be some phrases which are borrowed directly from Lennon, as we have shown. But 'Don't Look Back in Anger' is not a pastiche. It is a song of the 1990s (with 90s instrumentation and instrumental techniques), a vocal style for the 90s (with punk influences), and a depth of texture and a hardness of edge that goes beyond their 1960s models. Important though the influence of The Beatles is, it is impossible to ignore other influences on Oasis' musical style. They were influenced by the whole Manchester music scene of the 1980s and early 1990s, including the music of The Smiths, The Stone Roses, and the kings of 'Madchester', The Happy Mondays.

Further work and listening

- Listen to more songs by The Rolling Stones and The Beatles, and to other Britpop groups such as Blur and Pulp as well as Oasis. Compare and contrast the compositional and performance styles of the two generations.
- Compare and contrast 80s/90s cover versions of British hits from the 1960s. Try 'All Day and All of the Night' by The Kinks (1964) and The Stranglers (1988). What are the differences in performance style, and which do you prefer?
- Listen to other Manchester-born rock and pop from the 1980s and early 1990s: The Smiths, The Stone Roses and The Happy Mondays. Which aspects of their musical styles did Oasis inherit?
- What are the major influences on your own compositional style? Have you ever consciously imitated the works of others in your own 'original' compositions? What can be learnt from composing pastiche?

Dance and club styles

In the introduction to this section on popular music, we noted that 'what is essential to the understanding of the way in which popular music has evolved over the past 100 years is a realisation that recordings and technologies have enabled the cross-fertilisation and fusion of musical styles'. Technological advances led to the development of disco into the acid house and rap styles of the 1980s. These advances continued at an increasingly frenetic rate in the 1990s. Central to the plethora of dance styles of the late 1990s – amongst them trance, trip-hop, ambient, garage, jungle, and rhythm 'n' bass (confusingly sometimes abbreviated as R'n'B) – is the development of three technological tools:

- the sampler, where timbres or short extracts from existing works can be digitally recorded and then integrated into new compositions
- the portable multitrack recording studio, allowing compositions to be made in a variety of locations. Digital recording portastudios allow for easier editing, and for integration with digital samplers
- the spread of the Internet, allowing virtually unlimited access to all styles of music and giving composers the opportunity to promote their music to a world-wide audience.

With the cost of this equipment diminishing all the time, a much greater number of musicians have been encouraged to engage in composition. This, together with the increasing cross-fertilisation of musical styles, has led to greater diversity of musical style. Inevitably, all this has given rise to a number of important musical and even ethical questions. The 'borrowing' of samples from existing works has led to some really exciting and creative sound-collages, but many people have raised issues of musical copyright concerning these 'borrowings'. It has also been argued that the power and high availability of the new technology has led to the production of a disproportionately high level of inferior music amongst some clearly creative and imaginative work. Finally, it is argued by some that the high dependence on technology has led to a dehumanising of the music.

The answer to these criticisms of contemporary dance music may be found in the rise of the disc jockey as performer. Today's DJs are more than simply turntable operators. They have become creative artists in their own right. Not only do they create new 'mixes' of sounds, using the full gamut of technological devices including samplers, multi-track recorders, computers and vinyl disks on 'decks'. They also make these mixes live, on the dance floor, making the DJ a creative performer as well as a composer.

Television signatures

New digital and satellite technology has caused

a huge expansion in the number of television channels and, consequently, the number of television programmes made and broadcast. This has meant an increase in employment for musicians, with opportunities to compose incidental music (with the aid of MIDI technology), and 'signature tunes', signalling the start and end of a programme.

Composing a television signature tune is a refined art. Like a jazz standard, a Eurovision Song Contest entry, or – in the days of vinyl records – a hit single, the television signature tune is a formulaic process and a number of unwritten compositional conventions have developed in the genre. The success of a theme tune depends on the ability of the composer to achieve success in every element of this formula.

As a rule, successful television signature tunes display the following characteristics:

- The signature tune matches the mood or ethos of the programme that follows through tempo, pitch, texture, dynamics.
- Metre (time signature) can also set mood; a square 4/4 metre is comfortable, whereas an irregular metre (5/8, 7/8) can portray unrest or urgency. Similarly, unsquare melodic phrasing – syncopated or across bar lines – can also signal emergency.
- The choice of key can also set mood; neutral or flat keys can give a comfortable, familiar feel to signature tunes. 'EastEnders' is in E♭ major, 'Coronation Street' is in A♭

major and 'Brookside' ends in C major after flirting with several keys, including F major.
- These factors must be contained within a strictly limited time period, usually of twenty to thirty seconds. In this short time span, there is no room for confusion or contradiction – the message and mood must be conveyed directly.
- Because of the short duration of the theme, musical material must be punchy and to the point, and there must not be too much of it. Short two- or four-bar phrases, repeated exactly or with a little variation, help to make a signature tune memorable.
- The use of a distinctive motif – such as a scale pattern, an arpeggio or a quirky rhythm, also helps to make the tune memorable. This is often paired with distinctive orchestration/instrumentation.
- The very first thing that the listener hears in a signature tune is vitally important, and should be as distinctive as possible.

Simon May and Leslie Osborne
Theme music for 'EastEnders'

This music has been the signature tune for the BBC soap-opera 'EastEnders' since the first episode in 1985, and was specifically commissioned for the series. Simon May has also composed a number of other successful signature tunes for the BBC, including 'Holiday' and 'Howard's Way'.

Theme music for 'EastEnders'
Simon May and Leslie Osborne

Melody

The melody is constructed out of square two-bar phrases organised into antecedent and consequent phrases. Note the way in which Simon May has made use of the six-note scalic idea – ascending in the antecedent phrase, descending in the consequent phrase.

Form

In this extract, the phrases are organised in an A: A1: B: A: A2: Coda pattern. The versions that open and close each episode of the programme are slightly truncated versions of this. Listen for yourself and note down the form!

Tonality and harmony

The key chosen is Eb major – a 'flat', comfortable key. 'EastEnders' is a soap opera, seen three times a week, and, although featuring some extraordinary storylines from time to time, has a homely, everyday feel to it. All of the chords used are diatonic, with no chromatic alterations (not even secondary dominants). This adds to the directness of the music.

Instrumentation

Although the orchestration of this tune may seem quite ordinary at first hearing, there are one or two subtleties to the arrangement which contribute to the music's flavour. The main melody is scored for a piano which, whilst not quite having a honky tonk timbre, has the feel of the 'pub sing-along' to it as, perhaps, you might find in the Queen Vic. This tune is doubled by a whistle intended, perhaps, to sound reminiscent of a Cockney barrow-boy whistling cheerfully. Listen carefully and you might hear the sound of Bow Bells as well!

Viewers associate a particular sound or orchestration with the style and feel of their favourite programmes. Television companies will change or re-score a signature tune if they want to give the programme a new image – perhaps in keeping with the changing times, or changes to the viewing audience. A good example of this is the 'Blue Peter' theme tune which, in its 40 plus years has undergone a number of metamorphoses to reflect the changing attitudes of children. On the other hand, long-running adult shows like 'Coronation Street' have kept the same theme tune arrangement for 40 or 50 years, emphasising the programmes' traditional values and traditional audiences.

Rhythm

Apart from the rhythms of the melody – including the crotchet-triplet-group figure – there are two distinctive rhythmic ideas that permeate the 'EastEnders' theme. One is in the bass – a dotted crotchet-quaver idea, which moves the music forward – and the other is a two-quaver hand-clap that comes on the fourth beat of every other bar. Finally, of course, there is the rhythmic idea that instantly makes the music identifiable, and which calls us to attention. This is the triplet-crotchet/quaver/semiquaver tom-tom signal at the very start.

Further work and listening

- Choose two contrasting television theme tunes – from a news/current affairs programme and a comedy show, for example. Analyse both tunes in the same way that 'EastEnders' is analysed here. How are the musical styles of the two tunes different? What have the composers tried to achieve through their music?

Film music

Even before the first 'talkies', where sound in films was integrated with moving image, music played an important role in cinema. The silent movies were accompanied by a single pianist or organist, or in special cases, a pit orchestra. The skill for these players was to perform whilst watching the film, ensuring that the music was played at moments appropriate to the action. Even when sound recording was added to the film, the incidental music was added or 'synched on' by the conductor and other performers watching the pictures played back before them as they recorded the music. The advent of MIDI, and SMPTE – the Society of Motion Picture and Television Engineers' standard procedure – has meant that music can be recorded and synchronised digitally with a video image, using a complex and extremely accurate time code.

Pastiche or influence?

Over the course of the twentieth century, incidental film music has developed as a hybrid of art music and popular styles. Although one of the most important aspects of the film music composer's brief is to match music with mood, both generally in terms of the whole film and specifically in terms of specific events within the film, many film music composers have regarded their art as symphonic, producing scores which have a musical unity through the use of leitmotifs and leitmotivic development. An excellent example of this is John Williams' scores for the 'Star Wars' series of films. Williams matches the characters and narrative themes of good and evil that run throughout the series with a similar set of musical motifs matched to characters and narrative themes. Inevitably, working in an art form which is all about recounting events, times and places, many film scores are written in pastiche or quasi-pastiche styles. It is also fair to say that composers have chosen to write in musical styles which substantially borrow from the styles of previous composers where appropriate. And it is not surprising that some of the great composers of dramatic, emotional orchestral music – Tchaikovsky and Stravinsky amongst them – have been reflected in the musical styles of some of the most successful 'studio' composers. Listen to John Williams' score for 'Jaws' and you will hear more than a hint of Stravinsky's 'Rite of Spring'! At the same time, composers who have earned their reputations as major art music composers in their own right, like William Walton, managed to enjoy studio success without diluting their normal, personal compositional style.

Another option for film producers is to use existing music or songs alongside newly-composed music for their film soundtracks. An early example of this was the use of Rachmaninov's *Piano Concerto No. 2* as the soundtrack for David Lean's film 'Brief Encounter' in 1945; similarly, in 1991 the film 'The Commitments' used classic Atlantic soul songs as a soundtrack. Many films from the 1990s use a varied, sometimes unrelated collection of songs where the music or lyrics or both seem to capture perfectly a time, place, or emotion – 1960s London or the Vietnam War, for example.

The underscore

An important aspect of the film composer's art is creating an 'underscore' – music that is played discretely underneath dialogue. Composers creating underscored music, sometimes known as non-diegetic music, are faced with important decisions about the role that the music will play in conveying the drama to the audience. These decisions will undoubtedly be made with the director and/or the producer of the film, but ultimately it is the composer's responsibility to make the music work both for the film and musically in its own right.

The composer needs to decide:

- if there is any doubt in the audience's minds about what is happening visually, can music tell the audience how they should be reacting to the image?

- if there is no doubt about the nature or emotion of the image, how can music reinforce this feeling?
- how music can be structured or created to reinforce the physicality of an event or a series of events on film. (For example, how can music reproduce in sound the rhythm of an axe being repeatedly brought down on a log?)
- how music can be used to identify or create individual characters in a film. (For example, could individual characters or emotions be given leitmotifs, as in opera?) How can these themes be metamorphosed to reflect changing character or situations?

Just as a successful television programme needs a striking theme tune (see page 172), successful films invariably have a song which plays across the opening and closing credits. Again, this could be a pre-existing song (sometimes re-recorded especially for the film), or it could be especially composed for the film. In the case of newly-composed songs, the lyrics usually sum up the narrative or emotions of the film – 'You've Got a Friend in Me' from Disney's 'Toy Story' is a classic of this type. Alternatively the music itself is constructed from motifs used and developed in the incidental and non-diegetic music.

Leonard Bernstein at work

Further work and listening

- Watch a film which uses a collection of pre-existing songs as the soundtrack. Why have the songs been chosen, and how successful is the choice?
- Watch a film with specially commissioned non-diegetic music. What is the composer's aim in each scene? (Refer to the checklist given previously.) How successful is the music in the context of the film?

The musical

With the advent of films with sound, it was only natural that stage musicals, which had been popular throughout the first three decades of the twentieth century, should transfer on to the big screen. One of the most important aspects of this transfer was that a much bigger and more diverse audience was exposed to the composer's work, making the musical styles extremely popular.

Many films merely served as an opportunity to incorporate a number of set songs into the storyline. In the 1930s and 1940s, these songs were often in the classic thirty-two-bar standard form and composers such as Jerome Kern (1885–1945), Irving Berlin (1888–1989) and George Gershwin (1898–1937) enjoyed great success. Many films employed a team of musicians to assist with the musical production, with house arrangers taking care of matters such as the lush, full orchestrations that were required. This is still the practice today for both film and stage musical composers.

Encouraged by the success of the film musicals, interest in live, staged musicals increased in the middle of the century through the work of Rodgers and Hammerstein ('The Sound of Music'), Lerner and Loewe ('My Fair Lady'), and Frank Loesser ('Guys and Dolls').

Leonard Bernstein and 'West Side Story'

Arguably the greatest of all stage/film musical composers of the second half of the twentieth century was Leonard Bernstein (1918–1990). Like William Walton, Bernstein was a classically trained musician and composer of symphonies and choral works who also worked in the media of film and the theatre. On 'West Side Story', one of the most famous musicals of the 1950s, Bernstein collaborated with Stephen Sondheim a prolific composer of stage musicals in his own right, but who in this instance acted as lyricist. The musical score for the show contains many of the stylistic features typical of opera – solo arias, duets, complex ensembles where contrasting lines weave polyphonically, interacting with and sometimes opposing each other. What's more, Bernstein's score brings together a unique blend of high musical craftsmanship

(reflecting his musical training), the rhythms and melodies of mid-twentieth century jazz, and a high sense of the drama of the play being brought out through the musical score.

Leonard Bernstein and Stephen Sondheim
'Something's Coming' from *West Side Story*

The song 'Something's Coming', which appears early in 'West Side Story', is an excellent example of Bernstein's style. Listen to the song on CD2, track 31.

This is a solo song for Tony the tragic hero of 'West Side Story'. In the song, he soliloquises about the events that he is anticipating might happen at the dance that evening. Will he meet the girl? Will there be some 'action' (in the form of a fight)?

'Something's Coming' from West Side Story
Leonard Bernstein and Stephen Sondheim

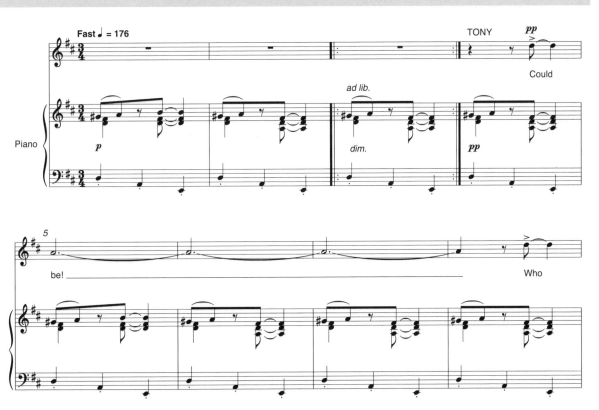

Matching dramatic and musical tension

Bernstein expresses Tony's tension and excitement through a number of musical devices. First, there is a cross-rhythmic tension throughout the song. The bass line pumps out the three-crotchet beat pattern of the 3/4 metre, whilst the vocal line – doubled in the orchestra – has a rhythm which suggests a 6/8 feel. This hemiolic rhythm is a feature elsewhere in 'West Side Story', most notably in 'America'. Later in this song, the hemiola is reversed when the accompaniment goes into 2/4 time and the melody carries a three-beat cross rhythm. The unsettled feeling that these rhythms create is added to by the pitch of the bass line, which features a strong tonic-dominant axis on the first two beats of the bar, followed by the supertonic on the third beat.

Melodically, the vocal line is characterised by opening on the note a tritone (the *diablous in musica*) above the tonic (G♯ against D). This is perhaps a sign that the something that's coming might not be very pleasant. Again, this is a feature found elsewhere in this score: 'Maria', Tony's hymn to his femme fatale, starts with exactly the same motif.

Further work and listening

- Study the songs 'America', 'Maria', 'I Feel Pretty' and 'Somewhere' from 'West Side Story'. How does Bernstein use music to convey the emotion and/or action of the drama?

Folk music today

Throughout the pop, rock and jazz section of this book, there have been many references to the way in which diverse musical and cultural elements have blended together to create a wide variety of musical styles. In the twentieth century, the United States was the world's cultural and racial melting pot, with peoples of all races migrating there through force or through choice. We should not therefore be surprised that the States was the birthplace of pop, rock and jazz.

Neither should we forget that before jazz and rock, America had a tradition of country folk music that originated with the folk music of the early English, Scottish, Irish and French settlers. The hillbilly and square dance styles owed much to the British jig, reel and fiddle traditions, whilst the foot-stomping Cajun sound had overtones of French folk music.

Over the border, Canadian folk music – and the music of Quebec, in particular – typically features elements of Irish music, such as the jig rhythms and fiddle tunes, as well as characteristics of French folk and café music, such as the ballad form and the use of the piano accordion for accompaniments.

La Bottine Souriante, players of Canadian folk music

Composing Renaissance Vocal Counterpoint

Introduction

The Renaissance was a time of intense activity, great exploration and discovery. Voyages of discovery and advances made in science and astronomy had their exploratory parallel in the arts. One of the major characteristics of the Renaissance was the revival of classical art and learning. Influenced by the spirit of the age, composers began exploring ways of increasing the expression of human emotions in music. This exploration marked the beginning of an entirely new musical world.

One of the most significant changes in music between the Medieval and Renaissance style involved changes in the basic structure of the fabric or texture of music. Early fifteenth century composers contrasted separate strands of music one against the other, and sometimes all singing different texts. Composers usually composed by adding on lines to a tenor cantus firmus line – a descant or soprano as a countermelody and a contratenor, which had a 'filling in' part. Late fifteenth century composers began to make individual lines of music blend together, developing a compositional style which involved equalizing the voice parts by each part singing the same texts, and through creating a different kind of texture – polyphony.

The change in style was developed and perfected by Josquin des Prez (c.1440–1521) widely regarded as the first of the great composers. Josquin combined polyphonic mastery with a profound emotional expression of the text, in both sacred and secular music. The desire for greater expressive musical sonorities led to his, and other composers, writing for four voices instead of the usual three. This resulted in a greater attention to the combined sound of four voice parts – to harmony and the ensuing dissonance and consonance. This combination of chordal and imitative polyphony, perfected by Josquin and others was refined by Palestrina (1525–94) in particular, and also Lassus (1532–94), Byrd (1543–1623), G. Gabrieli (1555–1612) and Victoria (1548–1611) among many others.

Secular forms of Renaissance music are enormously varied in style and in emotional mood and expression, reflecting the exploratory excitement and revival spirit of the age. The main forms are the madrigal, the ballett, the ayre and the chanson. Texturally, some songs are predominantly contrapuntal, others mainly chordal but many combine the two textures. Notable composers include Monteverdi (1567–1643), Lassus, Byrd, Morley (c.1557–c.1603), Weelkes (1576–1623), Gibbons (1583–1625) and Dowland (1563–1626).

Further work and listening

- Try exploring the different Renaissance genres, looking closely at the range of polyphonic styles. Listen, sing or play works to gain a first-hand knowedge of the style. Madrigals and balletts in particular were intended for participation like a musical game rather than to be listened to.
- To understand the enormous contribution of Josquin des Prez to the development of polyphony, listen to and sing his motet *Ave Maria* in which the imitation between the parts is clearly seen. Each part has the same text and the same music.
- Listen to the 'Kyrie' from Palestrina's *Pope Marcellus* Mass which shows some marvellous polyphonic writing. Any of his motets are also well worth studying. Listen to Byrd's motet *Ave Verum*, noting the characteristic false relation in his style.
- For a look at secular Renaissance music try singing a range of different madrigals, balletts and ayres by composers such as Gibbons – 'The Silver Swan', Morley – 'Now is the month of maying', Weelkes – 'As Vesta was from Latmos hill descending' from *The Triumphs of Oriana*, and any Dowland lute ayres.

Key considerations

- Renaissance polyphony is characterised by a rich, smooth, flowing texture, an intricate musical web, the seamless silken flow of the lines creating a unique expressive musical clarity. The style is well worth exploring by listening, playing and singing polyphonic works of the age.
- Renaissance vocal polyphony involves writing for two, three or more parts.
- Each line of the Latin text is composed to different music. All vocal parts sing the same text. Sections or phrases are not repeated. Thus the music can be said to be 'through-composed'.
- The imitative style which characterises Renaissance polyphony is created in a variety of ways and according to individual compositional styles. The texture comprises horizontal melodic intervals and vertical harmonically conceived intervals. There are certain stylistic points which need to be taken into your composing to be stylistically authentic.

  i)   The melodic lines derive from plainsong and are based on the modal system.

  ii) Phrases rise and fall as gentle curves.

  iii) The melodic range tends to remain within an octave, moving smoothly with mainly stepwise movement.

  iv) Any movement other than stepwise comprises leaps of a major 3rd and perfect 4th, followed by stepwise movement in the opposite direction. To maintain the smooth flow melodies only rarely leap twice in the same direction and then do not exceed an octave or add up to a major 7th.

  v)   Leaps of a major 6th, major and minor 7ths, all augmented and diminished intervals do not occur.

  vi) Quavers must be used very sparingly except at cadence points or in a decorated suspension, usually in pairs, worked in stepwise movement and between strong beats.

  vii) Melodies are characteristically decorated by passing and auxiliary notes which always move by step and harmony notes which can leap to another note consonant with the melody.

  viii) Rhythmically, individual lines are characterised by a seamless irregular and unrepetitive flow. Syncopation is a common feature, produced through tied notes, suspensions and the individual irregular accents of the lines.

- Melodies were based on plainsong which was based on the modal system. During the Renaissance period the increasing use of *musica ficta* – the practice of adding accidentals in performance which involved sharpening leading notes and other notes to sweeten dissonances and to avoid augmented 4ths and diminished 5ths – began to blur the individual qualities of the modes, and eventually only two modes came to be in common use – the major Ionian and the minor Aeolian – which we still have today. As *musica ficta* was a performance practice, composers regularly forgot to include the accidentals in the written music and there remains confusion amongst scholars as to how widespread and uniform the application of *musica ficta* was.

Vertical melodic construction

- **Texture**: To compose stylistically convincing polyphony the texture needs to have a quality of transparent clarity comprising smooth, flowing individual lines. Imitation between parts usually occurs within about 4 or 5 notes of the first vocal part leading, usually at an interval of a 4th or 5th and occasionally at the octave. Imitative parts must have flow and direction. Parts should always complement each other, moving in contrary motion as much as possible.

- In his treatise *Gradus ad Parnassum* (1725) J. J. Fux devised a system known as 'species' counterpoint which set out in detail the contrapuntal style of Palestrina. The treatise was codified as a type of graded guide to composing polyphony which moved from the 1st species – a simple note-against-note counterpoint, through to the 5th species – an elaborate free and florrid style using imitation and dissonance – each species in-between gradually adding two or three notes against one note, then four and so on until the 5th. Some of the basic rules set down in this treatise have governed contrapuntal writing since. Notably:

a) The intervals created between the voices on every beat must be a consonance. For this reason the most common intervals were 3rds and 6ths. 5ths and octaves, although also consonants were usually only on weak beats due to their thin sound.

b) Consecutive or exposed 5ths and octaves were not used.

- Thus, in general, your part-writing must be based on writing consonances – 3rds and 6ths on the strong beat and 5ths and octaves on weak beats. Octaves often start a phrase or are heard in cadences. In three-part writing the 3rds were frequently doubled but usually quitted in contrary motion. Watch that the 3rd is not also a leading-note, which cannot be doubled.

- **Dissonances**: dissonances on strong beats occur as suspensions which need to be prepared and resolved appropriately. Dissonances include intervals of a 2nd (9th), 4th and 7th. Double suspensions are possible, particularly in 3rds and 6ths. Take care to introduce unprepared dissonance such as accented passing notes, the 4th, the 'nota cambiata' and notes of anticipation only on weaker beats of the bar.

- **False relation**: where a sharpened or flattened leading note is sounded either simultaneously or in the ear proximity used particularly in the music of Byrd and also in madrigals occurred frequently for added expression and to heighten the meaning of the words.

- **Cadences**: cadences should always be decorated by a suspension and prepared and resolved appropriately. Perfect and imperfect cadences are common, plagal cadences occasionally and the interrupted cadence very rarely. In two-part writing one part falls in step to the final note and the other rises a semitone to the final note. In three-part writing the upper parts move as above and the lowest part rises a 4th (or falls a 5th) to the final note. The final cadence is always major.

- **Word-Setting**: Each phrase of the text should have its own musical motif and each motif should overlap with the next at the cadence point. At the first four or five notes of a phrase the text is usually set one syllable to one note. This develops into more melismatic phrases, with several notes to a syllable. Melismatic phrases should not include repeated notes. Rests should never break up a word.

Approaches to writing Renaissance vocal counterpoint

- First 'read' through, sing or play the whole extract.
- Analyse the given part(s), working out the character, shape, rhythm, word-setting and melismas.
- Mark on the score the points of imitation and the intervals at which the parts will work at the start of the phrases.
- Assess the cadences and work out what kind of suspensions you are going to write in each.
- Start creating your musical line. Movement between parts tends to be predominantly in 3rds and 6ths with intervals of 5ths and octaves at cadences and the beginnings of phrases. Your added part should form appropriate intervals with the other part(s), avoiding augmented 4ths, major 6ths, 7ths and intervals greater than an octave.
- Introduce accidentals appropriately in keeping with the *musica ficta* conventions of the time.
- Make sure that your melodic line moves in curves, forming a series of arch shapes with predominantly stepwise movement. Take care to adhere to the conventions regarding leaps within a melodic line. Look for ways of decorating your lines with idiomatic suspensions, passing notes 'nota cambiata' and so on.
- Phrases of text in each individual line should be complete. Phrases should end with a longer or same value note as the penultimate one, never a note of shorter value.

Benedictus from the Missa 'Descendit Angelus Domini'
Palestrina

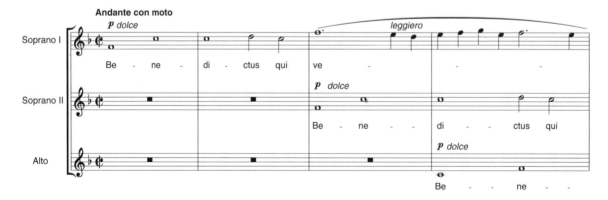

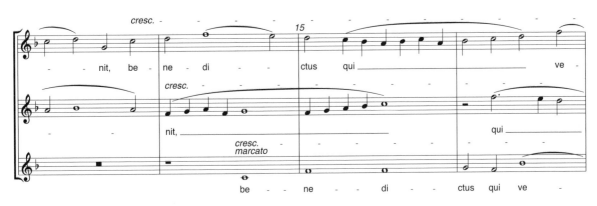

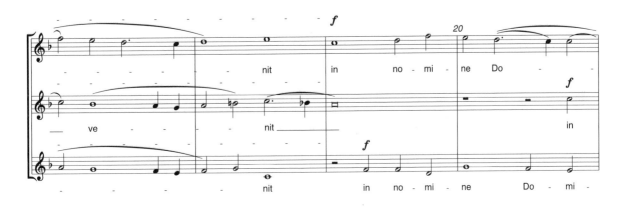

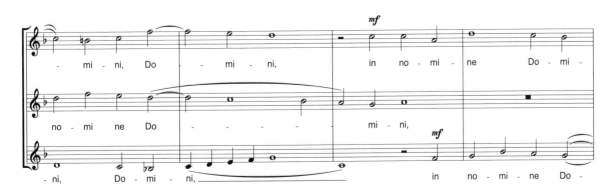

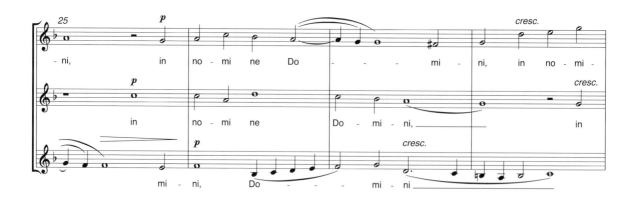

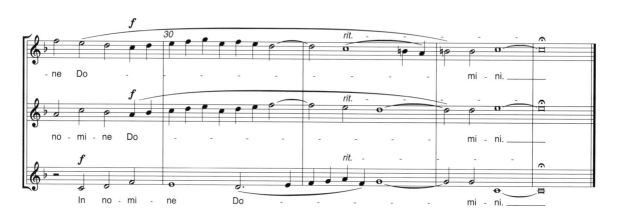

Palestrina's works are recognised as supreme models of Renaissance polyphonic style. His music is characterised by restrained serene beauty and contrapuntal transparency. His treatment of melodic shape and dissonance is stricter than that of his predecessors and many of his contemporaries.

Melodies

The melodies in the Benedictus are characteristic of plain-song. The shapes comprise long gentle curves in an arch form. Stepwise movement dominates with leaps of a 5th only at the beginning of some phrases. The range of the lines remains within a 9th. Note the continuous flow of the lines, with few repeated notes.

Polyphony

The music is in Common Time, two semibreve beats per bar. The quality of the polyphony lies in its serenity, transparency and kaleidescopic 'colour' changes as the spacing and grouping of notes continually alters. Note how only in the final phrase does the rhythm of the lines combine. Up to this point, shorter notes – crotchets – are balanced against longer notes. The passing movement and flow of the lines is almost continuous, moving gently between the lines. Part movement occurs in contrary and parallel motion. Intervals between the lines follows the conventions of 3rds and 6ths and avoidance of dissonant intervals.

Dissonances

Characteristically, the lines are almost devoid of any chromaticisms apart from those essential leading note accidentals, determined by the *musica ficta* conventions. However, the lines are suffused with suspensions which are always prepared on a weak beat with the dissonance occurring on the strong beat and then resolving down by step. This regularity of the dissonance, or tensions on the strong beat and resolutions or relaxations on the weak beat gives Palestrina's music its characteristic gently pulsating direction.

Composing Two-part Baroque Counterpoint

Introduction

Counterpoint is the term used to describe the art of combining two or more simultaneous melody lines. The term literally means 'point against point' or 'melody against melody'. In a very simple form, singing a round such as *London's Burning* is counterpoint, as, although the same melody line is sung in all parts, the texture is made up horizontally of lines of melody, all working effectively together making musical sense within a harmonic framework. This is the opposite of a hymn, for example, where the texture is conceived vertically – the melody line takes all the interest, accompanied by chords. Between these two kinds of textures there are endless variations and combinations, ranging from 'blocks' of contrapuntal passages juxtaposed with 'blocks' of chordal passages such as in the 'Hallelujah' chorus from Handel's *Messiah* to the intricate weaving of contrapuntally conceived lines within a chordal, or vertical structure, such as can be seen in many of J.S. Bach's works.

The terms counterpoint and polyphony are now used interchangeably, although there remains a tendency to apply the latter term to sixteenth century Palestrina style and counterpoint to early eighteenth century.

Counterpoint in Baroque music suffused all genres of music of the period and indeed lies at the heart of the musical style and character. The two main categories of Baroque counterpoint comprises the strict form such as that found in fugues, and a freer form of melodic counterpoint of melody supported by the continuo such as in sonatas, preludes, and dance suites.

Key considerations

As a preparation to writing two-part Baroque counterpoint, you may like to consider the following points:

- There is no real substitute for experiencing at first hand the character and style of two-part counterpoint. Make sure that alongside starting composing you develop a good grasp of the style through actively studying relevant works by composers such as Bach, Corelli, Handel and Telemann. Play through and sing works in two-part counterpoint style, looking closely at the idiomatic figurations and getting a real 'feel' for the character and style. For example, bass lines have a particular forward direction energy based on figurations so thoroughly intrinsic to the Baroque style they are almost formulaic – an Alberti bass would be quite out of character!

Analysis

Harmonic structure

- The key to successful counterpoint writing lies in underpinning the lines with a solid and coherent harmonic structure based on characteristic Baroque harmonic schemes and cadential progressions.
- Dissonance is a significant feature and needs to be an integral part of your harmonic structure. Dissonance can occur in the form of dissonant chords such as dominant and diminished 7ths, and in figurations as suspensions, unaccented and accented passing notes, appoggiaturas, cambiata notes (figurations involving a particular pattern of 4 notes), notes of anticipation and échappé notes, as illustrated opposite:

Suspensions: Bach's *French Suite No. 3 in B minor, Sarabande*

b: I   VIIb   Ib   VIIb   I   V   IVb   V7

* signifies suspensions

Unaccented/accented passing notes: Bach's *French Suite No. 3 in B minor, Sarabande*

* Unaccented Passing notes
• Accented Passing
  Note the suspensions in the `tenor' line

Appoggiaturas: C.P.E. Bach's *Duet for Flute and Violin*

Flute

Violin

* Appoggiaturas

Cambiata notes: Bach's *French Suite No. 2 in B minor*

The dissonance is quitted by leap

Échappé notes: Bach's *Two-part Invention No. V in E♭ major*

Échappé notes involve upward movement by step away from the harmony note, then usually leap down a 3rd.

Notes of anticipation: Bach's *Two-part Invention No. VII in E minor*

＊ note of anticipation

- Remember that in contrapuntal writing cadences are often dove-tailed, that is, while the bass may clearly indicate a perfect cadence followed by a rest, the melody will often not pause for breath and continue straight on to the next phrase, with new melodic figurations. This can also occur vice-versa with the bass continuing at a cadence.

Contrapuntal lines

- Contrapuntal lines are characterised by an abundance of idiomatic figurations and motifs – imitation, imitative figurations, sequences, specific melodic and bass patterns and combinations and so on. Effective composing involves using a full range of idiomatic figurations.
- Melody and bass lines frequently move in 3rds and 6ths, in parallel and contrary motion. Keep your contrapuntal writing fresh, clear and fairly simple. The lines need to show stylistic fluency and have a sense of musical direction – not 'meander' around particular notes or figurations. Avoid plunging randomly from very high to very low within a short space, unless this is part of a designed contrapuntal interplay. Take care not to write a melody which is consistently too low. Remember to let your music breathe by including rests appropriately.

Rhythm

- Rhythm is very important in emphasising the independence of the melodic lines. It is the life-blood of counterpoint, regulating the flow, tensions and relaxations, energy and vitality of the music. Rhythmically, both lines play an equally important part in driving the music forward. It is the conflict of the different musical stresses built in the figurations, rests and so on, both between the individual lines and together within the steady pulse framework of the piece which gives robust energy and vitality to contrapuntal music.
- Harmony is also an indispensable part of rhythmic life in counterpoint. Chord progressions comprising a series of tensions and relaxations – as with an accented passing note followed by an unaccented passing note – create the forward drive because of the need of the dissonant note(s) to resolve. For example, the level of tension created by a dominant 7th in one phrase can be stepped up a gear in another phrase by including a stronger dissonance such as a diminished 7th or other chromatically altered chord, thereby further increasing the tension level and therefore the drive and momentum towards resolution. This is why certain dissonant chords, for example, ♯iib7 are often used at a cadential approach. The music then passes from a chord of strong dissonance – ♯iib7 – to medium – V(7) – or less dissonance – V – to resolution – I –, a gradual attainment of relaxation.

Grammatical errors

- As in chorale harmonisations, take care to avoid those grammatical errors which can substantially weaken your music such as:

    consecutive 5ths and octaves

    incorrect doubling of the leading note (Unlike chorale harmonisations, leading notes in two-part counterpoint must rise to the tonic)

    false relation

    crossing and overlapping of parts

    awkward intervals both within and between melody and bass lines

    2nd inversion harmonies, except in a cadential 6/4–Ic–V–I progression.

Further work and listening

- There are numerous works to listen to, study and play or even sing through, which show the endless variety of contrapuntal forms and techniques. Try listening to some of the following:

- Any sonatas by Corelli or Telemann. Corelli's *Sonata Op. 5*, for example, synthesizes counterpoint with soloistic violin writing, and is an excellent example to study for how to write sequential progressions and suspensions.

- Listen to and look closely at the compositional techniques in some of Bach's *Preludes*, or in the dance movements of his *French Suites*. Some illustrate contrapuntal writing in which the melody is independent of the bass and others work to a close imitative relationship between melody and bass.

- For a closer look at more equal-voice writing, study some of Bach's *Two-Part Inventions*, perhaps advancing your study to the strict contrapuntal techniques of his fugues in the *Well Tempered Klavier*. Try composing some of your own inventions, perhaps using the opening of a Bach invention as a start.

- If you are interested in seeing how contrapuntal techniques work in larger, complex forms, try listening to Bach's *Art of the Fugue*, a great contrapuntal masterpiece which shows all the principal devices of full strict counterpoint. The complex choruses of his *St Matthew Passion* and *B minor Mass* are marvellous works of contrapuntal art.

Prelude No. 6 in E minor
J. S. Bach

E minor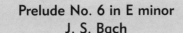

5 modulating sequence

to G major _____   to C major _____

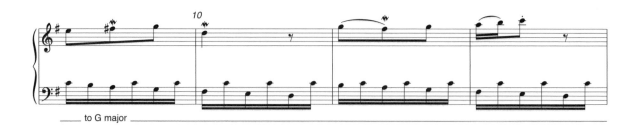

to G major

modulating sequence

to E minor   to B minor

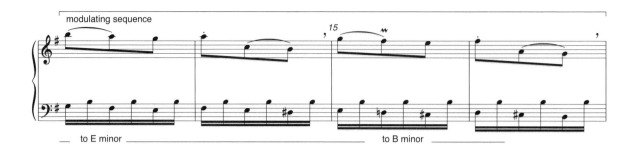

imitative sequence

Structure

In this prelude the melody and bass lines are independent of each other. While contrapuntal techniques of imitation and sequences are clearly integral to the style, the parts do not move in imitation of each other. The extract is twenty bars long with modulations and therefore cadences as follows:

Modulations:	E minor>	G major>	C major>	G major>	E minor>	B minor
Cadences in bars:	1	7–8	8–9	10–11	14–15	15–16

Note that the only 'full stop' cadence point occurs at the end of the section.

The harmonic scheme is based on a predominantly tonic/dominant relationship as the music moves through different keys, with 7th dissonances and supertonic and subdominant chords occurring at cadential approaches.

The phrase structure of 4 + 6 + 6 + 4 is interesting. Bars 9–10 act as a cadential ending to the sequence of the previous four bars while bars 11–12 act as an opening to the sequence in the succeeding four bars

Figurations

As marked on the score, two-bar descending modulating sequences occur in bars 5–8 and in bars 13–16. A one-bar sequence occurs in bars 17–18, thereby quickening the rhythmic pace towards the final cadence. The harmonic framework supports very typical figurations throughout, notably the way that semiquavers and quavers work together in bars 5–6, 11–12 and 16 –17. The bass line from bar 11 to the end is absolutely typical of the Baroque freer contrapuntal style.

Part movement

The extract comprises continuous rhythmic vigour through semiquaver passages and accompanying quaver movement. These alternate quickly between melody and bass in the first four bars, and through longer phrase lengths in succeeding phrases. In the final phrase the rhythmic action is heightened with both parts in semiquavers, adding impetus to the drive to the cadence in bar 20.

Note the variety and contrast of the part movement in this short extract. In bars 5–13 the parts move broadly in contrary motion, in bars 13–17 in parallel motion and in the final phrase, bars 17–20, in contrary motion. Characteristically there is much movement in 3rds and 6ths between the lines. Note the contrast of the close relationship of the bass passage work from bars 11–16 with the spacious melody line.

Approaches on how to start writing two-part Baroque counterpoint

The following points are designed to provide guidance for pieces which either provide a figured bass or melody.

- Work out the basic structure: is it in binary or ternary form? Work out the phrase structure, the cadence points and the modulations.
- Actively analyse the given instrumental lines, starting from the opening *incipit*. Is the type of counterpoint imitative – that is with one-part beginning followed by the other in imitation – or are the lines independent of each other, possibly beginning both together?
- As you analyse the lines, plan out and mark on the score your harmonic structure – particular progressions, harmonic sequences (recognisable by a particular pattern rising or falling) and cadential progressions.
- Start creating your musical line. Movement tends to work predominantly in 3rds and 6ths, with intervals of 5ths and octaves at cadences and the beginnings of phrases. Make sure your phrases have melodic shape, purposefully rising and falling as they correlate with the harmonic direction, for example rising towards a point of tension and so on.
- If the piece is in binary form, with sections A and B very similar but in different keys, look for stylistically imaginative ways of varying section B. You may wish, for example, to make the middle of this section the climatic high point of the piece, resolving slowly down to the final cadence.
- Look for places in the piece where a new point of imitation starts and work out which part leads. Such an occurrence often happens after a cadence point. Remember that in contrapuntal writing cadences are often dove-tailed. Whichever line leads, the other follows, imitating to the point when the imitation can no longer harmonically work. Note that imitation between parts may involve exact repetition or begin on a different note – commonly at an interval of a 3rd, 5th, 6th or octave.
- Imitative patterns can often be recognised by their idiomatic short, rhythmical phrases, sometimes separated by rests.
- The direction of a continuously rising or falling line is usually paralleled by the other part, as are sudden registal changes.
- If one line is 'busy' with continuous semiquavers, the other part is usually less 'busy' with slower paced notes such as quavers.
- In approaches to final cadences sometimes both parts combine in increased complexity or synchronise rhythmically to draw the piece or section to a close.
- Remember to keep your counterpoint vigorous and fresh with lots of rhythmic energy.
- Always make sure you realise the figured bass appropriately.

Sonata VII Op. 5, No. 7
Corelli

Study the partially completed score considering throughout from a composer's view-point how you would go about completing the work in an appropriate style. Before looking at the music and analysis marked on the score opposite, ask yourself the following questions:

1 What is the structure of the piece?
2 Are there any sequences?
3 What idiomatic figurations are used?
4 How should the phrase endings be treated?

Now study the music and analysis, and the points given on page 196.

Analysis
Sonata VII Op. 5, No. 7
Corelli

What is the structure of the piece?

The extract here is only twelve bars long, comprising one section of the sonata. The harmonic framework is predominantly diatonic and very much based on characteristic progressions involving chords I, V, II and IV and their inversions and the dominant 7th chord. Study the given figured bass as you follow the analyses here. The movement begins in D minor and modulates through G minor and F major in a modulating sequence in bars 4–5. It remains in F major until bar 10 when a pivot chord – vi – leads the way for the change of key to D minor. The section ends with an imperfect cadence.

Are there any sequences?

A sequence occurs in bars 5–6. The cadence in bar 5 leads us to assume that the melody line will 'lead' the sequence here, dove-tailing the cadence, thereby maintaining the lead set up in the opening bar. Sequences often have a particular character and here the sequence motif is defined by octave leaps working in 3rds and 6ths between melody and bass.

What idiomatic figurations are used?

As can be seen by the analysis on the score, the music is very much built on imitative figurations from the opening bar. The short phrases in bars 7–10, each with similar rhythm and separated by rests clearly indicate idiomatic imitation figurations. There are numerous ways to write in a free imitative style. As long as the basic harmonic or rhythmic shape, or phrase length is maintained, imitations can, for example, start on a different note as in this case, or invert the phrase shape or vary the rhythm pattern slightly. Imitative phrases between melody and bass frequently move in parallel motion.

How should the phrase ending be treated?

All phrase endings here are dove-tailed, apart from the final cadence. Note the rhythmic propulsion in bars 8–10 as the bass each time 'overlaps' the melodic phrase, giving impetus towards the cadence. Note also how the semiquavers are left out of the last phrase, thus allowing a natural rhythmic slowing of pace, further emphasised by the gradually descending line.

Composing Chorales in the Style of J. S. Bach

Introduction

The chorale held a significant position in German music in the Baroque period. The importance of the chorale dates back to the Lutheran church of the sixteenth century and the compositions of Martin Luther. Luther considered the chorale, or hymn, a central part of church worship. He used existing melodies and texts adapted from pre-Reformation hymns, plainsong and even secular songs as the basis of his chorale compositions. The chorale reached its highest point in the chorale harmonisations of J. S. Bach.

Chorales were also used as the basis for other vocal compositions, notably cantatas, oratorios and passions, and as the basis for works for organ, notably the chorale prelude, fantasia, fugue and partita.

Key considerations

When starting to write chorales in the style of J.S. Bach, you need to consider the following points:

- It is very important to think of chorale harmonising as writing music. Try not to approach your harmonising as a set of 'rules' to be followed or as a kind of puzzle to fill in the missing 'bits'. Although it is necessary to be grammatically correct in terms of the harmonic language, rather than approaching chorales as technical exercises they are more a musical art form and need to be treated as such. They can even be quite exciting!
- Some parallels can be made with learning a language. Consider learning to speak fluent French, for example, by only using lists of vocabulary. The flow of a phrase or sentence would be stilted, uneven and lack any real meaning.

- The chorale needs to be harmonised throughout for a four-part choir – soprano, alto, tenor and bass. To grasp a good understanding of chorales, you need to practically explore a broad variety of chorales. Sing through each vocal line of a chorale, changing the octave register as appropriate. Then in your group, sing the full chorale, listening carefully to the harmonic movement, idiomatic progressions and the impact of the modulations. Note the effectiveness, musical shape and flow of the passing notes, the expressive 'colour' created by suspensions and the moments of tension of the dissonances and their resolutions.

Linear flow

- Think of your composing in terms of linear flow. Each line – soprano, alto, tenor and bass must make musical melodic sense. The most important line is the bass.
- The **bass**: writing a musical, mobile and directional bass line is crucial to successful chorale harmonising. The bass provides the harmonic foundation and plays an important role in the harmonic scheme in determining the changes in pace and flow, and the tension and resolution within chorale phrases. In general, the bass is the most active part, often including leaps of an octave, particularly at the cadence points and the beginning of phrases.
- The **alto**: the alto line characteristically moves most frequently by step to the nearest note, or remains on the same note. Although some leaps do occur, they tend to be within the broad framework of a flowing but predominantly smooth line.
- The **tenor**: the tenor line is usually more adventurous and can add much expressive interest and melodic colour to a chorale. The tenor line frequently lies around middle C, often rising as high as G above.
- The **soprano**: having their roots in plainsong, *melodies* are usually fairly simple with

predominantly step-wise movement built on crotchet and quaver movement. Leaps occur most often in between phrases and at the beginning of phrases. Any longer notes usually occur at cadence points. Melodies also include repeated notes and can be quite stationary, with the 'action' happening in the inner parts, the bass and through the harmonic scheme.

- **Part movement**: in general the melody and bass move in contrary, parallel or oblique (if the melody comprises mainly repeated notes, the bass has more movement, rising and falling to maintain interest) motion, illustrations of which are given on pages 201–5.

- Avoid consecutive 5ths and octaves between any parts. Note that while 5ths and octaves are allowed, as is the interval of a diminished 5th followed in the same part by a perfect 5th, moving consecutive 5ths and octaves are considered weak progressions, due to the bareness of the intervals and are not allowed. Similarly, avoid false relation – a chromatic contradiction where, for example, an F♯ is heard in one chord and an F♮ is heard in the next, in different voices such as soprano and tenor.

Harmony

- A good understanding of the expressive power and function of harmony is essential for good harmonisations. This means not only knowing the harmonic 'vocabulary' – the notes of the chords, their inversions, the technicalities of 7ths and so on, – but the real musical function and expressive power of different chords and chord progressions. The key to good harmonsations lies in fully recognising and understanding how the music really works and eventually to be able to hear the sounds in your inner ear.

- Harmonic schemes need to be stylistically convincing with characteristic progressions, both within phrases and at cadence points.

- In brief, the strongest chords are the tonic, dominant and sub-dominant chords in root position. In both root position and 1st inver-sion these chords form the diatonic basis of chorale writing.

- Integral to this harmonic basis are the minor chords ii, vi, the diminished chord viib, and, occasionally in appropriate circumstances, iii/iiib.

- The strongest progressions involve progressions of 5ths, sometimes called the circle of 5ths, whereby the bass movement fundamentally progresses in falling 5ths, (and therefore rising 4ths), for example, I to IV, vii to iii, vi to ii, V to I and so on. This circle of 5ths also works if some chords are in 1st inversion. For this reason, one of the strongest and most common cadential progressions is vi ii(7)b V I. Due to their tonal strength, root position chords can firmly establish a tonality, or establish a modulation to another key. 1st inversions can also do this, making for a less strong, more subtle process.

- The dominant 7th chord in all inversions is very common and frequently takes the place of the straight dominant chord in cadences, in modulations and within the course of a phrase. The 7th is always treated very carefully particularly in root position where it is usually prepared, introduced in stepwise movement or 'staggered' as a passing note.

- The diminished 7th chord and other chromatically altered chords such as ♯ii(7)b and ♯IV(7)b act as a driving force in the directional flow of a chorale, often as part of a modulation to a new key, or to enhance a particular cadence. Diminished 7ths in Bach chorales usually occur in the minor key. The strength lies in the dissonant tensions of particular notes which need to resolve into a succeeding chord. It is this tension which creates added 'grip' to the music.

- Neapolitan 6th and augmented 6th chords are very rare in Bach's chorales, as is the passing 6/4 progression, although the cadential 6/4 is quite common. Diminished triads in root position are also rare, as is vib unless in a sequence of 1st inversions or before chord ii.

- **Harmonic pace**: chorales are usually harmonised with four chords to a bar, and with two, three or even four chord changes per bar. Frequently the chord itself does not change but changes in inversion, for example from a root position to a 1st inversion.
- Chorale are generally in 4/4 or C (Common) metre, with a few in 3/4.
- Minims in the melody line should be harmonised with two chord movements. Quavers in the melody line are often treated by:
    i) harmonising the first quaver only
    ii) moving in parallel 3rds or 6ths with the bass or alto
    iii) full harmonisation, changing the chord or inversion of the first quaver harmony.

Cadences

- Cadence chords are always in root position with very few exceptions.
- All chorale phrases end with a cadence, usually indicated by a pause sign ⌒ over the last note. The pause chord is, with very few exceptions, a straight chord without suspensions or passing notes.
- There are some very common cadential progressions which characterise the Baroque style, notably:
    vi iib(7) V(7) I
    Ic (or 6/4) V(7) I
    V with a 4:3 suspension I
    IV7 V(7)I
    (Upper case chord numerals, such as I IV V, stand for major chords and lower case, such as iv ii, stand for minor chords. The 7 is bracketed as it is optional.)
- The leading note does not always have to rise to the tonic of the chord and indeed is better falling a 3rd to the 5th of the chord or rising to the 3rd of the chord in order to complete the chord.
- The final chord of the chorale is always major. In a minor key chorale this means writing *a tierce de picardie* chord (chord with a major 3rd).

- Perfect and imperfect cadences comprise almost all chorale cadences. Interrupted and plagal cadences are used very rarely.

Modulations

- Modulations are an integral part of the chorale harmonic structure and as a compositional process reveal much about a composer's style. Changing key in a piece of music moves the directional flow of a piece and can alter the very character and mood of a piece. Modulations can be dramatic, exciting, abrupt or can move subtly and slowly, gently easing into a new key.

- Modulations in chorales are always to a closely related key, i.e. one having the same or very close key signature in terms of the number of flats and sharps. There are five most closely related keys to any key. For example, those closest to D major are its relative minor, B minor with the same key signature, the dominant, A major and its relative minor F♯ minor with 3 sharps, and the subdominant G major and its relative minor E minor with one sharp.

- Modulations occur in Bach chorales at least once, either passing through a key within a phrase or firmly established at a cadence point. In many chorales some keys are revisited, sometimes more than once.

- To change key or modulate, the 'new' note of the new key needs to be introduced into the music. This necessarily means a chord of the dominant group – V, V7, viib, or vii7 which includes the 'new' note – firmly established by a usually perfect cadence. For example, in modulating from D major to the dominant A major, the 'new' note is G♯ as it does not belong in D major. Similarly if modulating from D major to G major the 'new' note is the flattened C.

- There are several ways to modulate in characteristic Baroque style:
  i) A gradual or ambiguous modulation is very common and is effected through a pivot *chord*, a chord common to both the key of the music at the point of modulation and the key of the music from this point onwards. The pivot chord acts as a gateway to the change of key. It is followed by a chord from the dominant group as explained previously, and firmly established by a perfect cadence.
  ii) Modulations can also be accomplished by a pivot *note*. The principle is the same as that of a pivot chord, but in this case one note forms the link from the last chord in the old key to one of the dominant group in the new key.
  iii) Dynamic, abrupt modulations may be achieved by simply beginning a new phrase in a new key, a frequent occurrence in Bach's chorale harmonsations.
  iv) By introducing the 'new' note through chromatic movement in the bass.

Summary

A good, stylistic harmonisation of a Bach chorale will show:
- a thorough understanding of how harmony works with idiomatic harmonic progressions and when appropriate, musically adventurous chord selection
- a mobile and directional bass line
- a good understanding of harmonic pace
- a sense of tonality – when to modulate and to what key
- imaginative and stylistic part writing
- characteristic use of dissonances
- distinctive features of chorale textures
- good technical assurance, avoiding the pitfalls of consecutives, missed or wrong accidentals, false relation, unresolved or inappropriate dissonance treatment.

Further work and listening

- There is really no substitute for singing through a range of chorales and experiencing at first hand the harmonic expression, the varying textures, the nuances of varying dissonances, the pull of the 7th chords and the musical satisfaction inherent in tension and resolution. Bear in mind that when Bach wrote these chorales, Mozart, Beethoven and beyond hadn't happened!
- Study, sing and play chorale lines individually. Explore the different pairings of lines, the contrapuntal flow and then the full chorale texture.
- Practise listening and if possible, playing through lots of different kinds of chorales, from straightforward hymns to Bach chorales. Look at other conventionally harmonised melodies such as the national anthem. The more you explore, the greater your ability to 'read' the music implied by the symbols.
- Explore composing chorales using idiomatic harmonic progressions, even at first copying particular progressions exactly, perhaps in a different key. Plan harmonic schemes for chorales and explore harmonising phrases in different ways.
- Even though some Awarding Bodies allow the use of a keyboard in harmonising chorales, this does not replace a thorough inner ear knowledge of what different chords in progressions sound like.

Analysis

Chorale bass lines

It is essential to get a good grasp of how to write a musically convincing solid and directional bass line. The following examples show characteristics of good bass lines.

- The bass frequently moves in contrary motion with the melody line. The example below also shows some very typical bass movements that make for a musical flow and give forward movement towards the cadence. As in this example, bass lines often include strong movement such as octave leaps, particularly at the beginning and ending of phrases, but also within phrases:

- The bass also frequently moves in oblique motion (the melody comprising mainly repeated notes with some stepwise movement), rising and falling to maintain interest:

The bass line also frequently moves in parallel 3rds and 6ths with the melody:

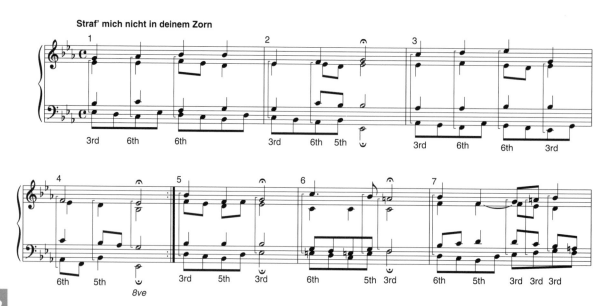

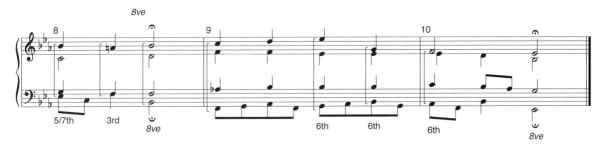

- Bass lines can be very active, as the example below shows. Note how the bass often moves from a root position to a 1st inversion of the same chord and vice-versa. Characteristic parallel 3rds and 6ths between melody and bass are common.

Note the high tenor line in the last phrase. It is worth noting also the characteristic treatment of the suspensions in the alto line in bar 2 which create a familiar syncopation pattern. Unaccented passing notes are common.

This is another example of a chorale with a flowing bass line full of very typical bass figurations. Note how the bass and the melody complement each other in contrary, parallel or oblique motion. Points to look at closely are as follows:

Herlich lieb hab' ich dich, o Herr

1. the contrary motion between melody and bass in bars 1–4 particularly but also in several other phrases

2. the varied and adventurous bass line in oblique motion passages. This happens in bars 7–11 particularly, and also in bar 2

where the bass typically moves from root position to 1st inversion of the same chord. Note how the 3rd of the major chord is doubled here. This is a regular occurrence in Bach chorales, and, as in this case, the two 3rds proceed in contrary motion

③ the parallel motion in bar 5, the interval of a 3rd taking prominence between melody and bass

④ how bass leaps of a 5th or octave occur predominantly at cadence points and at the beginning of phrases to thrust the music forwards or to abruptly introduce a change of key, as in bars 2–3 and 4–5

⑤ the modulatory pace quickens in bars 10–11 moving rapidly through the key changes.

Bach further enhances this forward drive by the imitative contrapuntal interplay here between the melody and bass, then followed in pairs – soprano/alto, and tenor/bass

⑥ the path for chromatic notes is smoothed through being in step-wise movements, as between bars 7–10, thus avoiding any awkward leaps

⑦ the treatment of leading notes in the bass which always rise by step, as in bars 7, 10 – 11 and 17.

Analysis in brief

Jesu Meine Freude

The following short examples, taken from different harmonisations of this chorale, show how the same melody can be harmonised and treated in stylistically varied ways.

E minor I   iii⁽⁷⁾   IVb   I   ii⁷b   V⁷   I

A idiomatic harmonisation, showing the typical cadential progression ii7b V7 I, the 7th of V falling as a passing note. Note here the motion of almost continuous quavers running through all parts.

A more complex, chromatic harmonic scheme with dominant and diminished 7ths and a chromatic ii7b. This extract is taken from the end of the chorale, and thus the final chord is major. Note the treatment of the rising 6th (C♯) and 7th (D♯) moving to the tonic E. Note also how the sequential relationship between melody and bass in the first four beats is varied. This short phrase is also a good example of doubled part writing moving in 3rds and 6ths.

In this example we see chord IVb in bar 1 now substituted with the diminished 7th vii7b chord. This is a common exchange and adds dissonant 'spice' to an otherwise diatonic phrase. Diminished 7th chords, mostly used in minor key chorales, regularly substitute chord V7b and, as a version of the dominant with a minor 9th, enhance the chorale with harmonic adventure and expressive 'colour'.

Note the suspensions here. The purpose of suspensions is to create an expressive moment of tension through dissonance, and directional drive through syncopation, often for greater resolution impact at the cadence. While a tied note suspension creates a gentle dissonance, a more emphasised dissonance would involve repeating the note to create the 'clash' before resolution.

An example of a more complex texture, with a highly decorated cadence:

Approaches on writing your own harmonisations

If you are harmonising a chorale from a given *incipit* (first two or three bars) or from a given melody or bass line, you may find the following approaches useful:

- Analyse the overall structure of the chorale, the phrases, cadence points and the given melody or bass part, interpreting any figured bass appropriately.
- Mark in precisely the keys and points for modulation. A new key can be introduced during a phrase, then firmly established at a succeeding cadence point. Identify where to modulate by working out the tonic key of the chorale and then each cadence point. Remember that a phrase can pass through one key to another. Note that almost all cadences are perfect, some imperfect and rarely, interrupted or plagal.
- If you are given the melody line as an incipit, plan and mark in your harmonic and cadential progressions on the score under the bass line. Similarly, if you are given a figured bass, work out the underlying harmonies and then compose your melody appropriately. An 'At-a-glance' guide to bass figuring is given in the Baroque listening section.
- As you consider the rise and fall of the musical shape, make sure you work out where the tension points are, and thus where dissonant chords such as diminished 7th or other chromatic chords or suspensions, will be most musically placed. These usually occur in phrases in the minor key when modulating or on the approach to cadence points. Make sure that when writing suspensions, the most common being 4:3 and 7:6 suspensions, they are prepared in the previous chord.
- When you first start to write your melody or bass line, compose in terms of writing melodic, directional lines using idiomatic progressions and patterns. Work to contrary, oblique or parallel movement between melody and bass lines. Frequent melody and bass intervallic structures are based on 3rds and 6ths, with intervals of 5ths and 8ves appearing commonly at cadence points. However, there is much variation to this broad characterisation. Avoid possible consecutive 5ths and 8ves, false relation and other grammatical errors. Remember that in general (but there are exceptions) the largest leaps tend to occur most frequently at the beginning of phrases or at cadence points.

- Actively consider the part movement, the texture and the spacing of the parts. Bear in mind the vocal ranges of each line.
- Once finished, always remember to check for consecutive 5ths and octaves, that dissonances have been resolved appropriately, that your vocal lines do not contain any ungainly jumps and you have remembered accidentals – particularly the 6th and 7th notes when harmonising in the minor key. Most importantly make sure your modulations include the essential accidentals. Without the accidentals the modulation simply can't happen.
- Be prepared to make changes once you have completed your choral harmonisation. Look particularly at how well your harmonic structure works and if the lines flow and make musical sense.

Analysis

Now study the following chorale, considering throughout what you would write if you were given just the melody or the figured bass line. How would you go about harmonising the complete chorale?

The structure

The chorale is twelve bars long, is in Common or 4/4 time, and has six phrases and cadence points. The modulations are as follows:

Phrase 1: D major

Phrase 2: modulates to the relative minor, B minor

Phrase 3: modulates from B minor to A major – a supertonic minor relationship. A major is also, of course, the dominant of the opening key

Phrase 4: modulates back to B minor ending this time with an imperfect cadence

Phrase 5: modulates to D major

Phrase 6: modulates back to B minor with a brief passing glance through A major.

The structural basis:

Phrases 1 and 2 are repeated in phrases 5 and 6. The melody is mainly step-wise apart from two rising intervals of a 4th and the leap between phrases 4 and 5. The bass comprises leaps and stepwise quaver movement, both ascending and descending. Note how melodic the bass line is. Try singing this line through. Note that there are no awkward leaps, just typical leaps of a 5th or 8th. Chromatic notes always are treated gently, in step-wise movement with no crude leaps.

How do the melody and bass lines interact?

Where the melody has repeated notes as in phrases 1, 3 and 5, the bass has more movement, usually idiomatic quaver passages. The intervals between the melody and bass are 3rds, 6ths, 5ths, 8ves, the 8ves occurring mainly at the cadence points.

How should the cadences be harmonised?

Of the six cadences, five are perfect and one imperfect. The cadences in bars 2, 6 and 10, have the same tonic – leading-note – tonic melodic shape and are harmonised Ic V(7) I. Note that the 7th is 'staggered' – placed on the 2nd quaver beat. The cadences in bars 4 and 12 involve a long supertonic to tonic and are harmonised basically V(7) – I in bar 4 with a more complex harmonisation of V – ii7b – V7 –

I in bar 12. Note the decoration and the implied suspensions in these cadences.

How does Bach harmonise the rest of the chorale melody?

Throughout, the basic foundation is chords I, IV and V and their inversions. The dominant 7th appears regularly in bars 3, 4, 6, 7 and 10 (twice) and 12 either to modulate to a new key as in bars 3, 7 and 10 or as part of a cadence, as in bar 4, 6, 10 and 12. Note the subtleties here, for example the modulation from A major to B minor in bar 7 by the crucial note, A♯, being placed as a passing note only within a basically dominant/tonic structure, which proceeds to an inconclusive imperfect cadence.

Points to watch out for:

1 Look carefully at how the cadences are decorated. No cadence is just two bare chords.
2 Make sure your 7ths always fall, and to raise the 6th and 7th notes to the tonic as in the ascending melodic minor scale, otherwise you will create an unmusical augmented 2nd between the unsharpened 6th nd the sharpened 7th. See bars 3–4 to illustrate this point.
3 Avoid writing very low tenor lines.In this chorale the lowest tenor note is F♯ and then only briefly, the main registral span lying between A and rising to F♯ above middle C.
4 Remember to include passing notes and suspensions in characteristic style. If you follow the travel of passing notes in this chorale, note that leaps only occur at cadence points, and how the quaver movement is maintained almost continuously throughout, travelling through all parts. In particular, look how in bar 7 the lovely descending bass line is immediately imitated in the tenor line and the moves to the alto line. There are many examples of similar beautiful subtleties of part writing in Bach chorales.
5 Note how high the tenor line is written at some cadence points, increasing the expressiveness of the moment.
6 If some phrases are repeated, as are phrases 1 and 2, and 5 and 6 in this chorale, the phrase repetition needs to be harmonised differently.

Composing String Quartets in the Classical Style

Introduction

The string quartet consists of two violins, viola and cello. The open strings of the violin, viola and cello are as follows:

In the Classical period, composers wrote little for the upper registers of stringed instruments, although the late quartets of Haydn and Mozart and certainly Beethoven extend at least the upper ranges of violin I and cello.

The Classical string quartet typically comprises four movements, the first movement being a sonata-Allegro, followed usually by a Minuet, Adagio and quick Finale. In his *Op. 33* quartets, Haydn introduced the Scherzo into the genre instead of the Minuet. As the string quartet developed, the slow movement was placed as the second movement in the four-movement scheme. Beethoven's string quartets considerably expanded the four-movement scheme. His late quartets illustrate marvellous innovations, radically altering the original four-movement scheme and straining the boundaries of the four-movement form.

Tone colour

The normal tone of the violin, viola and cello is obtained by passing the bow smoothly over the strings, agitating them and causing them to send vibrations through the bridge to the belly and through the sound-post to the back. A great variety of bowstrokes and other techniques are used to enable players to produce notes of differing smoothness and detachment. The most common requirements in the Classical quartet style are:

- a down bow to stress a beat and/or accent a strong beat, to play *sf* marked notes, and to make sudden musical surprises
- slurring – the playing of two or more notes in a bow to achieve a *legato* effect. The effect of slurring creates a less marked, more expressive 'nuanced' tone, often used in slow movements. At this time notes were rarely slurred across a bar line
- notes with a *staccato* and slur across, sometimes called *portato*, necessitates the bow being stopped on the string. Again, this type of playing is often associated with slow movements in the Classical period.

Vibrato

An effect produced by rocking movements of the finger on the string. A slow rocking movement creates a more languid, expressive tone, very characteristic of solo 'romantic' string melodies, while a quick, sharp *vibrato*, as used in the Baroque and Classical periods, makes the tone more vibrant but with less of an expressive overlay.

Pizzicato

This relates to the plucking of the string or strings, usually with the right hand. The direction, *pizzicato*, abbreviated to *pizz* on scores, indicates that this way of playing continues until the word *arco* appears which signifies that the bow should be used again. *Pizzicato* is a form of *staccato*; the sound dies away almost immediately. The difference between *pizzicato* on the violin and *pizzicato* on the cello is that on the smaller instrument, the violin, the strings are shorter and less resonant, while on the cello, the quality of tone is more vibrant and resonant because the strings are longer.

Multiple stops

This refers to the pressing of two, three or four strings simultaneously to produce double, triple or quadruple stops, also know as double-stopping. In the Classical period, two notes were usually played simultaneously, while three- or four-part chords were usually played as a quick arpeggio, with increased emphasis on the melody note, usually the highest note.

Dynamics

The most prevalent dynamic markings in the Classical period ranged from p – *piano* to f – *forte*. Other common markings were *crescendo* and *dimuendo*, sf, mp and mf. Beethoven expanded the dynamic potential to previously unknown levels. His works frequently range from ppp to ff, and demand many more sudden, dynamic and robust contrasts from musicians.

Writing string quartets in the Classical style

Key considerations

When starting to compose string quartets in the Classical style, you need to consider the following points:

Tonality and harmony

You need to write a solid harmonic scheme with characteristic harmonic progressions, both within phrases and at cadence points. This is in part produced by a good, directional cello line with a sense of forward movement. Classical harmonic schemes are constructed in a simpler harmonic style than in Bach chorale harmonisations, based predominantly on tonic, dominant harmonic schemes with added dissonances in the form of dominant 7ths, 9ths and 13ths, and diminished 7th chords, suspensions and appoggiaturas. Dominant 7th chords held a significant position as they defined keys clearly and could firmly establish a modulation. During the Classical period they were used in all inversions.

Chromatic chords are mostly found in minor key pieces which lend themselves more easily to expressive writing. Augmented and Neapolitan 6th chords need to be used sparingly, and usually either just before a cadence or to modulate to another key. The Neapolitan 6th chord is normally in the Ist inversion, often replacing chord II in the progression II(b) Ic V.

Characteristic progressions include passing and cadential 6/4 patterns, a particularly common progression being V/I IIB Ic V7 I.

Think carefully about chords you choose in your harmonic scheme. It is only a part of the procedure to know which notes go in which chord. The important point about good harmonic schemes is that they are devised through an understanding of the function and expressive power of harmony. For example, root position and dominant 7th chords can firmly establish a tonality, while Ist inversion chords are less strong. Diminished 7th chords can be used in appropriate places instead of dominant 7th chords, particularly in the minor key, in modulating sequences and as secondary dominants.

In general, the harmonic pace is slower than that of the Baroque period.

Modulation to close key relationships are an integral part of the style; to be stylistically convincing, pieces cannot remain in one key throughout

Texture

Texture in Classical quartets constantly changes. There are endless variations which include melody and accompaniment, pairing of instrumental lines, contrapuntal writing, all of which affect the spacing and grouping of instruments.

Idiomatic accompaniment

Use idiomatic accompaniment patterns. Accompaniment patterns used are many and varied and include broken chord and arpeggio figurations, repeated notes, sustained chords, syncopated figurations and pizzicato patterns.

String writing

Your writing for strings needs to be characteristic of the genre, for example instrumental lines often move in intervals of 3rds and 6ths. For dramatic contrast, the melody line is often doubled at the octave. Unison or octave passages frequently occur at the beginning or end of sections. As the form developed, equally significant parts were written for all four instruments, with less dominance of the violin I. Virtuosic passages as well as sustained *cantabile* passages were a feature of the Classical style as well as contrasts of mood, texture, and accompaniment figures. It would be wise to take a cautionary approach in writing in the extreme upper ranges for all instruments.

Stylistic fluency and originality

- Show stylistic fluency, in terms of sectional divisions, phrase divisions and how and when to introduce new thematic material.
- Show an ability for originality, for example through unexpected turns of phrases, suspensions and appoggiaturas.

Approaches on how to start composing a string quartet

If you are composing your string quartet from a given *incipit* (first two or three bars and possible subsequent bars on a skeleton score), or from a given violin I part throughout the extract, you may find the following approaches useful:

- 'Read' the opening given phrase and any other given bars in the extract
- Work out the structure: the tonic key, modulations (usually highlighted by accidentals); where the cadence points are (many are Ic-V(7)-I, or IIb-V(7)-I)
- Work out the phrase structure, by adding up the bars, marking in the cadence points, analysing the opening phrase, places where a new texture is implied or given and so on. Phrases usually fall into some kind of balanced 2+2+4, or 4+4, sometimes sequentially splitting into derivations of 1+1+1+1
- Look for points of imitation and identify which instrument 'leads' and how others are to follow
- Identify if there is a change of character during the extract; the given melody line should show this
- Actively look at and analyse the idioms used in accompaniment parts; work out how long the particular accompaniment patterns will go on for by identifying any changes in the melody, cadence point or textural change
- Look out for changes in the texture; there is a great variety of continually changing textures in Classical string quartets
- Be prepared to include some movement, usually in one or all parts, where the violin I has long sustained notes
- Be prepared to include some contrapuntal techniques, often occurring in passages where a given part is more motific, or where parts seem to move towards imitation instead of straightforward melody and accompaniment patterns
- If the given violin I line looks to be an accompanying, more decorative line, (often recognisable with semiquaver passages, sometimes separated by rests), consider if another instrument is to take the melody, or introduce a new melody, or develop motifs from the melody
- Let the music breathe; remember to use rests appropriately.

Further work and listening

- Listen to some works mentioned in this section, comparing and contrasting the different styles and the way that the genre developed. For example Haydn's *String Quartet Op. 2, No. 3* and Mozart's *String Quartet K465*.

- Explore the compositional style of Beethoven, comparing an early quartet such as one of the *Op. 18* quartets with a later quartet such as one from *Op. 127*. Look closely at how Beethoven develops the motifs, varies the textures and uses the full range and capacities of the instruments within the Classical style.

Identifying compositional techniques

In order to develop your ability to construct string quartets, you first need to understand and be able to identify characteristic compositional techniques, patterns and stylistic features.

Haydn
String Quartet Op. 2 No. 3, 3rd movement

Below is an analysis of a part of the slow movement of one of Haydn's earliest quartets, *Op. 2 No. 3*. Study the score below noting the key analytical points which relate directly to compositional features.

String Quartet Op. 2 No. 3, 3rd movement
Haydn

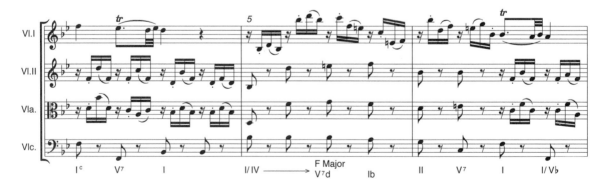

Analysis

Harmonies and harmonic progression

Cello line
The cello plays a combination of diatonic leaps, repeated notes and gradually rising step-wise passages, often working in contrary motion with violin I. It has a steady pulse of four notes in each bar, changing in bar 9 to a more prominent motif, as part of the lower strings dialogue with violin I.

Accompaniment
The accompaniment patterns are characteristic of the genre. The cello provides the harmonic framework while the inner parts play a lilting broken-chord motif, the last two semiquavers of which are slurred to create the lilting flow.

Cadences and modulations
The movement has frequent cadence points, and modulations fluctuate between the tonic key of B♭ and the dominant, F major. Note how the modulation at bar 5 is subtly introduced with the E♮ first heard in the violin II part and gently reinforced on the off-beat violin I semiquavers, before being more firmly presented at the cadence point. The brief return to B♭ in bar 7 is more strongly emphasised by the E♭ in the violin I part, against steady repeated B♭s in the cello line. The passage begins in B♭ major and ends in the dominant, F major.

Texture
The texture in bars 1–5 is a characteristic melody and accompaniment. Violin I takes the melody while the inner parts play a flowing, arpeggio accompaniment and the cello provides a *pizzicato* bass, underpinning the harmonic scheme. At bar 5 the texture changes and now the semiquaver figurations are played by violin I while all the other strings play chords; the texture again alters in bar 9, as discussed above to create a dialogue between violin I and lower strings. At bar 11 a more contrapuntal texture elaborates the cadence point.

Other points

Bars 7–8

The basic shape of the melody line is one of two descending phrases. This is counterbalanced by the steady rising bass line, in contrary motion with the melody, and the quite stationery inner lines.

Bar 9

Texture – individual instrumental lines and the shape of the melody line contrasts with the previous two bars, the unity being maintained by rhythmic similarities throughout; the melody includes rests at this point which often indicates that other parts have more significance. In this case, a dialogue is created between violin I and the lower strings. The effect is heightened by the cello being marked *arco*, the dynamic marking f, and the octave leap in the cello motif. This bar also stands out as it is based on repeated notes, in contrast to the preceding and subsequent phrases.

Bar 11

The long note in the violin I part and ornamentation at the end of the bar, moving the line towards the final bar, is a common feature in slow movement cadences, as is the appoggiatura in the final bar. Long notes in the violin I part often implies more movement in the lower parts.

Key features

Look closely and analyse other Haydn and Mozart quartets as you prepare to write your own. Key features of Haydn quartets are:

- as the genre developed, the four instruments made an increasingly individual contribution, the emphasis changing away from the dominance throughout of the violin I part
- the violin 1 part usually takes the more virtuosic line

- there is much use of contrapuntal techniques
- a typical format is the statement of a theme, followed by a 'looser' passage when motifs or fragments of a theme are passed from one instrument to another
- Haydn often marks **forte** in unison or octave passages to announce new sections
- some quartets are infused with a light hearted, witty humour, especially in Minuets
- melodies are more motific than lyrical
- Haydn enjoyed including 'surprise' tactics – sudden dynamics, pauses, rests, or changes of register
- The later quartets explored more minor keys which allowed for increased expressive feelings to be conveyed. With violin II, viola and cello now equally as important as violin I, the variety of textures increased to include contrapuntal techniques and increased motific development passing between all instrumental lines.

Mozart
String Quartet in F Major K590, 2nd movement

Now study the following extract, considering throughout what you would write if you were given just the opening phrase, followed by the violin I part, and were asked to complete the extract.

Read through the given analysis from a composing view point, keeping in mind the approaches given above. Remember, this is one interpretation, albeit Mozart's! When you have a go at composing your own quartet, while composing 'in-style', you can explore all possibilities.

String Quartet in F major, 2nd movement
Mozart

Analysis

In the opening eight-bar phrase, the texture is chordal and in close harmony. The melody is in the violin I part and the phrase structure is 2+2+4.

The structure

The extract is 46 bars long and begins in C major. It has a 6/8 metre and is marked Andante. In bars 21–22 the music passes through G major, in bars 23–27 modulates to D major, and in bars 29–36 to G major/C, touching through A minor at bar 37 before ending in G major. Hints of D minor appear in bar 4, hints of G major appear in bars 7–8, and of D minor in bars 12–13. When working out the modulations, look at broad sweeps and overall phrases, taking in the cadence points. Work out whether the modulations are established by an end cadence or are transitory modulations – passing through keys on travels back to the 'home' or another key.

The phrase structure

The main section breaks occur at bar 16, bar 24, bar 33 and bar 46. Less clear cut phrase endings, punctuated by cadences occur almost every eight bars, following the phrase structure of the first eight bars. This whole section is based on varied repeats of bars 1–8.

The Detail

The opening phrase
The opening eight-bar phrase is perhaps not fully characteristic of the usual lyrical Mozart style. There is much use of repeated notes in the melody, and the overall melodic line is broken up into short motifs. The phrase, however, is typically based on a diationic harmonic framework, consisting of tonic/dominant progressions. Note the transitory modulatory cadence into D minor at bar 4–5 and G major at bar 8–9.

What makes the opening phrase appealing?
The close harmonisation, with all instruments

playing melodically constructed lines, the balanced phrase structure of 2+2+4, the sequence in the first four bars; the sense of direction to the cadence point in bar 8.

How is the sense of direction created?
Again, a combination of musical elements: the balance of the phrases, the rising sequence, in particular the harmonic progression and movement of the cello line in bars 5–8 in which at the end of bars 5 and 6 the lyricism in the phrase works over the bar line, gently driving the music forward. This contrasts with the first four bars where the two phrases are separated by rests at the end of each phrase.

The violin I part from bars 9 – 16
As violin I now plays continuous decorative semiquaver figurations, it is clear that the melodic interest will lie in one or more of the lower parts. Here, the melody is now taken by violin II accompanied in close harmony by the lower strings, as in the opening phrase. The decorative figurations of violin I follow the shape of the melody. Note the subtleties in these passages: the scalic passages parallel the phrase endings in bars 10 and 12. When there is less movement in the melody – repeated notes – the violin I passages in contrast are more expansive, playing arpeggio-like passages, and when the melody is more lyrically conceived, Mozart enhances the lyricism with subtle contrary motion; when one line leaps, the other is more step-wise. In the second half of the eight-bar phrase, Mozart varies the melodic line.

The violin I part from bars 16 – 24
The rests in the violin I part in bar 16, together with the cadence point here, usually imply that some action needs to happen in another part. This section, built on the first eight-bar phrase, is this time accompanied by a rising semiquaver figuration which begins in the cello and gradually moves up through the instruments, finally returning to violin I for the cadence point at bar 24. Again the first phrase is varied, now being heard with violin I playing one octave higher and the cello playing two octaves higher. The texture is additionally altered as the semiquaver passages move through the instrumental parts.

The violin I part from bars 24–32
The decorative violin I part indicates thematic interest elsewhere in one or more of the other instrumental parts. Here, the inner strings play a varied repeat of the opening phrase while the outer strings imitate each other with sweeping semiquaver and repeated-note passages. Note the texture change from the previous eight bars; also the characteristic suspensions in bars 30-32 in the stepwise descending violin I line and the subtle dissonances thus created with the cello part.

The final section from bar 33
Compare the first four bars of this section with the opening four bars. By 'staggering' the viola and cello lines, Mozart not only varies this phrase from the opening but also, through drawing the quaver movement across all four bars, creates increased momentum. The sudden contrasting dynamic markings at bar 37 emphasise the change of treatment and also of key. Decorative figurations in the violin I part which begin on an off-beat, as do the rising arpeggio motifs in bars 40-42, will often imply other instruments playing on the beat. The descending stepwise line to the final cadence is characteristic of this typical cadential progression. Note how the bass underpins the harmonic progressions, rhythmically working in alternation with violin II, while the viola keeps the momentum going with rising semiquavers, imitating the previous bars of the violin I.

Summary
The 'material' of this extract is fairly straightforward. Basically, it comprises the eight-bar first phrase, scalic and arpeggio semiquaver accompaniment figurations and typical cadential progressions. The interest lies in the changing textures; the individual instrumental contributions in alternately taking the theme and accompanying, small variations in the repetition of the main melodic theme; the modulations, all of which maintain close key relationships with the 'home' key of C major; and the increased harmonic tension points which give the extract its sense of direction.

String Quartet K590, 1st movement
Mozart

Characteristic features of Classical string quartets

Allegro movements

The opening of this movement presents an octave announcement of the theme, followed by the theme repeated but now harmonised. This opening, with its contrasting textural treatment of the main theme is very common. The melody continues in the violin I, the harmonic framework in the cello, accompaniment in block repeated harmony by the inner strings.

String Quartet K458, 1st movement
Mozart

Predominantly, the melody is played by violins I and II in 3rds, the cello provides the harmonic bass and the viola plays an inner melodic line, as a counter-melody.

String Quartet Op. 76 No. 2, 1st movement
Haydn

This has a characteristic Classical melody and accompaniment, with the melody clearly in the topmost part in the opening phrase. The accompaniment comprises jogging repeated notes, maintaining the harmonic scheme.

String Quartet K465, 1st movement
Mozart

Extract 1: bars 22–32

This is an example of a more lyrical opening melody, again with the repeated jogging accompaniment patterns. Note how lyrical all the instrumental lines are, including those with repeated notes. The phrases are very regular and clear cut, again typical Classical features. In the final two bars of this extract we see a different, but characteristic textural melody and accompaniment arrangement.

Extract 2: bars 107–134

Later in the quartet the melody is developed as shown above. The harmonic scheme here is maintained in the cello, the other three instrumental lines are contrapuntally derived, a common development technique. Consider the interplay of these lines, the way in which they fragment at bar 117, and the concluding octave arpeggio passage. This extract also illustrates the melody now being played by the cello, the other strings responding with answering phrases from bars 121–125. The extract also shows how syncopation can stimulate movement in a passage. Notice the two-part imitative counterpoint between the violin I and the cello from bar 125.

String Quartet Op. 18 No. 6, 1st Movement
Beethoven

Extract 1: bars 1–16

Extract 2: bars 92–100

These two extracts are taken from one of Beethoven's early quartets and illustrate his characteristic development method of introducing a small motif unobtrusively in an opening which becomes the central core in the subsequent development section. In this case it is the short semiquaver motif. The first extract (bars 1–16) shows the opening of the movement, the arpeggio, motific theme in typical Beethoven style. The example also illustrates the increased prominence of the cello with its answering phrase to the violin I opening. Note how the semiquaver motif is taken out of the arpeggio theme and used as a link to the next section.

In the second extract (bars 92–100) – the opening of the development section – we see how this motif is now the centre from which the development begins. The motif is passed through all instruments and Beethoven typically uses this fragment of the main theme with the energetic quavers, now in the bass.

Slow movements

This is an example of a clear melody and accompaniment texture. The melody is in regular phrases and the accompaniment is a characteristic slow movement lilting pattern, marked staccato, but played semi-staccato as opposed to legato playing.

In this extract the melody is now accompanied in a different way, with an arpeggio-like accompaniment.

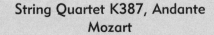
String Quartet K387, Andante
Mozart

This shows the use of a syncopated accompaniment pattern, common in slow movements to keep the momentum going. Note the repeated bass, now with the octave leap. The melody is characteristically ornamental.

String Quartet K465, Andante
Mozart

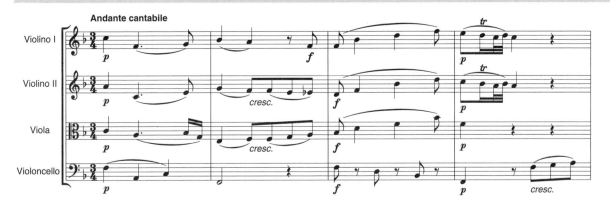

This is an example of the start of a warm, expressive slow movement, conveyed through the composer writing full lyrical lines with chro-matic moments, which makes for a rich texture. The cello takes a significant, melodic role.

**String Quartet Op. 76 No. 3, Variation 4, Andante
Haydn**

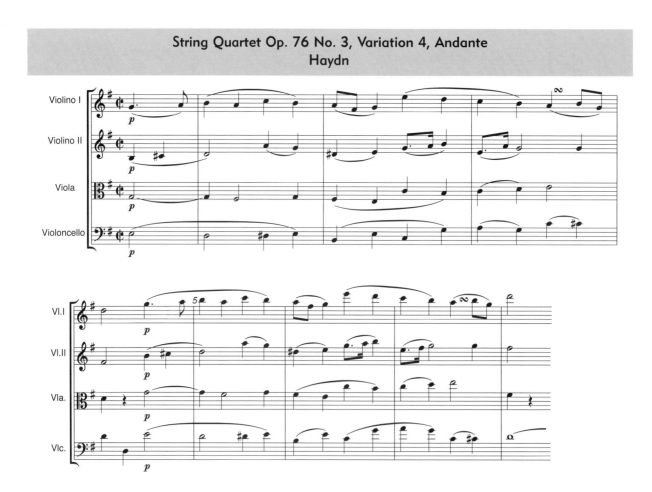

In this extract from Haydn there is again a full, rich, sustained texture with all the instruments playing melodic and significant lines. The repetition of the first four bars is an octave higher.

String Quartet Op. 74 No. 3, Largo assai
Haydn

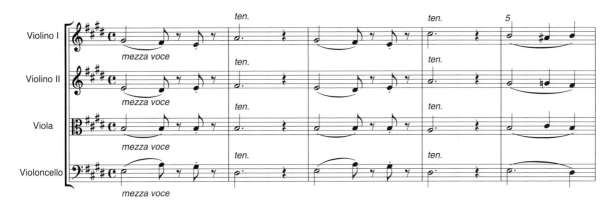

This is another example of rich, textural expressive writing, but this time the theme comprises ten bars, builds up to a tension point and resolves into the dominant key. Look closely at the way Haydn develops and expands the first two-bar motif, increasing the interval on the last two notes, and then writing a melody which ascends higher and higher in each bar to bar eight, before coming to resolution in bar 10.

String Quartet Op. 131, Adagio
Beethoven

The intensity of the Adagio in this late Beethoven quartet is clearly apparent in the expressive, chromatic instrumental lines, all of which now play an equally significant role. The extract also illustrates the range, rhythmic diversity, and sheer richness of the composer's innovatory string writing.

Minuets and trios

String Quartet Op. 76 No. 1, Minuet
Haydn

This is an example of typical rustic minuet writing with all the interest being in the violin 1 part, with chordal flourishes at the cadence point. Look closely again at the shape of the two ten-bar phrases. Shape plays a key role with the harmonic framework in giving the music a sense of direction.

String Quartet Op. 74 No. 2, Menuetto
Haydn

This is an example of a more complex minuet style, shown in the more elaborate melody line and in the rhythmic variety between the instrumental lines. The character of this minuet is of a less rustic nature than the previous example.

String Quartet K458, Trio
Mozart

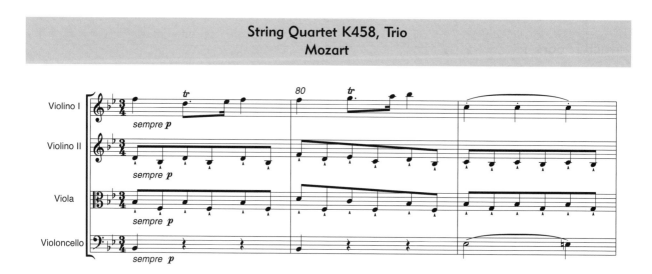

This is an example of a typical Mozart trio section in a minuet. A lyrical, balanced melody is played by violin I, with the inner instrumental lines playing a typical accompaniment quaver pattern and the bass providing the harmonic framework.

Finales

String Quartet Op. 77 No. 1
Haydn

Extract 1: bars 1–8

This finale has an octave, presto beginning and the melody is adventurous, covering a good range in a short phrase space. The use of two-note slurs, *staccatos*, sudden *sf*s, short semiquaver motifs and regular balanced phrase lengths are all common finale features. The second example shows how the music is developed at the start of the next section.

Extract 2: bars 100–108

String Quartet Op. 18 No. 5
Beethoven

Contrapuntally derived, the opening to this finale shows the ways that Beethoven drives a movement forward, the independence of the instrumental lines, the textural contrasts and the robust energy in the music

Introduction

The variation principle of composing has long been a favourite with composers and dates back to the instrumental music of the sixteenth century.

Sixteenth century variation form

There are many examples of sets of variations on dances and popular tunes in the sixteenth and seventeenth centuries. A frequent composition method involved improvising variations over simple bass line *ostinato* patterns. The melodies used were usually short, simple, and tuneful with regular phrasing, either in binary or ternary form and with clear cadences.

Chaconne and passacaglia

The *chaconne* is a Baroque dance and variation form which originated as a dance-song in Latin America and was popular in Spain and Italy in the seventeenth century. The *chaconne* can be recognised by its strict *ostinato* ground bass and it is usually in triple metre and at a slow tempo. The ground bass is relentlessly repeated throughout the composition with little or no melodic variation. Chaconne basses were governed by the interval of a 4th. A typical *chaconne* ground bass comprises a descending four-bar formula based on either a major, minor or chromatic scalic pattern, covering the interval of a 4th. Another type of *chaconne* bass consisted of a sequence of 4ths and a cadence formula. While the harmonic scheme and progression is fixed, in each variation the figuration or some other feature changes to produce the variation.

The *passacaglia* originated in Spain as a *ritornello* – a repeated passage with a fixed pattern of guitar chords which was played between the verses of a song. It also evolved into a variety of bass formulas, usually in triple metre and slow tempo. Since the eighteenth century, the difference between the *chaconne* and *passacaglia* has become confused, with composers using the terms indiscriminately, although some

theorists maintain that the *passacaglia* bass originally had no recognisable *ostinato*, but just recurrent patterns and harmonies.

Theme and variations

In the sixteenth century, dances were frequently used as frameworks for instrumental variations. The art reached a high form in the keyboard works of Cabezon. The English virginalists, notably Byrd, also excelled, their works influencing composers such as Sweelinck and Scheidt. A characteristic technique of composers writing at this time involved repeating the melody almost exactly in each variation, but varying the contrapuntal schemes. Other composers maintained the same harmonic scheme in each variation but embellished the melody, which was almost always the top voice.

The variations of Frescobaldi in the seventeenth century illustrate a further technique – that of fixing the bass and harmony framework as the constant factor, with the melody being less important. Chorale variations for organ developed at this time, notably by Sweelinck and Scheidt who varied each verse of organ chorales, often with motifs related to the text. The form of free variations was perfected by Buxtehude, particularly in his chorale fantasias. In contrast, strict variation forms were developed by Pachelbel.

J. S. Bach used almost all variation types: *passacaglia* and *chaconne* in works for organ and solo violin; grounds in several vocal movements, including the 'Crucifixus' in the *Mass in B minor*; chorale partitas and canonic variations for organ. The *Goldberg Variations* represent the highest artistic development of the bass-framework variations.

Variation types in the Classical era

Although C.P.E. Bach and Haydn continued to cultivate the ground bass type of variation, from 1770 the melodic type dominated. In the Classical period, variation techniques occur in three broad situations:

- as an independent theme and variations composition
- as a theme and variation movement of a symphony, concerto or sonata
- as a technique within a large formal plan – a rondo, or sonata, where, on the repeat of a section, the first theme is varied.

The form

The theme, usually harmonised, is first stated and then followed by a number of varied restatements. Variation technique can involve melodic, rhythmic, textural, harmonic and instrumental changes, and include various altered settings and characters. Up to the time of Beethoven, the same key, or its parallel minor or major, was usually retained as well.

Further work and listening

- **Sixteenth century variation methods** – listen to some of the keyboard works of the Spanish composer Cabezon, the English virginalists, notably Byrd's variations on Dowland's air 'Flow, my tears'. Try incorporating some of the techniques used here in your own compositions.

- **Chorale variations** – listen to works by W Sweelinck, Pachelbel, and J.S. Bach; for example, Bach's variations for organ on *Von Himmel hoch*. Look carefully at the way in which the chorale melody is maintained with a range of contrapuntal techniques. You could, for example, explore composing a variation with your theme placed in the middle of a four-part contrapuntal texture. Try writing variations on a hymn tune, using imitative, contrapuntal and *fugato* techniques.

- **Chaconne and passacaglia** – listen to J.S. Bach's *Passacaglia in C minor* for organ; the *Chaconne* in his *D minor Partita* for solo violin; for a ground bass, listen to Purcell's final aria from the opera *Dido and Aeneas*, 'When I am laid

in earth'; and the 'Crucifixus' of J.S. Bach's *Mass in B minor*. Try composing your own ground bass, as a bass to an instrumental or vocal piece.

- **Theme and variations** – there are numerous works to listen to and study in this form, but perhaps most significant include the following:

– J. S. Bach's *Goldberg Variations*, which represent the highest artistic development of bass-framework variations. All thirty variations preserve the bass and the harmonic structure of the theme. The work is a masterpiece of magnificent proportions
– Haydn's second movement from *Symphony No. 94 in G*, the 'Surprise'; second movement of the *String Quartet Op. 76 No. 3 in C major*. For examples of his art of varying two themes alternately, listen to the second movement of Haydn's *Symphonies Nos. 53 and 63*, and the *Variations in F minor* for piano
– Mozart's sets of variations for piano, his *Sonata in A major K331* for piano; and variation movements in his string quartets
– Beethoven took the art of variation technique to previously unseen heights, and particularly so, in his late works. His *Thirty-three Variations on a Waltz by Diabelli Op. 120* represent a microcosm of late Beethoven variation style and technique; the finale of his *Symphony No. 3*, the 'Eroica'; the slow movements of *Symphonies Nos. 5 and 7*; the finale of *Symphony No. 9* which begins as a set of variations, the 'Appassionata' *Sonata Op. 57*; *Sonata Op. 111*; the slow movements of the *String Quartets Op. 127 and 131*.

Before you start writing your own theme and variations, it is important to listen to a range of works in this form and to actively look at the composing processes and approaches used. Then, try incorporating some of the methods into your own compositions. Some suggestions of specific approaches are given in the following illustrations.

Writing variations

Key considerations

When starting to compose variations, you need to consider the following points:

Structure

Your chosen theme needs to be suitable for variation form. Themes need to be tuneful or memorable in some way and be capable of being varied both as whole themes and broken up into fragments. Fragments should each present a particular interesting feature, such as an emphasised leap or colourful motif.

The possibilities for variations are many and varied, but always in the overall scheme a comprehensible plan can be followed. There are many examples of sets which begin with variations on the whole theme, and gradually both transform and fragment a theme as the set progresses.

The theme section is usually in simple ternary form – A B A – with the middle section presenting a different theme, often in a different key.

Variation techniques

i) Variation sets often start by varying either the whole theme or accompaniment using Alberti bass-type semiquaver patterns in the first variations, followed by variations based on triplets, sometimes changing the metre, and progressing through to more dramatic variations using octave patterns, or *maestoso* variations featuring dotted rhythms and a march-like style. Other characteristic variations include expressive variations using more flowing part movement; variations in the upper register only, or those in which the theme is played in the bass and accompanied by a decorative line in the treble; variations focusing on chordal passages, or contrapuntal techniques.

Almost all sets include a decorative ornamental variation and a variation in the minor key, or the relative major if the tonic key is a minor key. The penultimate variation is very frequently an Adagio followed by a substantial Finale.

ii) Contrapuntal techniques such as imitation, sequences, inversions and *fugato* sections are common.

iii) Variations can be written focusing on a particular motif of the theme while maintaining the overall phrase balance and structure.

iv) Variations can be written based on the harmonic structure only, with the theme being fragmented and only one or two particular motifs used.

v) Common accompaniment patterns based on semiquavers, or triplets or arpeggio passages are generally based on characteristic Alberti bass figurations.

Harmonies

The harmonies are generally based on tonic, dominant and dominant and diminished 7th chords, with chromatic chords such as augmented and Neapolitan 6ths being used sparingly to increase points of tension, to modulate, or just before a cadence.

In general, the harmonic pace is one or two chords per bar, often changing to four per bar in the approach to a cadence.

Character

As well as variations focusing on melodic, rhythmic, harmonic, timbral, tempo and textural elements, they can also be composed in different moods or characters; for example, Scherzo or 'elfin-like', wistful, or deeply expressive, or other moods as described above.

Your variations could have a particular theme running through the set, for example particular aspects of nature, or characters of people.

Approaches on how to start writing variations

- Choose your theme for variations carefully. Almost any tuneful and interesting melody can be used. Beethoven, for example, wrote variations on *Rule Brittania*, and Mozart often used popular tunes of the day, or melodies from operas. Start, for example, with an eight-bar theme, and progress to a longer theme section in A B A form comprising sixteen or twenty-four bars
- Analyse the harmonic structure of the theme, the tonic key, the modulations, the cadence points and the harmonies used
- Work out the phrase structure of the theme, considering the balance, if there are any sequences, and how any rests are built in to the structure
- Plan your overall scheme, working out the number of variations you are going to write and how each is to be varied
- Look for ways of varying the texture, both between and within variations
- Remember to use rests. Not all parts need to be active continuously
- Include contrapuntal techniques in your variations
- Your writing for keyboard or ensemble should be playable. Make sure you consider carefully what works well for different instruments and what types of writing are typical of the genre. For example, variations for piano need to be pianistic, and take into account the limitations of ten fingers, the span and the tempo of the music.

Identifying compositional techniques

It will help you a great deal in your composition of variations if you develop an understanding of compositional techniques and stylistic features through listening and analysis.

Mozart
Twelve Variations on 'Ah vous dirai-je, Maman' K265

Mozart's independent sets of variations for piano were popular in his lifetime and well into the nineteenth century. He also used variation form in his divertimentos, serenades and concertos, occasionally in string quartets and piano sonatas, but not in any of his symphonies.

Nearly all Mozart's variations are of the melodic-type with fixed harmony. Characteristics of his variation style include a penultimate Adagio variation, often with a great deal of embellishment, a contrasting minor key variation and a fast final variation, very often in 6/8 metre. Within the variations themselves there are many remarkable, characteristic features, as we shall see below.

The *Twelve Variations on 'Ah, vous dirai-je, Maman'* were an early set of variations, written in 1781–2. They are pleasant, simply constructed and never vary far from the melodic outline or from the original harmonies. The extracts which are scored below show how the first eight-bar phrase of the theme is varied. The variations are characteristic of Mozart's early variation technique.

Analysis
Theme

Variation 1

This variation elaborates on the theme with simple semiquaver passages. Mozart incorporates appoggiaturas on the strong beats of each bar, sometimes above the main melody note on each first beat and below on each second beat, and vice versa at other times. Note the rhythmic change in the left hand in the second half of the phrase, where Mozart introduces some gentle syncopation.

Variation 2

In Variation 2 the movement is created in the bass with continuous semiquaver passages, based on the fixed harmonic framework. The single line melody is now filled out with chords, and further heightened by suspensions running throughout much of these first eight bars. Note the contrast here between this variation and Variation 1, in which the texture is far more linear.

Variation 3

The device of changing a theme by using triplets is very characteristic of Mozart, and much used in sets of variations in the Classical period. In this variation the registral span is widened through arpeggio-like passagework and extended intervallic leaps in the melody in the second half of the phrase, thereby expanding the restrained dimensions of the original theme. The articulation markings in the second phrase contrast with the *legato* first phrase.

Variation 4

As if to balance Variation 3, the triplet figurations now appear in the left hand. Again the shapes of first and the second four bars vary, following the basic patterns of Variation 3. The appoggiaturas in the chordal right-hand line are another favourite Mozart device.

Variation 5

After the full sound of the previous two variations, Mozart now lets some light into his variation set. Here, the theme is divided between the right and left hand as an interactive dialogue. At the same time, the rests allow a breathing space, a breath of fresh air to perpetrate the variation. Mozart also brings into the scene some gentle syncopation. Although the balance of the phrases is still 4+4, the phrases are again treated in contrasting ways in the second phrase.

Variation 6

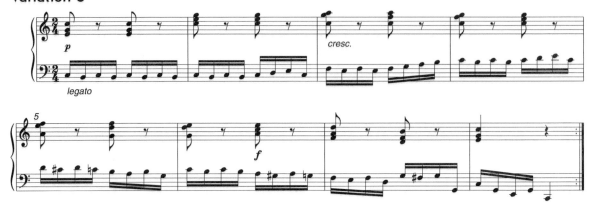

The tight, continuous semiquaver patterns in the left hand in this variation illustrate another favourite Classical device. Note the implied appoggiaturas in the chordal right hand, bars 3–8, and the characteristic octave leaps at the cadence point.

Variation 7

Now the movement is transferred to the right hand, this time in sweeping semiquaver scalic phrases. The second phrase contrasts these passages by short, motivic, leaping thrusts. Note the transitory V7 I cadence in A minor in the second phrase, a slight deviation from the fixed harmonic framework.

Variation 8

Many variation sets include one or more variations in the minor key. Very often, as in this case, they are in the tonic minor. Note the detailed articulation and dynamic markings.

The expressive character of the variation is created through almost continuous appoggiaturas, often comprising minor 2nds, to create added poignancy.

Variation 9

The common feature of hand-swopping can be seen here, as the left hand now plays the melody, accompanied by arpeggio motifs in the right hand. Note the registral and textural contrast between the first and second phrases, and

the way that Mozart introduces a series of diminished 7th chords in the second phrase, marked *forte* in contrast to the *piano* marking of the first phrase.

Variation 10

Marked Adagio, this variation is placed in its usual position, as the penultimate variation in the set. It is generally one of the more expressive variations, with more lyrical melodic leaps. A characteristic feature of many Adagio varia-

tions is the demisemiquaver ornamental passagework decorating the original theme, with lingering appoggiaturas, often, as in this case, at the cadence point. Imitation between the parts is also a feature in the first phrase.

Variation 11

This final variation illustrates the change to triple metre, a common feature for the final variations, marked Allegro in contrast to the preceding Adagio. The left-hand pattern is also very common – that of spiking the first note in each bar while the rest of the semiquavers take on a rolling pattern. Note the infusion of a more final 'feel' with the full chords, the trills, the wider span between right and left hand lines and the low bass notes.

Other characteristics of Mozart's variation sets

The characteristics common in other Mozart variation sets are illustrated as follows. Examples for analysis and comparison are taken from Mozart's *Ten Variations on Les Hommes Pieusement from La Rencontre Imprévue by Gluck K455*, and *Nine Variations on a Minuet from Sonata for Violoncello, Op. 4 no. 6, by Duport K573*.

> ### Mozart
> Ten Variations on Les Hommes Pieusementfrom La Recontre Imprévue, by Gluck K455

Theme

This is bars 1–4 of a theme in ternary form. The whole theme is twelve bars long, divided into three four-bar phrases. The key is G major, and the second phrase modulates to the supertonic minor, A minor, for bars 5–6 before returning to G major. The phrases are balanced – 2+2 – throughout. Note the simplicity of the melody line. The final four bars repeat the first, but one octave higher, with double octaves.

> ## Mozart
> Nine Variations on a Minuet from Sonata for Violoncello Op. 4 No. 6, by Duport K573

Theme

Again in ternary form, this is bars 1–8 of the theme material on a larger scale, comprising 24 bars. Note the similarities with the previous theme: both have tuneful melodies, both have balanced phrases.

Variations techniques

Below are examples of variations techniques of bars 1–4 of the *Gluck* theme and of bars 1–8 of the *Duport* theme.

Example 1: Gluck

Example 2: Duport

In Example 1, the theme is embodied in semi-quaver passages in the right hand. Although the octave passage alters considerably bars 3–4 of the theme, the overall phrase structure and cadence are the same.

In Example 2, the semiquavers create an appoggiatura effect as the main theme notes appear as the second note of each four-note pattern. As a further variation, each four-note semiquaver pattern in the second four bars begins on the note below, rather than above the main theme note. The bass scheme is the same as the original.

Example 3: Gluck

Example 4: Duport

As a typical progression from the above variations, the next variations now introduce semiquaver passages in the left hand. Although both left hand figurations begin with the same pattern, they continue with different figurations, with split octaves in Example 3 and arpeggio figurations in Example 4. Both are very typical Classical accompaniment patterns, as is the cadential bass pattern in Example 4.

Example 5: Duport

Characteristic features of this minor key variation are the decorations featuring turns, rhythmic alterations, underpinned by the harmonic scheme of the original theme.

Example 6: Gluck

The penultimate variation is generally much more elaborate as shown in this example. Note the wider note range throughout, but perhaps particularly noticeable in the first phrase. The decorations of the melody include triplets, trills, chromaticisms and suspensions. Again, the harmonic scheme remains the same as the original theme.

Haydn
String Quartet Op. 76 No. 3, 2nd movement

Haydn wrote few independent sets of variations but included variation movements in several chamber and orchestral works. He is particularly noted for developing a special variation form in which he had two alternating themes – a major and a minor – which are both stated before either one is varied. Haydn's *Variations in F minor* for piano is a good example of this variation technique.

Haydn's *String Quartet Op. 76 No. 3* is one of six string quartets composed in his last period, in 1797. It contains perhaps the best known and most outstanding example of slow movement variation form. Haydn's use of this form decreased in the late quartets. Now the German national anthem, Haydn composed the melody of this movement as a birthday hymn for Kaiser Franz Joseph 1.

Look closely at the expressive string writing opposite, the parts often moving in 3rds and 6ths, the instrumental groupings. Also, analyse the bass line and the harmonic silence.

Theme

The variations are worth studying in the way that the theme is passed from instrument to instrument through the variations, bringing about timbral, textural, and registral changes. Haydn's use of appoggiaturas, suspensions and changing notes are worthy of equal investiga-

tion. The following extracts from each of the following four variations illustrate lines 1, 2, 3 and 4 respectively of the national anthem, showing how the texture varies through the set. A brief analysis of the first half of Variation 1 is also given.

Variation 1

Variation 2

Variation 3

Variation 4

Variation 1: brief analysis

This is a good example of characteristic Haydn decorative accompaniment over the main theme, played by the 2nd violin. The variation gives an immediate timbral contrast to the statement of the theme as it is played by just the two violins. The linear, contrapuntally conceived texture also contrasts with the chordal harmonisation of the theme.

Note the detailed articulation markings for the accompaniment and the contrast between the wide-ranging arpeggio-like passages and tighter, more chromatically inclined passagework. Haydn creates 'breathing spaces' in the music by carefully placed rests, and by taking the accompaniment below the melody to emphasis significant notes of the melody line so as to fully penetrate the texture. Indeed, the dialogue interaction between the two violins, particularly the continually contrasting registers are all significant features in this variation.

Beethoven's variation technique

In Beethoven's late compositions, variation technique became the spiritual centrepiece of his style. Beethoven didn't just treat the theme as a foundation to be subjected to different forms of elaboration, but as a framework on which a series of musical entities could be built. He used different variation approaches including:

- varying the melody
- varying the tonality, harmonic schemes and progressions; adding chords, altering chords
- using particular rhythmic features taken from the theme, or harmony motif or the rhythm of the phrase structure
- creating different points of tension and resolution between variations
- making contrasts between easily recognisable variations and more obscure ones
- redefining the character of the theme.

Beethoven
Thirty-three Variations on a Waltz by Diabelli, Op.120

The *Thirty-three Variations on a Waltz by Diabelli Op. 120* stand alongside J. S. Bach's *Goldberg Variations* as a pinnacle of artistic achievement in the variation genre. The story goes that Diabelli, an Austrian music publisher and contemporary of Beethoven, had an idea to send a simple waltz theme to every notable Austrian composer, asking them each to write a variation on the waltz. The result was 50 variations, published in 1824 and Beethoven's *Diabelli Variations Op. 120*.

The variations are recognised as a microcosm of Beethoven's variation style. They are all built on motifs derived from some part of the theme, but altered in rhythm, tempo, dynamics and content. They are particularly significant in that, unlike earlier themes and variations, many of them also transform the character of the theme. The *Diabelli Variations* strongly influenced Schumann, and in particular, Brahms in his *Variations on a Theme of Handel*.

Analysis

Theme bars 1–16

	Character	Melodic Outline	Phrase Structure	Harmony/ Tonality	Texture	Tempo/ Rhythm
Theme	Waltz; characteristic musical humour	Waltz theme based on interval of 4th begins in right hand, immediately taken into bass	4 + 4 + 2 +2 + 4	Tonic key C major established bars 1–4; dominant chord G emphasised bars 5–8 Sequentially modulating cadences – F maj – G maj – A min – bars 9–12	Chordal melody and accompaniment	Waltz

Variation 1

	Character	Melodic Outline	Phrase Structure	Harmony/ Tonality	Texture	Tempo/ Rhythm
Variation 1	A majestic march	Maintains original shape and intervallic structure in 1st, 2nd and 3rd phrases. In 4th phrase the climax point is taken a 3rd higher	As original theme	In C major, tonic chord emphasised; harmonic framework maintained. In the 3rd phrase, instead of passing through F – G – A min, modulations move from F – B♭ – – A min. Instead of dominant 7ths in the up-beats to each one-bar phrase, acting as modulatory cadences, diminished 7ths in bars 12, 13, 14, increase the dissonance	Chordal; full bodied, chordal	Marked *alla marcia maestoso*. In common time with the beat emphasised by the *sf* markings on 1st beat of each bar

Variation 2

	Character	Melodic Outline	Phrase Structure	Harmony/ Tonality	Texture	Tempo/ Rhythm
Variation 2	Contrasting; lighter, marked *semi-staccato*	Melodic shape implied through harmonic framework	Maintained, a crucial part of recognition	In C major, harmonic framework of bars 1–4 in C major; bars 5–8 emphasising the dominant, G. Note pedal B in left hand of the second phrase, giving sense of less stable tonality. Also the play of F♯ and F in this second phrase – a destabilising juxtaposition of C major and G major. Bars 9–12 more chromatic and includes aug 6ths and dim chords	Chordal but full chords heard simultaneously are avoided	Quick, continuous quaver motion split between right and left hands

Variation 3

	Character	Melodic Outline	Phrase Structure	Harmony/ Tonality	Texture	Tempo/ Rhythm
Variation 3	Tenderly passionate; ethereal, *cantabile*	Melodic shape maintained both horizontally and vertically; expressive use of the 6th interval; four-bar descending phrase followed by second four-bar descending phrase. In the 3rd phrase, one-bar phrases are varied, emphasising intervals of diminished 5th, augmented 4th instead of original rising semitonal figure	As original theme	Much more chromatic bars 1–4: C major. Bars 5–8: the dominant, G emphasised. Bars 9–12: dim 7th – I in F major; Aug 6th – G major; Bars 13–16 dim 7th chromatic harmony ending in G major	Loosening of chordal structure in first eight bars. Left hand emphasis on 2nd beat gives more lilting feel; hints of melodic interest in left hand of bar 5 as counter-melody. Bars 9–16 resume the one-bar modulatory sequential cadential pattern in chords	Marked *L'istesso tempo*, this variation deliberately goes for gentle, less energetic rhythmic emphasis

Variation 4

	Character	Melodic Outline	Phrase Structure	Harmony/ Tonality	Texture	Tempo/ Rhythm
Variation 4	Still marked *dolce*, but now with more movement; deeply expressive	In contrast to Variation 3, phrase bars 1–4 now ascend with bars 5–8 ascending more chromatically; 3rd and 4th phrases now ascend to the higher octave register; suspensions; appoggiaturas; chromatic octave ascending step-wise movement	Now only 15 bars long: 4 + 3 + 4 + 4. Phrases less clearly divided, emphasis being on chromatic lines	Expressive chromatic harmony; 1st and 2nd phrases: as original theme; 3rd phrase: A min – G major; use of dim 7ths; introduction of new note – Ab – Aug 6th 'just missed', but implied in bar 12	Imitative counterpoint, based on opening motif. 1st and 2nd phrases linearly conceived; 3rd and 4th phrases more chordal	Less marked; predominating rhythmic phrase from 1st motif present throughout

Variation 5

	Character	Melodic Outline	Phrase Structure	Harmony/ Tonality	Texture	Tempo/ Rhythm
Variation 5	Extremely quick, one-in-a-bar, similar character to Scherzo	Not melodically conceived. Melodic shape maintained through intervallic structure based on 4ths of original theme	As original theme	Diatonic, C major but with added dim 7th on C# in 1st phrase; 3rd phrase, modulatory sequence now descends, moving from A minor (bar 12) – G major (bar 13) – E minor (bar 14)	Chordal	Energetic, robust, based on rhythm of waltz motif with emphasis on 3rd beat

Variation 6

	Character	Melodic Outline	Phrase Structure	Harmony/ Tonality	Texture	Tempo/ Rhythm
Variation 6	Decorative, light, sprightly	Arpeggio-like phrases; ornamental – trills dominant feature; detailed articulation; as in original, first two phrases follow arpeggio outline, while 3rd phrase follows rising step-wise melodic shape	As original theme	As original theme until 3rd phrase which includes dim 7ths instead of dom 7ths	Dialogue between right and left hand, more contrapuntally conceived	Emphasis on rhythmic length at beginning of bars and quicker movement on last beats of the bars

Composing Piano Accompaniments in Early Romantic Style

Introduction

The Romantic movement of the early nineteenth century had a great effect on the evolution of song. The early Romantic period was a great literary age which gave rise to a prolific outburst of poetry. There was at this time a liking for nature, landscapes and the expression of intense emotions of love – in particular yearning and unrequited love. This and the enormous popularity of the piano, with its new possibilities for expressive accompaniments made the song reach a previously unprecedented status.

Schubert's Lieder

With his enormous output, Schubert effectively established the German lied as a new art form in the nineteenth century. His songs, which span his entire creative career, number over 600 and are enormously varied in style, character and mood.

Melody

Schubert's supreme lyrical gift is recognised as being amongst the finest of the art. His melodies cover a vast range, from simple folksong to declamatory, arioso and dramatic styles.

Harmony

The striking aspect of Schubert's harmony is his use of chromatic chords – diminished 7ths and augmented 6th chords in particular – for atmospheric and emotional expression. Also characteristic is his sudden introduction of a chord with a minor 3rd when a major 3rd is expected and vice-versa. His genius lies in the way he uses chromatic expression within a harmonic framework of tonic and dominant chords and their inversions, and familiar Classically based cadence progressions.

Tonality/modulation

An important aspect of Schubert's tonal schemes is his modulations. The most notable are usually abrupt, expressive modulations to the mediant or submediant, or even to a different tonality altogether. He frequently swaps between major and minor tonalities, particularly of the tonic key. Schubert's tonalities are often ambiguous, or kept in suspense. He liked to flirt with a key, blurring tonal distinctions by delaying resolutions, only partially resolving, or avoiding altogether a definitive cadence and instead turning to a new tonal direction.

Accompaniments

Schubert had a deep understanding of the resources of the piano. His imaginative and rich accompaniments are never merely pictorial, but are beautifully designed as an integral part of the character and mood of the song. Although idiomatic accompaniment patterns can be discerned, they are rich in musical subtleties and ingenious innovations individual to each song. Characteristic accompaniment patterns include arpeggio-like or broken-chord patterns, plodding quaver accompaniments, triplet figurations, running semiquaver idioms, long chordal phrases, tremelo agitations, bass scalic motifs, dramatic full chords and bass melodic lines.

Form

Broadly, Schubert's songs fall into one of three forms:
i)   strophic form (same melody for each verse)
ii) modified strophic form (slight variations to the melody, accompaniment or harmony)
iii) through-composed (unified through recurring themes, tonal/harmonic schemes or accompaniment patterns.

Schumann's songs

Schumann was the first important composer after Schubert. His songs are significant because of his ability to unify poetry and music. Probably the most striking characteristic of Schumann's best songs is the close relationship between the voice and piano. His piano accompaniments play at least an equal role with the voice; in some songs the vocal line appears almost less important than the accompaniment. In many of his songs the piano preludes, interludes and postludes play a major role. The preludes are usually short, the interludes play a significant role in unifying the song and the postludes continue and intensify the mood of the song after the singer has finished.

Harmony

Schumann's harmony lingers on non-harmonic tones for expressive moments and he makes lavish use of secondary dominants. He was fond of writing around, but avoiding, the tonic.

Melody

His melodies are warm and expressive, often seeming to evolve from the accompaniment. They are perhaps less suffused with the sweet melancholic lyricism characteristic of many melodies of Schubert, with fewer exquisite moments of musical piquancy.

Accompaniments

Schumann often writes expansive, gentle arpeggios aided by the sustaining pedal, or solid chordal accompaniments, often with bass octaves. Full octave passages and repeated block chords above a bass harmony note sustained by the pedal, often marked semi-staccato, are also characteristic Schumann accompaniment styles.

Rhythm

Rhythmic elements play a significant role in Schumann's songs. He was especially fond of syncopations and subtle emphases on second beats of bars, dotted rhythms, repeated chordal quaver passages, and of repeating a particular rhythm through long sections.

Form

Schumann wrote songs in strophic and modified strophic and declamatory forms. His strophic songs are generally simple and folk-like and his declamatory songs are melodious. In his late songs Schumann often composed songs in a chordal, hymn-like style.

Further work and listening

Listen to some of the songs suggested here:
- well-known classic Schubert songs such as 'Erlkönig', 'Gretchen Am Spinnrade', 'Die Forelle', 'Auf Dem Wasser', 'Der Tod und Das Mädchen', amongst many others
- other characteristic songs by Schubert and Schumann and also Mendelssohn. Try 'Der Atlas' for a declamatory, intense song; 'Der Wanderer' for a song with varying accompaniment patterns throughout; 'Der Doppelgänger' for a declamatory style and 'Am Meer' for chromatic harmony
- songs from significant song cycles, such as Schubert's *Winterreise*; and Schumann's *Dichterliebe*.

While you are listening, think about the following points:

- What is it that so beautifully captures the mood and character of the songs?
- How is this achieved? Listen carefully for the harmonic and melodic subtleties; the relationship between the voice and piano accompaniment.
- Consider why some phrases are so exquisite, or so intense, or depict light-heartedness, for example.

Approaches on how to start writing piano accompaniments

Listen to and analyse a range of early Romantic songs *that you like*, and are interested in, looking closely at how they work. Think about the words and the way songs convey character and mood. It will help you to write your own accompaniment if you understand the genre.

If you are given an opening *incipit*, or a full melody line, study closely the idiomatic accompaniment and the overall style of the opening. Then begin planning.

- On the score, work out and plan:

    - the phrase and harmonic structure
    - the keys and points for potential modulations
    - whether you want to change key, balance two tonalities ambiguously, and so on. Bear in mind the tempo of the song, which is important in deciding your tonal scheme and harmonic pace.

- Plan your idiomatic accompaniment. How long will the opening style continue? What changes are you going to make and where?

- If appropriate, will your song have a prelude, interlude or postlude?

Remember that the solution to your planning always lies in the character, mood and meaning of the text.

Schubert
'Du Bist Die Ruh'
(You Are Rest and Peace)

The song *Du Bist Die Ruh* (You are Rest and Peace) dates from 1823, composed when Schubert was 27. It is one of his most well known and popular songs, full of Romantic sweetness and melancholy and with marvellous subtleties of emotional expression. The text is from a poem by the poet, Ruckert.

Herz.

2. Come in to me, and silently close the gate behind you,
Drive other griefs out of my breast, let my heart be full of your joy.

Voice

Piano

3. Dies Au - gen - zelt,   von dei - - - nem Glanz   al -

1. Du bist die Ruh,
   Der Friede mild,
   Die Sehnsucht du,
   Und was sie stillt.

   Ich weihe dir
   Voll Lust und Schmerz
   Zur Wohnung hier
   Mein Aug und Herz.

2. Kehr ein bei mir
   Und schliebe du
   Still hinter dir
   Die Pforte zu.

   Treib andern Schmerz
   Aus dieser Brust!
   Voll sei dies Herz
   Von deiner Lust.

3. Dies Augenzelt,
   Von deinem Glanz
   Allein erhellt,
   O füll es ganz!

You are rest
and gentle peace
you are longing
and what stills it.

To you I consecrate –
full of joy and of grief –
my eyes and my heart
as a dwelling-place.

Come in to me,
and silently close
the gate
behind you

Drive other griefs
out of my breast.
Let my heart be full
of your joy.

This tent of my eyes,
lit solely
by your brightness –
O fill it wholly!

Analysis

Form

The song is in modified strophic form. The first two verses are set to exactly the same music, but the third verse is varied.

Opening

The scene is set in the opening piano introduction. The tempo of the song is Andante, the key Eb, and in 3/8 metre. The mood is one of peace, but not quite; there is from the very start an air of quiet unrest, conveyed in the seven-bar phrasing, the suspensions and the lingering dominant 7th resolution. This opening phrase is placed in the treble register only, the expected vocal line melody hinted at rhythmically, below a rocking broken chord accompaniment. The lingering dominant 7th chord draws us into the opening of the first verse.

Verse 1

The verse begins as the opening introduction, still in the treble range. The vocal melody, however, starts on Bb, the dominant, and rises to the upper tonic, creating a subtle quality of ethereal serenity. Following the repeat of the opening phrase, Schubert harmonises the third phrase, on the words 'Ich weihe dir' (to you I consecrate), 'Voll Lust and Schmerz' (full of joy and of grief), and 'Zur Wohnung hier' (as a dwelling-place) with diminished 7th chords on A, giving us momentary inclinations to B♭.

This diminished 7th chord heard three times is the only chromatic chord in the diatonic harmonic landscape of verse 1, which makes it all the more effective. However, Schubert keeps the tonality ambiguous with simple suspensions and a lack of a lasting definitive resolution. Suddenly the tonal mist clears. The direction is made clear by the A♭ in the fourth phrase, as if the song is returning back to E♭, but again Schubert maintains tonal unrest through his characteristic liking for alternating major and minor, in this case A♭ and A natural. Note here also the beautiful subtleties in the lines: where the vocal line repeats notes (bars 16 and 20), so does the accompaniment; when the vocal line is more flowing (bar 18), so too is the bass which descends in contrary motion.

Schubertean lyrical sweetness

The last phrase of verse 1 gives us one of Schubert's beautiful lyrical moments. How is it achieved? Is it possible to describe such moments in words? To technically or mechanically describe the moment could ruin it. However, we can look at a few inherent musical features:

The last phrase of verse 1 begins as if to repeat the third, but instead Schubert changes direction, bringing in an A♭ at bar 22 to reintroduce the tonic key of E♭, as discussed above. This second half of the last phrase is now twice as long – six bars – as the first half, thereby making the phrase linger on, gradually coming to resolution.

How is the beauty of the moment created? At first glance, the melody and accompaniment

seem almost too simple. However, with close, musical appreciation the following musical features all combine to create this beautiful, but simple moment, so characteristic of Schubert:

- the move to a flatter key, from B♭ to E♭
- the release from tension of the preceding diminished 7ths
- the contrasts between the restrained broken-chord rocking motion of the accompaniment and the slowly chromatically rising 'pull' of the melody line, followed by the sinking down effect of the two vocal phrases, the first descending an interval of a 6th followed by a smaller descending interval of a 5th
- the harmonic pace of one chord per bar
- the play on A♭ and A natural.
- Until the last phrase, the accompaniment broken-chord pattern gently supports the melodic shape, while the bass parallels the rhythm of the melody line. In the last phrase the accompaniment doesn't follow the melody, but leaves it to rise alone, thereby heightening the poignancy and expressive emotion at this point. The final E♭ is only reached finally as the last quaver note, the main thrust staying on the dominant, B♭.

Piano interlude

After such an ending of strained melancholic beauty, the piano interlude to verse 2 gives us a much needed gritty phrase to counteract the 'sweet pain'. Note the way the bass reaches its lowest notes so far in the song. The phrase brings in another reminder of inner unrest, playing on the flattened C♭, hinting at an augmented 6th but never taking it to resolution. Instead Schubert alternates the accented chromatic note with C natural. The musical effect is one of a deep sigh, in registral contrast to the higher tessitura of the verses – the compass in which the rest of the song lies. At the entry to verse 2 after the five-bar piano interlude, Schubert prepares us to return to the higher register.

Verse 2

Verse 2 is a repetition of verse 1, and as a repetition, makes the changes to come in verse 3 all the more effective.

Piano interlude

In the piano accompaniment link between verses 2 and 3, Schubert makes some slight changes. What reason would he have for doing this? It could be that the tied Eb in the bass very subtly take away the steady rhythmic motion of the preceding harmonic movement, in preparation for the emotional intensity of verse 3.

Verse 3

The words of verse 3 read as if the mood may change to one of increased animation. However, Schubert beautifully depicts the unsettled yearning behind the desire for peace and rest in almost surreal moments in this verse. How does he achieve this?

Schubert starts off verse 3 in the same way as the previous verses but instantly plunges us into a strong chromatic rising line, taking the melody to previously unheard heights. The ambiguous tonality of this line, which starts in Eb major and ends in Ab, with marvellous tonal travels in between, is very characteristic of Schubert, as is his use of chromatic chords for expressive purposes.

The passage is remarkable in the way that Schubert creates almost extraordinary 'brightness' in the words through chromatic chords, and the implied enharmonic cadential modulations; from a perfect cadence in Cb major/enharmonic B major, to Eb major and finally to Ab major. The suspensions running through the phrase move from Cb to Bb, Db/C#, resolving to Cb/B, and from Eb resolving down to D. A far-ranging implied modulation from the three flats key signature of Eb over to the five sharp key signature of B major!

The sudden 'false' brightness prepared so simply, yet occurring so unexpectedly and the tension heightened by suspensions running throughout the phrase creates a powerful moment. Note how this phrase is actually eight bars long, but shortened by one full bar rest as if to let the impact reverberate. Bar seven of the phrase, marked $\Longrightarrow$ to die away, is not convincingly resolved, and in some ways acts almost as an addition, a further perfect cadence, this time in Ab major. Phrase lengths generally have been shorter up to this point, so the long, now unbroken melodic line here further places it apart from others.

There is a bars rest and then Schubert repeats the last phrase of the previous two verses. But this still does not find the longed for rest and cannot yet finish in peace. So, the 'surreal' chromatic phrase is repeated, this time further heightened by the Fb on the words 'Von deinem Glanz' (by your brightness).

The final two phrases of verses 1 and 2 are repeated to close the song, the vocal line being embraced within the altered lines of the accompaniment. A final poignant moment is created as the vocal line ends on the dominant, open, waiting on the words 'O füll es ganz'. It is left to the closing bars of the accompaniment to finally fall to the tonic, Eb, and bring the song to rest.

Characteristic features of piano accompaniment

As you prepare to start your own piano accompaniments, study the following characteristic accompaniment extracts from a range of songs and styles composed by Schubert and Schumann.

Simple folk-like style

Wandering is what the miller enjoys, Wandering!

In this example, there is a lightweight simple broken-chord accompaniment, sustaining the harmony and creating rhythmic motion, independent of the vocal line. The four-bar piano introduction is complete in itself, ending with a perfect cadence.

rau - schen wohl __ aus dem Fel - sen - quell,

I heard a little stream rushing from it's source among the rocks

Here, there is a triplet accompaniment figuration, more complex than in 'Das Wandern', with a tonic dominant lilting motion created in the bass, independent of the vocal line. The piano introduction flows into the song.

'Haiden-Röslein' (Hedge-roses)
Schubert

Sah ein Knab' ein Rös - lein __ steh'n Rös - lein auf der Hai - den,

A boy saw a rose growing in a meadow

This time there is a phased chordal accompaniment between left and right hands, sustaining the harmony and giving some melodic support to the vocal line. The song begins straightaway, with no piano introduction.

'Die Krähe' (The Crow) from *Winterreise*
Schubert

A crow came with me out of the town

The opening four piano bars introduce the melody line of the song above broken-chord patterns which provide the harmony. When the voice enters, the broken-chord accompaniment pattern is split between right hand and left hand, the vocal line melody being played at the same pitch in the left hand.

'Frühlingstraum' (Dream of Spring) from *Winterreise*
Schubert

I dreamt of bright flowers that blossom in May;

This uses a simple broken chord accompaniment pattern in 6/8 metre, independent of the vocal line. The opening introduction comprises a four-bar phrase, giving the following melody line and ending with a perfect cadence.

Intense, declamatory style

'Der Wanderer' (The Wanderer)
Schubert

I come from the mountains, the valley steams, the sea roars

The pain of wandering is depicted in this song by the dark, plodding triplets, the gradually expanding chromatic harmonic colouring and the lingering tension of the diminished 7th chord in bar 5. The sombre mood is also con- veyed by the *lento* tempo, the dramatic dynamic markings, and the accented static bass F♯ below the vocal line. Strong chords characterise this passage, with a dismal, foreboding motif in the bass.

'Der Doppelgänger' (The Double)
Schubert

The night is still, the streets are at rest, my sweetheart lived in this house,
Long ago she left the town, [but the house still stands where it always stood]

A totally different kind of accompaniment can be heard in this song. Schubert marvellously depicts the ghostly horror of the poet meeting his double in the moonlight at the abandoned house where his sweetheart had once lived. Heavy, obsessively dark and sombre chords, which revolve around the tonic B throughout the song, are combined with a sinister recurring melodic motif in octaves, heard in the opening four-bar piano accompaniment. The declamatory voice line consists of short, dark phrases revolving around the dominant F♯. Only twice in the song, in between vocal phrases, is the accompaniment given any wisp of melody. Harmonically, note the characteristic play between A and A♯ throughout. This is a song well worth looking at in close detail.

'Der Atlas' (Atlas)
Schubert

I bear what is unbearable and my heart wants to break, Proud heart - you have what you wished

Here there is an intense, dramatic *forte* accompaniment, with tremelos, low chromatic octave passages doubling the vocal line, dramatically ascending against static tremelos, marked with a *crescendo* to **𝑓𝑓s** and **𝑓𝑧**. At **𝑓𝑝** the accompaniment pattern changes, introducing another typical, very agitated idiom. The bass again has more movement than the quaver pairs above. Dialogue between the vocal line and the accompaniment in such instances often occurs between the bass and the vocal line, in answering phrases, similar or contrary motion or melodic fragments.

Schubert: agitated, highly emotional passages

'Erlkönig' (The Earl King)
Schubert

Extract 1: bars 1–24

Who rides so late through the night and the wind? It is the father with his child.

This is an extremely well-known song. Agitation and anxiety are conveyed in a variety of ways, at first in the accompaniment through the pounding triplet chords, the menacing rising scalic passages in the bass depicting the swiftness of the galloping horse and the anxiety of the father holding the frightened child. The vocal line is independent of the voice.

Note the ways that in contrast, Schubert depicts still restless, but more sublimely agitated moods in the same song, illustrated in the extracts below. The corresponding key changes from G minor at the opening of the song in extract 1, to the Bb tonality illustrated in extract 2 and finally to an almost surreal C major, as in extract 3 show how Schubert emphasises changes of moods with changes of tonalities.

Extract 2: bars 57–61

Darling child, come away with me!

Extract 3: bars 86–90

`You beautiful boy, will you come with me? My daughters will wait upon you'

Landscape and music

It was the lyric poetry of landscape that was the chief inspiration in the development of the *lied*. The core of Schubert's artistic genius lies in his setting of short, lyric poems, most often sentimental descriptions of nature. Each song acts as a landscape, setting a particular pictorial image. But these are no mere imitations of nature in music; the landscape acts as a means through which deep feelings are expressed.

Memory plays a central role. Sometimes called the double time-scale, the representation of the past through the immediate emotional feelings of the present made possible one of the greatest achievements of the Romantic style – the elevation of the song from a minor genre to a vehicle of the sublime, giving vocal music the grandeur that had until then been reserved for opera and oratorio.

As well as many striking and notable songs, the magnificent song cycles of Schubert and Schumann, particularly *Winterreise* and *Dichterliebe* respectively, are marvellous cycles of images of character and mood. They are rather like looking through a kaleidoscope, slowly turning and revealing different landscape and emotional 'colours'.

'Auf dem Flusse' (On the River)
Schubert

Extract 1: bars 1–11

You clear wild stream that one rippled so gaily
How silent you have become! You do not bid me farewell

This is one of twenty-four songs which comprise Schubert's *Winterreise* song cycle, on poems by Müller. The landscape of songs express the feelings of a lover taking a melancholy nostalgic trip in winter back to the haunts of his failed summer love affair. In *Winterreise* all the events take place before the cycle begins, and we are not even sure what they were. We just have images of the affair through the lover's memories. In the extract above, the lover stands on the river bank looking at the ice on the river. Marked *pianissimo*, the opening piano chords depict the frozen state of the river, and again simultaneously the frozen state of the lover's emotions. The dynamic markings change to ***ppp***, the second phrase lurches down from E minor to D♯ minor, the grace notes in the vocal line depict the shakiness of his voice, while the accompaniment remains unmoved. The relentless plodding motion in the accompaniment together with a gently supporting bass line are idiomatic of accompaniments depicting such a mood in a slow tempo. The example below shows the song in its last phase, as the raging torrent beneath the hard crust of the lover's heart cannot be quelled.

Extract 2: bars 40–53

My heart, do you now see your own likeness in this stream?
Is there a raging torrent beneath *its* surface too?

'Auf dem Wasser' (Down from the Heavens)
Schubert

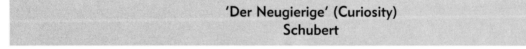

For from the sky, the last rays of the sun shine on the waves and dance about the boat.

The accompaniment here simultaneously depicts the image of the poet in his boat as he glides like a swan over the softly shimmering waves, and the inner joy and pleasure that the poet is feeling as his soul glides over shimmering 'waves' of joy. The subtleties of the partnership between the semiquaver accompaniment passages and the vocal line are well worth studying closely in this song, as is the tonal scheme, and the harmonic interplay of diatonic and chromatic chords. For example, on the word *tanzet* (dance) we hear a characteristic change from minor to major; a marvellous musical moment, almost physically giving an uplifting burst of joy and surging the music forwards.

'Der Neugierige' (Curiosity)
Schubert

Brook of my love, how silent you are today! I only ask one thing, a single word one way or another
One word is `yes', the other `no', These two words include the whole world for me.

It is not only with notes that Schubert enjoys the major/minor interplay, but also with tonalities, of which there are many examples in his songs. One example is in the song *Der Neugierige* from the song cycle *Die Schone Mullerin*, from which this extract is taken.

Here, the shift from major to minor is unprepared but then resolved as Schubert takes the D in bar 13 and uses it to modulate to the flattened submediant G major. This is a very characteristic modulation, particularly as it occurs at a turning point in the poem.

Schumann accompaniments

'Mondnacht' (Moonlight)
Schumann

It was as if the sky had quietly kissed the earth

This Schumann song has a deceptively simple structure, and is well worth studying. The accompaniment contributes equally with the vocal line to create the sense of stillness demanded by the poem, particularly with its slowly moving repeated patterns and disso- nances. Note at bar 8 the poignant clash of E♯ in the voice with E in the bass. Schumann's 'simple' accompaniments are never that inno- cent, and often there is an indirect disquiet or unease throughout, as in this song.

Preludes, interludes and postludes

'Der Nussbaum' (The Nut Tree)
Schumann

In front of the house stands a green nut tree fragrantly, airily it spreads its leaves.

The piano accompaniments in Schumann's songs are important. The interludes in this song 'Der Nussbaum' often act as a unifying feature throughout the song, the vocal line appearing to flow in and out of the accompaniment. This example is in typical Schumann style; long expansive flowing arpeggio patterns span continually varying ranges – sometimes starting very low in the bass and rising expansively, other times covering a more conservative range.

Particularly significant postludes can be seen in Schumann's song cycle *Dichterliebe*, especially the conclusion to the last song, as it leads back to the contemplative mood of the first song of the cycle.

Introduction

The Romantic miniatures or 'character' pieces, are generally short lyric pieces for piano which describe a mood or character, and usually have titles suggestive of a mood or scene. As in Romantic song, nature played a significant role in the lyric piano genre – many character pieces have titles depicting aspects of nature. Romantic miniatures are the piano equivalent of the vocal lyric song or lied. The genre gradually emerged through the development of the minuet into the characteristic piece of Beethoven, Schubert, Schumann and others.

The most common types of character pieces are bagatelles, impromptus, intermezzos, elegies, humoresques, études rhapsodies, ballads, scherzos, mazurkas, nocturnes, preludes, waltzes, and fantasias. Some composers grouped a number of short character pieces together into loosely organised cycles; as did Schumann, for example, with the piano cycle *Carnaval*. This shows another characteristic trait of the Romantics, that of depicting in music the characters of people.

The most important composers of the Romantic character piece are Schubert, Schumann, Clara Wieck Schumann, Chopin, Brahms, Liszt, Mussorgsky, Dvorak and Grieg. Although there are certain characteristics which are common to all, their individual styles are quite different.

Identifying compositional techniques

If you understand and are able to identify the characteristic compositional techniques of the genre, it will help you with your own compositions. In the following section we will look in some detail at the stylistic features of the music of three important composers of the Romantic miniature: Chopin, Schumann and Grieg.

Writing Romantic miniatures

Key considerations

When starting to compose miniatures in the Romantic style, you need to think about the following points:

Form

Form is usually but not always ternary.

Style

Decide on the style, character and mood of your piece. If you are writing in the style of a particular composer, incorporate appropriate stylistic musical elements.

Tonal/harmonic framework

Work out the tonal and harmonic scheme, the modulations, phrase structure and cadence points. Build the shape of your framework on ternary form ABA sections and consider the following:

1. The tension or climax points – your piece must have a sense of direction, largely determined by the tonal plan and harmonies. Dissonant harmonies – dominant and diminished 7ths, augmented and Neapolitan 6ths, altered chords and so on all create tension points

2. Tension points can be heightened by the length of time the dissonance is held before resolution, by changing chords, by modulating, or otherwise delaying a resolution point

3. You can appear to be moving towards resolution or the 'home' key, then take a different turn and move into another key

4. As we have seen, secondary dominants are very common in the Romantic era and very effective in changing the expressive colour of a piece. Try incorporating secondary dominant progressions based on the circle of 5ths in your piece

5. Remember that chromatic harmony works best within a predominantly diatonic framework.

Melody

Melodies must be in character: for example, long, lyrical and expressive, or in a dance form. Melodies are often phrased in regular eight-bar measures, and need shape and stylistic musical elements.

Texture

Work out your textural contrasts through the piece.

Chopin

Repertoire

Chopin wrote almost exclusively for piano. His principal works are two concertos, three sonatas, twenty-seven études, four scherzos, four ballads, twenty-four preludes, three impromptus, nineteen nocturnes, and numerous waltzes, mazurkas and polonaises.

Piano style

Chopin's style of composition is introspective and intimate. His own playing style was subtle and restrained with its exquisite delicacy in contrast with the contemporary virtuoso 'Titans' of the piano. Playing Chopin's piano works demands flawless technique, imaginative use of pedals, control of the full range of dynamic shadings, and subtle nuances of piano tone colour and musical understanding of *tempo rubato*.

Melodies

Chopin's melodies are highly expressive. Influenced by the Italian opera *cantabile* style, his melodies range from ornamental figurations and passagework, intimately related to the underlying harmonies, to long languid melodic lines, often with ornamentation derived from vocal music. His ornamentation is often chromatic, as it imitates the operatic singers' *portamento* and *rubato*. Expressive melodies can also be found in inner voice lines. His melodies are basically diatonic, and, like the Italian *bel canto* are constructed in regular eight-bar phrases. Chopin liked to displace the eight-bar feel of stable regularity by elliptical cadences. His melodies frequently begin *cantabile*, or are derivative of folk-song and quickly develop into ornamental arabesque-like decorative lines. The Polish Lydian 4th is often present in his melodies and in his mazurkas, polonaises and waltzes, in particular. (The Lydian scale is on the white notes and starts on F, with the raised 4th being the B natural.)

Counterpoint

Chopin was highly influenced by J. S. Bach, particularly his *The Well-tempered Clavier*. Chopin's music is rich in contrapuntal brilliance. We see free canonic writing, or voice leading, contrapuntal part writing, and harmonic and melodic dissonance treated contrapuntally. His melody lines often appear in contrapuntally derived arpeggio figurations.

Harmony

Chopin's harmony was conspicuously innovatory. His harmonic schemes are rich with chromatic chords, notably chord extensions, and chromatic and enharmonic inner parts. A favourite chord of Chopin's was the diminished 7th in second inversion, associated with the Lydian 4th – thus combining his loves of chromatic harmony with Polish musical characteristics. Typical chromatic harmonic progressions begin and end in the tonic key and use mostly tonic-dominant relationships to rapidly move through a series of keys. Through such excursions into passages of pure chromaticism, discreet melodic clashes, ambiguous chords, delayed or surprising cadences, and unresolved dominant 7ths, Chopin pushed the boundaries of dissonance and key into previously unexplored territory. It is important to remember that in much of his music, chromatic harmonies were intended to be glided over, the interest being in the changing tonal colour.

Tonality

Chopin was fond of remote or sliding modulations and of modulating using an unresolved dominant 7th chord in third inversion, followed by runs and scale passages. His pieces often begin on chords or chordal figurations other than the tonic. His tonalities are often ambiguous, with chromatic chords fluctuating around tonal ambiguity.

Rhythm

Although largely derived from Polish dances, Chopin's rhythms are flexible. Common features include various types of cross-rhythms, notably passages of figurations of irregular grouping of notes, fitted to a regular quaver accompaniment. The effect of the cross-rhythms is again to create an intimacy of colouring, rather than to energise rhythmic complexity. *Tempo rubato* is an essential part of Chopin's music. His rhythms, although written with specific accuracy, rely on the flexibility and fluidity which *tempo rubato* provides. Rhythms characteristic of Polish folk dances and songs are present in his mazurkas and polonaises.

Texture and form

Most of his works have a simple texture of melody and accompaniment. Many of the shorter pieces are basically ternary in form, with a contrasting middle section and with the return being varied, delayed, shortened or extended in different ways.

Analysis of Chopin's style

Nocturne Op. 27 No. 2, bars 1–9
Chopin

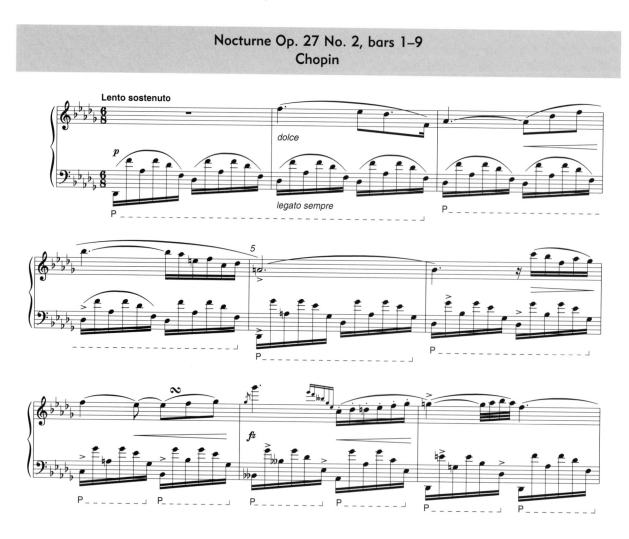

This is a beautiful example of Chopin's *cantabile* style, over characteristic arpeggio bass. Note the ornamentation and improvisatory style between bars 7 and 9; the meticulous articulation and the low bass notes, sustained by the pedal. The harmony of the passage is characteristically based on diatonic progressions, but includes dominant and diminished 7th chords, a long held appoggiatura in bar 5 and a chromatically altered diminished 7th in bar 8, marked *sf*.

Nocturnes Op. 72 No. 1
Chopin

Extract 1: bars 1–5

Again, this is an example of a characteristic flowing arpeggio bass with a long lyrical melodic line. It is selected here to show the different elaborations on the melody, as the piece progresses.

Extract 2: bars 31–34

A more elaborately decorated version, with trills, mordents, ornamental passagework and grace notes. Chopin subtly urges the music forward by crossing the rapid ornamental passages from the end of one bar to the beginning of the next. The bass harmonic scheme remains the same.

Extract 3: bars 39–42

The melody is now played in octaves, with some gentle but highly characteristic changes in the melody line. This is worth noting carefully as an example of Chopin's individual style.

Berceuse in Db Op. 57
Chopin

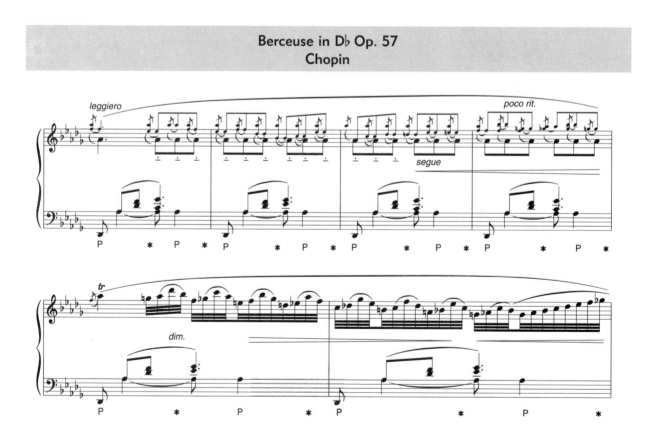

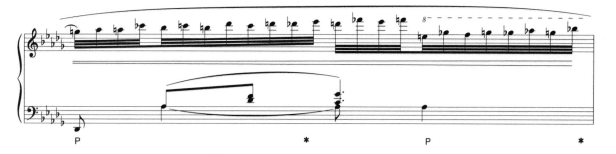

Over a harmonically and melodically static, repetitive bass, Chopin presents highly ornamental, arabesque-like passages in an improvisatory style, suffused with exquisite delicacy. Many of Chopin's most intimate ornamental characterstics are present in the *berceuse*.

Nocturnes Op. 9 No. 2
Chopin

Here the more complex broken-chord bass shows a typical fast harmonic rhythm modulation – not a true modulation – as it starts in the home key and returns to it.

Fantasie Impromptu Op. 66
Chopin

This extract shows Chopin's frequent interplay of cross-rhythms. Note the contrapuntally constructed lines, with the melody within, both in the lower and upper figurations of the passage. The bass arpeggio passages maintain the harmonc framework, but are also an intrinsic part of the *tempo rubato* required to effectively perform the piece. The middle section of this *Fantasie* contains one of Chopin's most well-known and popular melodies. It was set to the words 'I'm always chasing rainbows' in the early part of the twentieth century, transforming it into a popular song.

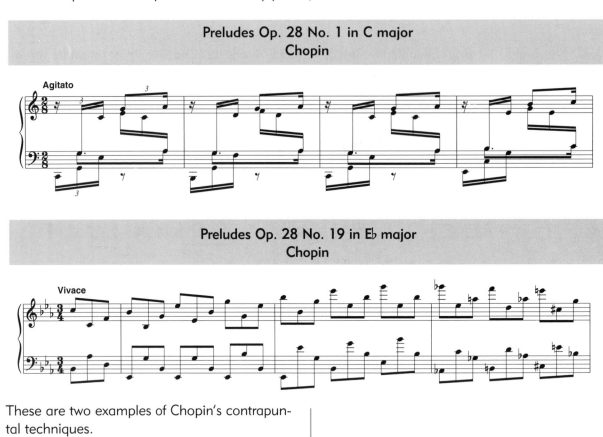

Preludes Op. 28 No. 1 in C major
Chopin

Preludes Op. 28 No. 19 in E♭ major
Chopin

These are two examples of Chopin's contrapuntal techniques.

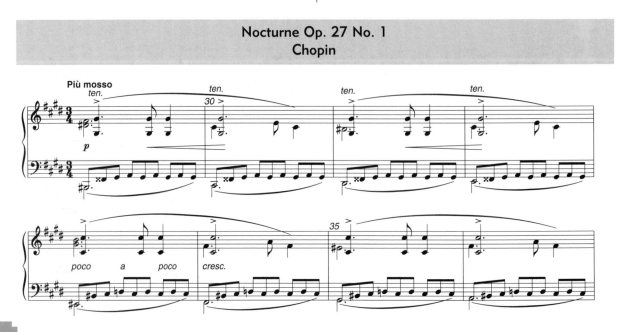

Nocturne Op. 27 No. 1
Chopin

Many of Chopin's nocturnes are in simple ternary form, with a contrasting middle section. This extract shows Chopin's fondness for introducing very contrasting, dramatic middle sections in his nocturnes. This middle section shows real passionate power. Marked *piu mosso*, the section builds up quickly to a passionate climax, which first peaks at bar 45 with a diminished 7th on A#. This is followed by an enharmonic modulation from C# minor to A♭ major, another dramatic moment which dies down only to build up again and introduce a new melody, before the reintroduction later of the first section.

Mazurka Op. 6 No. 1 in F# minor
Chopin

Chopin's mazurkas show great variety in mood and contain some of the most interesting melodic and harmonic ideas of any of his compositions. Within the constraints of the dance form, Chopin used Polish folk origins not as mere arrangements of popular tunes but as infusions of fragments of melody and hints of national rhythms into his own sophisticated style. The mazurkas show his marvellous contrapuntal skills, explorations of new harmonies, masterful exploitation of the emotional effect of obsessive rhythm repetition, and of course, *tempo rubato*. One of the most common rhythmic traits in the mazurka is that of strong accents unsystematically placed on the second or third beats, a rhythmic aspect inherent in his folk-like tunes, illustrated below:

The opening section of this mazurka also displays Chopin's characteristic combination of folk rhythms with melodic motifs in sophisticated counterpoint; the common eight-bar phrases which characterise much of Chopin's music and the beautiful effect of the change from F natural to F# in bars 13–15, combined with the variation in the melody line from the previous rhythmic repetition.

Schumann

Schumann had a highly individual musical style and was a true Romantic composer. His published compositions from Op. 1 to Op. 23 were all written for piano. Many of his character pieces are linked to literature. He used more descriptive titles and extra-musical connections than any other composer, apart from Liszt. His piano works contributed greatly to the change in public taste from sonata to character piece. The piano cycles, which are sets of loosely organised cycles of character pieces, built on forms of variation techniques, show Schumann at his most Romantic. The pieces include variations on the name of one of his lady friends, Abegg (the musical notes A-B-E-G-G), the character pieces *Davidsbündlertanze* (Dances of the League of David), *Carnaval* (pieces with literary or other allusive meanings, including one on the notes A-S-C-H after the place another girl friend came from), *Phantasiestucke* (a collection of poetic pieces around the character of a mad Kapellmeister) and *Kinderszenen* ('Scenes From Childhood'). Key features of his piano style are highlighted in the extracts below:

Carnaval Op. 9 Préambule No. 1
Schumann

This shows his powerful dotted-note march-like passages with full chordal weight in both hands.

Carnaval Op. 9 Marche des Davidsbündler contre les Philistins
Schumann

This extract features characteristic triple metre chordal passages which incorporate the melody, alternating parts of the chord in 3rds with a leaping waltz-like octave bass.

Album for the Young: A Stranger
Schumann

Featuring Schumann's octave, chordal style in both hands, with characteristic ascending motion, contrary motion and dotted rhythmic patterns.

Faschingsschwank Op. 26, Allegro
Schumann

In the opening of a piece, or new section, Schumann often writes full chords, with arpeggio to passages and rising full chords in short phrases.

Faschingsschwank Op. 26, Intermezzo
Schumann

This is an example of Schumann's characteristic sweeping arpeggio lines with the melody an integral part of the figurations.

Kinderszenen Op. 15, Traumerei
Schumann

Beautiful melodies, often song-like in conception, which derive from the simple, symmetrical shapes of the German folk-song are a key feature of Schumann's style.

As can be seen in this example, Schumann used chromatic harmonies for expressive reasons within a diatonic harmonic framework. Schumann's music reveals much use of first inversions, secondary dominants, dominant and diminished 7ths and 9ths and altered chords with added 7ths. Secondary 7ths can be often found in sequence in circle of 5ths and in wide-ranging modulations, all held within a tonal structure.

Romance in F# minor
Schumann

This is an example of an inner melody in arpeggio accompaniment.

Album for the Young: Sheherazade
Schumann

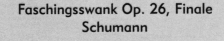

Look for the continuous rolling quavers in the middle of the texture.

Faschingsswank Op. 26, Finale
Schumann

This extract features spiky fragmented semi-quaver passages punctuacted by sudden *sf* chords emphasising phrase beginnings and endings. Note the frequency of the parallel intervallic rising and falling in 3rds and 6ths.

Grieg

Although Grieg's piano music shows the influence of both the Romantic piano writing of Schumann and the delicate ornamentation of Chopin, the overriding influence on his music is that of Norwegian folk-song and dances. Grieg was essentially a lyrical composer and his music encompasses a wide range of emotional expression and atmospheric colour.

The composer's Norwegian heritage is reflected both in his melodies with characteristic folk-like ornamentation and in his innovatory use of almost impressionistic harmony and piano sonorities, particularly those melodies and harmonies based on modal elements such as the Lydian raised 4th. Much of his piano music includes drone basses reminiscent of old Norwegian stringed instruments. Another common characteristic of his music is his liking for combining 2/4 and 6/8 rhythms. Grieg's miniatures are commonly in ternary or five-part form.

Norwegian Bridal Procession Op. 19 No. 2
Grieg

Of all his miniatures for piano, Grieg's ten books of *Lyric Pieces* represent his finest works in the art. They are his most important works for piano, holding a wealth of characteristic mood-sketches. In this extract from his *Lyric Pieces*, note the drone effect of the bare 5ths in the bass in the introduction, the ornamental folk-like melody and the wide leaps in the bass accompaniment.

Butterfly Op. 43 No. 1
Grieg

This extract is an example of Grieg's characteristic wide arpeggio lines, subtle sonorities and harmonies, embraced in a lovely lyrical line. The harmonies include altered chords, and non-harmony tones; altered major and minor 3rds, which are suffused with chromaticisms. It is a beautiful mood picture of a butterfly. The tonality fluctuates from A major to Eb major, to G major, and finally to F# minor through an array of chromatically altered chords.

Approaches on writing for the piano

When planning a Romantic character piece, or set of pieces, you must first consider effective ways of writing for the piano. If you are a keyboard player, you may find it useful to play parts or all of some pieces, looking particularly at the compositional procedures involved. If you are not a pianist, it would be worthwhile discussing with someone who does play the piano the particular nature and character of piano writing in Romantic short forms.

- Consider carefully what works well within the limitations of ten fingers, particularly when writing characteristic long *legato* melodies over expansive arpeggio figurations.

- Take into account the stretch, or span. Although Liszt, for instance, often writes chords spanning intervals of a 10th, as a guideline it would be best to work within a maximum span of a 9th or better, within an octave. It is more difficult to play a full three- or four-note chord spanning an octave than a series of bare octave passages. Wider chords, the notes of which cannot be played simultaneously are indicated by a ',' meaning 'spread the chord'.

- An important factor to take into account is the tempo of the piece. Wide leaps in the bass, running semiquaver passages, broad arpeggio sweeps – all typical Romantic characteristics that need care when writing to ensure they can be fitted in and actually played at the tempo you choose.

- The pedal is used extensively in Romantic piano music, often functioning as an integral part of a work as it maintains harmonic progressions, sustaining low harmony notes under long arpeggio passages and long *legato* melodies. It also maintains harmonies over wide leaping bass lines.

- Textural contrasts are achieved through varying the spacing of chords – both in individual chords and in chordal phrases; varying the spacing between melodic; inner and bass line part movement; voice leading; registral contrasts; and full use of the expansive tone colours and range that the piano offers.

Further work and listening

- **Chopin:** Listen to *Waltz Op. 70 No. 1* for a characteristic light, graceful, ornamental melody line and a typical waltz bass line. This piece has a contrasting middle section, again common in Chopin's waltzes, many of which were in straightforward ternary form. The melody in the middle section is in 3rds, again a common contrasting feature. The waltzes show the use of spread chords and Chopin's marvellous textural subtleties and contrasts. *Waltzes Op. 69 No 2, Op. 64 No. 1* and *Op. 34 No 2*. are well worth listening to and studying, as is the famous *'Minute' Waltz, Op. 64. No. 1*. For a more complex and powerful set of works, try listening to any of the polonaises, but perhaps especially the one in A major. Try comparing John Field's nocturnes with those of Chopin which served as a model for Chopin, but are not of the same quality. Chopin's nocturnes are marvellous miniatures, and again worth studying in detail. If you are considering writing a study or prelude, you may find listening to and studying the Op. 10 *Etudes* and *Preludes Op. 45 in C# minor* useful.

- **Schubert:** Listen to (and trying playing if you are a keyboard player) *Moments Musicaux D780* and the *Impromptus*. All are short, appealing pieces. They are easy to listen to and display many characteristic Schubert features.

- **Schumann:** Listen to and study Schumann's piano cycle *Carnaval*. The dominant idea is that of a masked ball where masked characters, portrayed in short character pieces, flit back and forwards. Each is a microcosom of a particular personality characterised in the music. Try working out how Schumann depicts the characters, and how he uses particular musical features. You may like to explore this approach yourself in your compositions. Also well worth studying are Schumann's *Kinderszenen Op. 15*.

- **Grieg:** Listen to the *Watchman's Song Op. 12 No. 3*. Inspired by a performance of Shakespeare's *Macbeth*, the piece succinctly depicts the watchman's call and the ghostly voices he thinks he hears. Look at the piano writing, in part influenced by that of Schumann but infused with Grieg's individual harmonic style. Try composing for similar circumstances.

- **Mendelssohn:** The composer himself was a virtuoso pianist. Listen to his *Lieder Ohne Worte* (Song Without Words). Some of these pieces have suffered from over-popularity over the years, but there are some lovely character pieces in the collection which are easily equal to the finest Romantic short forms, notably 'Spinning Song' *Op. 67 No. 4*. 'Album Leaf' *Op. 117* reveals particularly well the elfin-like lightness and clarity which characterises much of Mendelssohn's music.

Introduction

Serialism is a technique of composing in which one or more musical elements – pitch, duration dynamics – are arranged in a fixed specific order, or series. The most common element to be arranged in a series is pitch, in which all twelve tones of the octave are arranged in an order the composer chooses. This is called a tone row. The tone row is used both horizontally to construct melody lines and vertically to construct groupings of notes, or chords. Serial composition technique involves using the tone row in four ways:

- as the original row
- inverted (intervallically)
- retrograde (backwards)
- retrograde inversion (backwards and inverted).

A full illustration of these techniques can be found on pages 100–1 in the 'Listening' section. The row can also be transposed to begin on any note – thereby creating a possible 48 different forms – and different notes can be 'displaced' into different octaves while still maintaining the fixed order. Any note in the tone row can be repeated but the order must be maintained.

Approaches to serial composition

When starting to compose a serial composition you may like to consider the following points:

- Before starting to compose, it is important to first listen to and study a range of serial pieces, not only those of the 'Second Viennese School' – Schoenberg, Berg and Webern – but also the way Stravinsky composed using serial techniques, Lutoslawski and others. You must be interested in the music to be able to effectively compose in this style.

Tone rows

- First, construct your tone row, considering the character of serial music you want to write. Some tone rows can be structured in a tonal vein, whereas other tone rows may deliberately avoid any intervallic relationship which suggests a tonality or any conventional interval progressions.
- A tone row can be constructed with a tonal basis through planning the order of the notes to fall into groups of tonally based harmonies. For example, Berg's *Violin Concerto* is a very warm expressive work based on a tonally conceived row as can be seen below.

Berg generally used tone rows in a freer manner than Schoenberg or Webern, not always following exactly the order of the row. His music combines serial techniques with rich harmonies – made up from groupings of notes from his tonally designed row – with a lyrical quality which makes his music attractive and immediately appealing.

- The character of serial music in the works of Webern is completely different. In keeping with his extreme brevity and economy

of material, Webern's rows are cool, dry, concentrated and deliberately shaped to unlyrical intervals such as major 7ths, minor 9ths and so on which avoid tonal implications. In constructing a row in the style of Webern any reference to conventional melodic or harmonic progressions need to be avoided.

- All tone rows need to be composed with imagination and attention to the shape and intervallic structure of the line.
- Stylistically authentic compositions need to

include all forms of the row, some transpositions of the row, and include octave displacement for further variety when appropriate.

Texture

- Broadly speaking, three kinds of textures are prevalent in serial music. One type is a harmonically conceived texture characteristic of many of the works of Schoenberg and Berg.
- The second type, also in the music of Schoenberg and Berg but particularly characteristic of Webern's music is that of imitative counterpoint. Being based on tone rows, the horizontal structure of serial music lends itself to imitative interplay, canons, and so on. Webern's music is a good example of very sparse, bare counterpoint within a cool dry character.
- A third type of texture is known as 'pointillist' and is characteristic of many of Webern's works. The term pointillism is used in painting for a technique used by Seurat and other post-impressionists involving separate dots of pure colour. The term was borrowed by writers on music to describe passages where the notes seem to be dots rather than rounded musical phrases. In music, pointillist texture is extremely bare and sparse and made up of single notes, tiny motifs or wisps of sound. The texture is very open with numerous rests and in which each note counts as a microcosm of a full phrase. Such is the concentration and brevity of musical lines that a full symphony for Webern can last only nine minutes.
- Consider texture carefully in your composing, and whether you want your musical lines to be of a sparse nature or a more full texture, or perhaps a combination of both. The 'harmonies', or places where two or more notes are sounded together are based on organised groupings of the notes of the tone row, as can be seen in the analysis of the first phrase of Schoenberg's *Quartet No 4* (see page 302).
- How these groups are organised is entirely up to the composer. The closer the style is to that of Webern, the less the need to take into account any formal 'harmonic' conventions. However, to make your compositions work, the music still needs to have direction and flow through points of tension and resolution. This can be achieved through relative dissonance and consonance, rhythmic complexity and lack of rhythmic complexity, varying degrees of contrapuntal complexity, or phrases being largely dispersed, fragmented, separated through rests, pauses and so on, and variety of instrumental timbral combinations. The structure of the piece should act as a framework through which to plan the overall direction of the music.

Rhythm

- Rhythmic patterns are often complex, often regularly changing metre, pulse, accent or dividing parts of beats in intricate ways. The effect of the irregular accents and unrepetitive pulse integral to Palestrina's polyphonic style can be compared to the rhythmic irregularities in the highly complex lines of some serial music, particular that of Webern.
- Explore different rhythmic combinations and groupings in your composing, perhaps also moving through different time signatures. Note that in a sparse, bare texture, as in pointillist music, rests are used a lot in all instrumental parts, as the instruments are rarely heard all together.

Instrumental colour

- Webern's *klangfarbemelodie* method of distributing notes across all different instrumental lines, often with only one or two notes heard by the same instrument at any one time, creates a mosaic of abrupt timbral contrasts and is one of the most recognisable characteristics of Webern's serial style. Whereas Schoenberg and Berg regularly used instruments and instrumental combinations in a more conventional manner, Webern always composed in a concentrated economical manner using only tiny wisps of music. The effect is one of almost sporadically placed instrumental sparks or cells of contrasting colours flashing across the listening horizon.

- These contrasting cells of colour are emphasised by very detailed dynamic markings – sometimes on every note in a particular phrase – and articulation marks, for example, pizzicato, tremelo, muted, and even instructions as to how a particular note

should be played!

Structures

A range of structures are used, from simple binary and ternary forms to sonata form and Baroque dance forms. For a closer look at other structures in serial music, study the way that Lutoslawski in his *Funeral Music* composes in a serial style, described in the 'Listening' section of the Teacher's Resource File on pages 105–7.

String Quartet No 4, 1st movement
Schoenberg

This string quartet begins in a sharp, energetic mood with strong dynamic contrasts, biting chords and with a vigorous melodic line.

The work is based on the tone row, below:

D   C#   A   Bb   F   Eb   E   C
        Ab   G   F#   B

In the first phrase, bars 1 – 6, the violin I melody is constructed from the row in its original or 'prime order' (PO) form, below. Note the 3rd note A is repeated three times, as is the E in bar 3. The row finishes in bar 5.

The second melodic phrase, bars 6 – 9, is played by violin II and the third phrase returns to violin I, bars 9 – 14. In the second phrase, violin II plays an inversion of the row, transposed up five semitones, or a perfect 4th. The line therefore starts on G. Follow the grid on the line 15 to work out the order of the row. The third phrase is in retrograde version, the row in its original form moving from B to F# to G and so on. Study the grid overleaf and see how these various tone row permutations happen.

Allegro molto, energico

	I	I	I	I	I	I	I	I	I	I	I	I	
	0	11	7	8	3	1	2	10	6	5	4	9	
P0	D	C#	A	Bb	F	Eb	E	C	Ab	G	F#	B	R0
P1	Eb	D	Bb	B	F#	E	F	C#	A	Ab	G	C	R1
P5	G	F#	D	Eb	Bb	Ab	A	F	C#	C	B	E	R5
P4	F#	F	C#	D	A	G	Ab	E	C	B	Bb	Eb	R4
P9	B	Bb	F#	G	D	C	C#	A	F	E	Eb	Ab	R9
P11	C#	C	Ab	A	E	D	Eb	B	G	F#	F	Bb	R11
P10	C	B	G	Ab	Eb	C#	D	Bb	F#	F	E	A	R10
P2	E	Eb	B	C	G	F	F#	D	Bb	A	Ab	C#	R2
P6	Ab	G	Eb	E	B	A	Bb	F#	D	C#	C	F	R6
P7	A	Ab	E	F	C	Bb	B	G	Eb	D	C#	F#	R7
P8	Bb	A	F	F#	C#	B	C	Ab	E	Eb	D	G	R8
P3	F	E	G	C#	Ab	F#	G	Eb	B	Bb	A	D	R3
	RI	RI	RI	RI	RI	RI	RI	RI	RI	RI	RI	RI	
	0	11	7	8	3	1	2	10	6	5	4	9	

Prime: horizontal axis, left to right; Inversion: vertical axis, top to bottom; Retrograde: horizontal axis, right to left; Retrograde Inversion: vertical axis, bottom to top.

Grid guidelines

The tone row in its original form takes the top line, PO, horizontally across the grid. P1, P5, and so on in the far left hand column refer to the transpositions of the row. For example P2 is the row transposed up two semitones, therefore starting on E. Inversions of the row work vertically from top to bottom. Thus the inversion of the row in its original form (0) in the first column can be seen to move D, Eb, G and so on, inverting the intervals of the row in its original form. In the far right hand column the RO, R1 abbreviations stand for 'retrograde' (backwards). Retrograde transposed up one semitone is abbreviated as R1. R1 thus moves horizontally from right to left starting with C to G to Ab and so on. This is the original row backwards and transposed up a semitone. Along the bottom of the grid you will see RI. This stands for 'retrograde inversion' where the inversion is played backwards. Thus the row in retrograde inversion in its original form, detailed in the first column (0), starts on F and moves up the column from bottom to top.

The melody and accompaniment

It is interesting to note the way that Schoenberg has composed the spiky robust chordal accompaniments to the melody. In close analysis of bars 1 – 4 all chords are derived from the row in a special way, described as follows:

	Bar 1	Bar 2	Bar 3	Bar 4/5/6
Violin II:	4 9 11	7 12 2	10 1 6	2 2 6 7
Viola:	6 7 10	8 11 3	12 3 5	1 1 5 7
Cello:	5 8 12	9 10 1	11 2 4	3 3 4 8

Note how each 'chord' is made up of successive notes of the row, such as 1,2,3, or 6,7,8. Note also that those notes 'missing' from the chords are in the violin I part, apart from note 3 – A – in bar 1, as detailed below:

Bar 1: 1 2	Bar 2: 3 4 5 6	Bar 3: 7 8 9	Bar 4: 10 11 12

The texture is characteristic 'chordal' quartet texture with one part taking the melodic interest and the other parts accompanying. Note how the texture changes in bar 16 where the three upper strings combine to form a countermelody with the cello, with some imitation introduced in bar 21. Precise dynamic and articulation markings abound throughout.

Composing Using Minimalist Techniques

Introduction

Minimalism is a technique of composing which uses intentionally limited compositional means. Characteristic musical elements include:

- static or simple tonal or modal harmony
- ceaseless repetition of short motivic patterns
- the prolonging or gradual adding on of single notes to a melodic pattern
- concentrated, limited timbral contrast.

Broadly speaking, using the barest of material, short musical cells gradually permutate and transform into different 'shapes' of rhythm, pulse, or pitch relationships. These shapes gradually shift as the music works out, often creating an improvisatory or hypnotic, trance-like quality. The style is strongly influenced by African, Indian and Balinese music as well as electronic music and rock, popular and jazz styles. Due to the inherent non-western influences, minimalist music is often associated with meditation and non-western philosophies, particularly Zen Buddhism.

Notable minimalist composers include La Monte Young, Terry Riley, Steve Reich, Phillip Glass, John Adams, Michael Nyman and Arvo Pärt.

Approaches to minimalist composition

When starting to compose a minimalist composition you may like to consider the following points:

- As you start to explore composing in this style, listen to and study minimalist works of composers such as those listed above, to gain an understanding of the character of the music. Read the section on minimalism on page 137 which also gives an analysis of Terry Riley's work, *In C*.
- There is always a danger in composing in a minimalist style that pieces can end up being musically monotonous and lacking in any real interest. To avoid this, you need to have a clear aim in mind as to the character of your music, and work out carefully the construction of your piece, the kind of material it is to be based on, and how it will maintain direction in terms of pitch, rhythmic, textural and timbral relationships.

Minimalist techniques

There are several techniques used in creating a minimalist piece:

- A frequent composing technique involves gradual transformation of an initial cell or idea through adding or subtracting notes from a particular repeated musical cell. Philip Glass bases much of his music on one motivic cell comprising, for example, five notes which are first repeated several times, then followed with a note added to make six, repeated for a while then progressing to seven notes, then eight and so on. Terry Riley's *In C* uses a similar method of gradually building up a single motivic cell. Interest is often maintained through the melodic cell gradually getting longer while simultaneously transforming rhythmically.
- A short cell is repeated until the performer decides, or the composer indicates on the score when the cell should be changed. Cells often have a recognisable shape, for example with one or two notes higher than others.
- Two or more phrases or melodic cells begin in unison and gradually move out of synchronisation with each other, altering the regularity of the pulse to fall on different notes in the melodic pattern. This movement creates a type of counterpoint, with canonic, or echo effects between the two parts. In an almost surreal way, the music slowly evolves from the opening cell, through a series of perpetually changing patterns. This technique is used frequently

by Reich who based some of his music on tape loops to build large cumulative forms in this way, such as *Violin Phase* (1967).

- Some minimalist styles are based more on traditional phrasing and melodic structures, the repetition element enlivened by more melodic vocal, instrumental or percussion lines.

- The influence of the raga scales, rhythms and improvisatory style of Indian music influenced several composers including Terry Riley in his work *A Rainbow in Curved Air* (1970). Similarly the rhythmic organisation inherent in Indian music can be seen in the works of Philip Glass.

- Multi-layered rhythms, riffs, ostinatos, repetitions, conflicting rhythmic patterns, rhythmic transformations and syncopation are all common in this style. Glass, for example, used rhythmic cycles to create extended structures in his music by superimposing two or more different rhythmic patterns of different lengths.

- Make sure you work out whether you are writing for live performance, or recorded, or perhaps a combination of both as in Reich's *Violin Phase*, for example, a work for one or four violinists with three synchronous violin tracks on tape.

- As well as non-western influences, musical material is frequently derived from pop, jazz or rock styles. For example, Riley's *A Rainbow in Curved Air*, involves rock and jazz styles with rock amplification.

- Acoustic instruments – brass, saxophones, perhaps a solo violinist and woodwind, are frequently combined with electronic keyboards synthesisers and percussion.

Piano Phase
Steve Reich

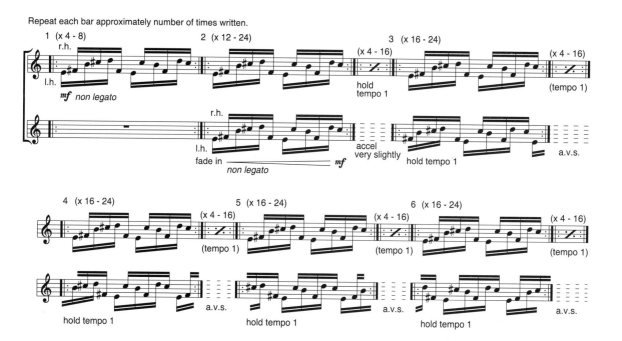

This music is written for two pianos, or two marimbas. In this piece, based on repetition, one piano repeats a fixed melodic pattern throughout until broken at phase 26–28, returning only in a fragmented form to end the piece. The second piano part gradually accelerates, creating a phase shifting relationship as can be seen in bars 3–6 in the music above. Note how each bar begins on a note further on in the pattern. After a number of repetitions the two piano parts play in unison again.

The piece is built on two sonorities – E B D and F# C#. The evenly marked phases are almost entirely consonant and the odd numbered phases are significantly more dissonant, with the interval interaction of 2nds, 4ths and 6ths. The first performer changes the basic pattern at bar 16 and the second performer gradually fades in with another pattern at bar 17. At bar 25 the first performer gradually fades out and

the second performer continues alone until bar 28. The second performer again slowly increases the tempo, making the last phases out of synchronisation with each other until returning to unison for the end in bar 32.

The texture continually permutates from absolute unison as in bar 2 and bar 6 to highly contrapuntal texture as in bar 4.

You will notice that the music instructs performers when to fade in and out of the piece, indicates the number of repetitions for each phase, and indicates when to gradually accelerate and when to hold tempo.

Introduction

Whether you're composing popular music in the reggae, punk, heavy metal, Europop or middle-of-the-road styles, or even if you're composing songs to be performed as part of a musical drama on stage or film music, there are a number of important principles that should govern the way that you work. Inspiration and originality is important, but you must not underestimate the importance of having a good composition technique and knowledge of musical conventions.

In whatever style you choose to compose, use the checklists given here as you work. Read the analyses in this book and go through the Listening section with your teacher. Take special notice of the techniques and conventions that different composers use. You'll be surprised to see how much different composers have in common, in terms of the devices and techniques that they use.

Key considerations
Form and Structure

Like Classical sonata form, the standard thirty-two-bar song has a balanced structure which is built from tonality and rhythmic/melodic motifs. The basic structure is an A-A-B-A form, each section representing an equal section of eight bars. Each eight-bar section is divided into (usually) equal phrases of two or four bars, arranged as antecedent and consequent phrases.

Like sonata form, the A sections are usually centred around the tonic key of the song, with the central section - known, for obvious reasons, as the middle eight – venturing into another key which may or may not be closely related to the tonic. Whatever key is modulated to in the middle eight, by the end of this section the music must be ready to start again in the tonic key at the beginning of the final A section. This modulation back to the tonic is known as the 'turnaround', and ensures that the final chord of the B section is the dominant of the tonic.

Other popular songs have a verse-chorus structure, often including an introduction, playout and instrumental break.

Harmony
Major keys

Whilst the harmony of popular music is firmly rooted in the hierarchy of primary and secondary chords, there are a number of ways in which the harmonies of a song can be embellished from their basic form. In a major key, these can include :

- sharpening the 3rd of chord II, III or VI, creating secondary dominant chords within the circle of 5ths
- flattening the 3rd of chord IV to create a 'flat IV' chord
- flattening the roots and 5ths of chords VI and VII to create major chords which are 'borrowed' from the descending melodic minor scale
- adding the 6th to a chord to create an 'added 6th' chord
- adding the 7th to a series of chords within the circle of 5ths to create a 'chain of 7ths', including the diminished chord VII7
- adding the 9th to a chord to create an 'added 9th' chord, or even the 13th!
- suspending the 4th in a chord (with or without preparation and/or resolution) to create a 'sus' chord
- adding a resolving appoggiatura to the top of the chord.

Minor keys

In minor keys, there is a greater range of harmonies for you to choose from within the range of the harmonic and melodic minor scales. This can mean that you can choose more expressive harmonies, but it can also lead to problems - for example, chords II, III, VI and VII can take diminished forms (use sparingly and with care!). Many composers opt for the major or minor versions of these chords to give a stronger feel to their harmony. The use of the major version of chord VII is a particular favourite, particularly as a substitute to chord V at a cadence. This gives a modal feel to the harmony.

Modulation

Whether you are making a passing modulation or a more substantial change of key, there are a number of cliched harmonic progressions to facilitate modulations within a song. These include:

- sharpening the 3rd of chord II, III or VI, creating secondary dominant chords. We have already explored the use of these within the circle of 5ths; it is more than likely that these will produce nothing more than passing modulations, the music progressing back to the tonic key without much delay
- adding the flattened 7th to chord I (particularly at a perfect cadence), thus producing a modulation to the sub-dominant key
- suspending the root of chord I into chord II#3, which in turn becomes the dominant 7th for a modulation to the dominant key
- modulating by tertiary shift - where chord I modulates suddenly to the key a minor 3rd above it. Such modulations tend to last longer; and the modulation back to the tonic is also enabled through a tertiary shift from the new key to the dominant chord of the tonic
- modulating up a tone after a perfect cadence by sharpening the root of chord I, adding the 6th, and treating this chord as the dominant 7th of the new key, which is a tone above the first. This technique is almost *de rigeur* in the last verse of Europop songs. Use it either with care or with irony!

Accompanying figurations

It is likely that your main accompanying instrument will be piano or guitar. Whichever you choose, remember that the accompanying instrument will fulfil a variety of roles. It will pro-

vide the harmonic bedrock for the vocal line; it must have rhythmic movement to drive the song forward (especially if you are not using a drummer or synthesised drumtrack); it must give support and guidance to the vocal line (doubling in places if you feel this necessary); and it must provide extra melodic interest at the ends of phrases and in counter-melody with the vocal line (especially if there are no other melody instruments in your arrangement).

There are two principles to bear in mind when writing your main accompaniment:
- make the part idiomatic – that is, the music must not only be playable on the instrument, but the music must suit the natural timbre and mechanics of the instrument.
- as has been stated often – you must be consistent. When you set up an accompanying pattern at the start of a song, you must maintain the accompaniment in that style throughout the song (unless, of course there is a clear and very sudden change of mood in the music).

Bass lines

If you are going to perform your song with the backing of a small group, it is likely that you will have a dedicated bass instrument playing – double bass, bass guitar or bass synth. Even if you are just writing a simple piano accompaniment for your song, you will have to consider your bass line.

There are a number of related issues for you to think about with regard to your bass lines:

- In the same way that you want to vary your harmonies, you will want to use a variety of inversions in your chord structure. You can use root position, first, second and third inversions as required to give you the bass-line shapes and characteristics that you require. These can be used freely, but remember that root position chords are strongest and should be used in places where strong harmony is required.
- Bass lines can be smooth – with the mini-

mum movement. Choose inversions that keep bass movement smooth. Remember that bass pedals – where the bass line remains static whilst the harmonies move above – can be very effective.

- A variation of this pedal idea is to keep the chord static, whilst moving the bass up (or, less usually, down) a step – a sort of upwardly-moving appoggiatura.
- Bass lines can also move by step or by leap. If your bass line moves by leaps of a 3rd, introduce passing notes in the bass to give smoothness. If the leap is a large one, it's often a good idea to return within that leap for the next bass note.
- Rhythm is important for a bass line in the same way that it is important for a melody. Choose a rhythmic motif for your bass line and stick to it – doing so will help to create a sense of coherence for your song.

Rhythm

For the harmony and bass lines of popular songs, the rule is consistency – consistent use and development of melodic motifs, consistent harmonic rhythm and accompanimental patterns. The same principle applies to the rhythm track of your song – once you've chosen your rhythmic style, you need to be consistent in its use. The rhythmic style of a song helps to create the mood and general feel as much as the melody and harmony. Moreover, the way in which the rhythm track is built helps to reinforce the melodic phrasing and the harmonic rhythm.

In the same way that cadences and melodic motifs define the ends of musical phrases, the fill-in can also help to define the sense of musical phrasing. Don't forget that just as there are different types of cadences, you should also invent a variety of fill-ins to end your phrases.

Remember, too, that rhythm is multi-dimensional. The drumkit has a number of constituent parts, all of which can do different things within the rhythmic texture but all of which need to work together when forming the whole rhythm style.

Realising your rhythms

When you start working on your song, you will probably find it useful to use one of the preset rhythmic styles on a keyboard or sequencer. However, when you come to refine and record/perform your work there is no substitute for writing your own bespoke drumtrack on the sequencer or employing a 'live' drummer to realise your rhythms.

Whatever option you take, you must be prepared to be absolutely precise about what you want. In the case of a 'live' drummer, come to the rehearsal session with a clear idea of exactly what you want to be played on each part of the kit and, if appropriate, on auxiliary percussion instruments. Don't be afraid to give your drummer a detailed score of what you want – but at the same time, be ready and willing for the drummer to 'contribute' with ideas about fill-ins and other technical matters.

Other instruments

When scoring your song for instruments, try the following:

Brass

Being potentially very loud, brass parts can be very effective when used to play 'stab' chords to punctuate the musical texture. This will enhance the rhythm of the song as well as the timbre and the harmony. Trombones can be used effectively to play bass riffs, perhaps against a more functional bass guitar line. Don't forget that there is a range of tonal effects, including various types of muting, that are available to use with brass instruments.

Strings and saxes

Strings and saxes have excellent sustaining qualities and can therefore be used as harmonic binding agents, playing long sustained chords which hold the musical texture together. This technique is known as a 'pad'. Alternatively, try exploiting the lyrical qualities of the strings in unison, or a single, poignant saxophone to play a counter-melody against the main vocal tune.

Thirty-two-bar standards
Identifying compositional techniques

The best way of finding out how the form, harmony, accompaniments, bass lines, rhythm and instrumentation of thirty-two-bar standards work is by studying the songs themselves. If you can, obtain lead sheets/piano scores and recordings of some of these songs to help you as you listen and analyse. This will help you when you come to compose.

Song	Composer(s)	Recommended Recording
'All the Things You Are'*	Kern and Hammerstein	Tony Martin (Decca F7645)
'Flamingo'+	Grouya/Anderson	Leslie Hutchinson (HMV BD 10003)
'From Me To You'+	Lennon/McCartney	The Beatles (Parlophone R 5015)
'I've Never Been In Love Before'+	Frank Loesser	Robert Alda (Brunswick LAT 8022)
'Lullaby of Birdland'	Shearing/Weiss	Ella Fitzgerald (Brunswick LAT 8115)
'Satin Doll'+	Duke Ellington	Duke Ellington and his orchestra
'Skylark'	Carmichael/Mercer	Hoagy Carmichael (Vogue VA 160112)
'Take the 'A' Train'+	Billy Strayhorn	Duke Ellington and His Orchestra#
'These Foolish Things'	Strachy/Link/Marvell	Leslie Hutchinson (Decca LF 1207)
'Will You Love Me Tomorrow?'	Goffin/King	The Shirelles (Top Rank JAR 540)
'Yesterday'	Lennon/McCartney	The Beatles (Parlophone PMC 1255)

* score included in the Student Book page 149
+ score included in the Heinemann Advanced Music Teacher Resource File, pages 349, 351, 338, 344, 132
# included on CD2, track 33

Harmonic resource

On a lead sheet, the chords to be played are indicated above the melody. The notation used is not the standard Roman numeral or figured bass systems that one would expect in art music. However it is just as straightforward to understand. For your reference, here is a chart of the most common chords in the harmonic repertoire of pop, rock and jazz. All chords are shown in the diatonic key of C major.

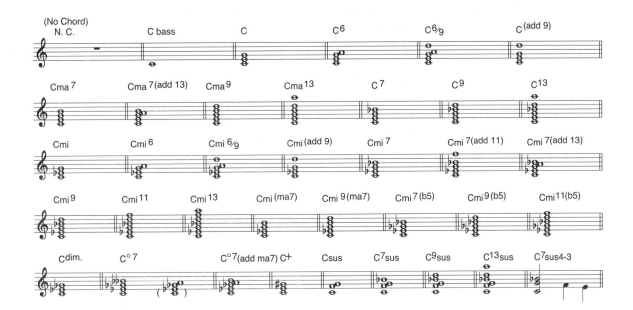

Using ICT to help you compose

Sequencing packages such as Cubase, Logic and Cakewalk are incredibly useful tools to help you work as you are composing. Here are some ideas for using MIDI sequencers in your composition work:

- When your teacher gives you a composition task which involves completion of a partly-worked score, start by playing in what is given. This is what is known as the 'incipit'. This will help you to understand the style of the music you are working with.
- Layering each part on separate MIDI channels means that you can hear melodies playing whilst you work on the harmony, and vice versa.
- When you are composing an original piece of music, it is incredibly useful to be able to layer the parts one by one, with realistic timbres, so that you can hear the whole sound of your piece and work on it without the additional complication of involving other musicans.
- You should try to use the MIDI keyboard to input the music in 'real time'. However, the drum-edit function of your sequencer will be useful in building drum patterns. If a drum pattern is repeated, the cut-and-paste function comes into its own!
- If you are working to a strict time-plan or deadline – in film music, for example – you can set the tempo and the MIDI clock to exactly the rate required to fulfil the task. A basic mathematical ability is all that is required!
- The score-writing facilities mean that you can concentrate on the practical business of composing, rather than the writing down of your work.

Ensuring accuracy

However useful sequencers are, there are a number of functions that you must be sure to apply if your sequenced composition work is to be musical and accurate in terms of both performance and printed score.

- Whether you are playing your work in real time or sequencing it in step time, you must set a suitable quantise in order to ensure that your work is played back accurately.

- Similarly, you must set a suitable score quantise so that your score is accurate. Remember that, in some styles of pop and jazz, it is conventional for 'swung' rhythms to be written 'straight'.

- Don't forget that there are 128 General MIDI voices to choose from, in addition to the plethora of drum and percussion sounds. On some programs, keyboards and sound modules, you will be able to edit these voices to give you an even bigger choice of timbres. Choose and use your instrumental voices with care, appropriate to the composition.

- You should use MIDI controllers to shape fundamental music elements such as volume, velocity and articulation.

- Any scores that you produce must be accurate, musical scores that live musicians could perform from. You will need to use the score quantise functions of their sequencer carefully and, perhaps, independently from the various performance quantise functions. You must always add the correct phrasing, articulation, dynamics and other performance instructions to your scores.

Choosing a 'free' Composition Topic

Whichever examination syllabus you are working to, it is likely that you will have to pre-select a genre or style for your own composition. Here is a list of some of the styles and genres that you could choose from:

- Theme and variations
- Piano miniatures – song without words, prelude, study
- Dances – minuet, waltz, allemande, gavotte, bourrée
- Minimalism
- Popular song forms – thirty-two bar song, twelve-bar blues
- Extended popular styles – reggae, heavy metal, punk
- Contemporary dance music – ambient, garage, hip-hop
- Jazz styles – blues, swing, bebop, cool
- Fusions – mixes of pop, jazz and/or non-western musical styles
- Incidental film music
- Television and film theme music
- Music for the theatre – opera, ballet and stage musical styles
- Music inspired by folk culture
- Sacred vocal music
- Chamber music styles – the string quartet and more . . .

This list is not exhaustive!

When you consider your choice, you should take a number of important factors into consideration. If you can answer 'YES' to all of the following questions, then you have found your own personal composition topic!

- Am I interested in the musical style/genre?
- Do I enjoy listening to this type of music?
- Do I have access to the instrumentalists/singers who could perform my music for me? (You can include yourself here, of course!)
- Does this type of music require any special music technology? If so, do I have access to and the expertise needed to make good use of this technology?
- Am I going to be able to produce a composition assignment in this style in the time available and to the highest possible quality?

The *Heinemann Advanced Music* student book is full of examples and analysis of different musical styles to help you as you compose in your chosen style. You'll also find useful information about important matters such as harmony, stylistic writing and orchestration/effective instrumental writing.

Once you have made your choice of composition topic, your teacher will guide you through the process for managing your work and ensuring that you meet the all-important submission deadline.

When you are giving a performance, it is important to give careful attention and thought to preparing your recital programme. Aim to create a well-balanced, coherent and varied programme that will show your capabilities and musicianship and will provide opportunities for you to demonstrate a range of technical skills.

Preparing your recital programme

The following points are to help you effectively prepare your recital programme for both formal and informal concert recitals, or for an examination or audition.

Understanding your instrument

Know your instrument well. This means having a confident, practical understanding of the range and technical capabilities of your instrument, knowing the characteristics of different sounds and how each is produced and the techniques specific to your instrument. For example on a string instrument, this would include the different bowings, vibrato speeds and fingering styles.

Choice of pieces

Choose pieces that you like and will be capable of practising thoroughly in preparation for your recital. To give yourself the best possible chance of choosing the right pieces, explore as much of the repertoire as you can for your instrument. As well as listening to CD recordings, take up opportunites to see live solo and ensemble performances. Look at the radio listings and try to make time to listen to those you select. Explore playing through different pieces or parts of pieces. This will not only expand your knowledge of the repertoire, but will also help your sight-reading skills.

Be imaginative in your choices. In your exploration of different styles, look particularly at how composers have written for your instrument. Why does some music work well for your instrument (for example, Weber for the clarinet) and

other music not so well? Look critically at why certain passages are good to play. Each instrument has its own particular characteristics, and a composer who writes well for a particular instrument will exploit the full potential of the technical and expressive capabilities of the instrument.

Choose pieces that are:
● within your technical grasp. If there are passages that you feel you will only just master and can only just get through in rehearsal, even with lots of practice, then the piece is possibly not going to work well for you in the performance situation

● within your interpretative grasp. You must feel comfortable in meeting the expressive requirements of the piece and in communicating the character and mood of the piece in a convincing manner.

Always remember that it is quality of performance rather than diversity that counts.

Pacing yourself

Maintaining stamina is important in a long recital and needs to be practised to ensure that you pace yourself appropriately. Prior to the recital performance, practise performing the full programme from start to finish, with no breaks. Include tuning up and presentation.

Constructing your recital programme

Your choice of pieces should reflect the nature of the recital. For example, if the recital is for a more informal setting, a well-balanced programme should include items likely to have immediate appeal as well as others that are more challenging. Or a recital for a young audience might include one or two pieces which describe a scene or animal.

A formal recital programme needs to include a

varied selection of pieces that provide good opportunities for you to show your technical skills, musicality, control of the instrument and overall musicianship in communicating your performance to an audience.

Suggested below are some approaches to help you design your recital programme.

A range of styles

Select one piece from each of a range of styles, moving chronologically from Baroque to the twentieth century. Choose pieces by those composers who are recognised as having contributed to the repertoire for, or technical advancement of your instrument.

For example, a formal **vocal** recital could include music by some of the following composers, all of whom have contributed significantly in different ways and in different styles to the vocal solo repertoire:

Renaissance: Dowland
Baroque: Carissimi, Stradella, H. Purcell, Handel
Classical: Mozart – an aria from *The Marriage of Figaro*, *Don Giovanni*, *The Magic Flute*
Romantic: Schubert, Schumann, Donizetti, Rossini, Hugo Wolf
Twentieth century: Britten, Fauré, Head, Howells, Vaughan-Williams, Warlock, Gershwin, Kern, Bernstein, Sondheim, Cole Porter, Kurt Weill

End with a flourish

Consider ending your recital with a short humorous piece, rather like an encore. For example, if you are a **trombonist** you might choose:

Baroque: a J.S. Bach cello suite
Romantic: 1st movement from Rimsky-Korsakov's *Trombone Concerto*.
Twentieth century: R. Strauss, Edward Gregson, Alan Ridout, Derek Bourgeois
Encore: J. A. Greenwood's *The Acrobat*

In this example, the recital finishes with J. A. Greenwood's *The Acrobat* – a lively comical piece originally written for the Victorian music hall. It brings out the more amusing side of trombone playing, particularly *glissandi* and low notes. Such pieces are usually short and often provide opportunities for more virtuosic elements.

A well-balanced programme

If you are performing on an instrument for which the repertoire is less expansive than for others, think carefully about how your programme can be broadened to make for a well-balanced programme. In the case of the **saxophone**, look for opportunities for an improvisatory section, for example:

An unaccompanied, atmospheric piece: Debussy' *Syrinx*
A Classical piece: Haydn's *Gypsy Rondo*
A more virtuosic piece: any well chosen technical jazz study or piece
Improvisation: a blues/jazz piece

Choose pieces from one period

Select a varied range of pieces from one particular musical period which demonstrate contrasting techniques, styles and moods. For example, you could choose the twentieth century:

Clarinet
L Berkeley, Ridout, Stravinsky, Lutoslawski, Arnold, Milhaud, Poulenc, Hindemith, Paul Harris

Recorder
Reizenstein, Arnold, Hindemith, Hans Martin Linde, Badings, Henze, Berio

Themed recital

Recitals could also be built around a particular theme, as long as your choice allows full potential for you to demonstrate your technical capabilites and musicanship. For example, you could choose dances composed for the **piano**:

Baroque: dances from J. S. Bach *French Suites*, Handel
Romantic: Chopin waltzes, mazurkas
Twentieth century: dances from Bartok's *Mikrokosmos Vol. 6*, Martinu, any jazz-influenced dances

Playing a single work

Choose one longer piece – a single work such as a whole sonata which includes variety and contrast.

Time limits

In your programme construction, make sure it keeps within the prescribed time limits. This is particularly important if you are preparing for an examination. If the programme is too short, you may lose marks, and if it is substantially over-length, the last part of your recital may not be counted in the marks. Your choices for a well-balanced programme should also take into account the following:

- the contrast of unaccompanied and accompanied pieces
- the varying lengths of pieces, for example balancing one long piece with two or three shorter ones
- including a range of moods and character as well as different styles
- including unusual, imaginative choices as well as those in the standard repertoire
- creating the running order of your programme carefully, perhaps with the longest and most demanding work first or last. Consider the balance of length, and accompanied and unaccompanied pieces and of contrasts of character, moods and styles. Work out whether, for example, you will be performing your pieces in date chronological order, starting with the earliest composition first, or whether the programme will follow a different format. As the soloist think about the adjustments you will have to make with the changes of character and mood in your programme.

Programme notes

Decide whether or not you are going to distribute programme notes, and if so, what you are going to write. Programme notes usually contain a short paragraph about you as a performer, and notes on the music. Generally, these are not deeply analytical, but tend towards a light informative tone, often supported with interesting anecdotal comments on particular pieces or circumstances of composition. In certain examination situations, you may be asked to include your own responses to the pieces you have chosen, to give reasons for your choices and why you enjoy playing the pieces.

Programme notes to accompany songs by Purcell, Handel, Schumann, Britten and Schoenberg selected from the example on page 317 could look particularly at the ways in which composers set words to music. Purcell's renowned word-setting could be compared to the style of Handel, both writing in the Baroque period. A Schumann *lied* requires the singer to sing in German, and could promote discussion in the programme notes on singing in a foreign language, diction problems to encounter and so on. Britten's gift of setting words to music has long been recognised as one of the finest, and programme notes could again compare his style with that of Purcell and Handel. Finally, singing a song from a musical such as Schoenberg's *Les Misérables* provides another stylistic contrast. As with singing songs from any musical, the singer needs to be able to convey the degree of emotion at the point from where the song is taken in the musical, as well as the overall compositional style.

Performing
Practising performing

To be able to perform successfully you need to practise performing regularly in front of an audience. While some people thrive on performing in public, others dread the experience. It is important to remember that *performing* is different from just *playing through* a piece (see 'Communication' on page 320).

Take every available opportunity to practise performing. Try first in informal surroundings, to friends or family, and in small concert environments, gradually building up to more formal and larger occasions. If you are more used to playing or singing in ensembles such as bands or choirs, make sure that you give yourself or find opportunities to perform regularly as a soloist.

Venue
Acoustics

Investigate the venue where you are playing. They differ considerably, not only acoustically but also in the feel of the performance when you are on stage. If possible, take a rehearsal in the venue so that you can hear the sound and the extent to which it may reverberate. The capacity, the formality or informality of the venue and the balance between the instruments all count in performance. For example, if your recital is in a large church, the reverberations may be much longer than in a theatre and you may need to take account of this in your playing. Amplification is another important factor to take into consideration and you may want to practise with a microphone beforehand. It can be a very exciting, thrilling experience to become familiar with the amplifed sound you are making.

Stage set and lighting

If possible, rehearse your performance on the stage with the lighting that will be used for the performance. Stage lights can be very off-putting in unfamiliar circumstances. If you are sharing the stage area with other performers, ensure that you have sufficient space to perform effectively, and that the lighting will not hamper your reading of the music on the music stand. Familiarise yourself with the proximity of the audience, and whether or not you will require more distance to feel comfortable. Find out where the stage door is, the backstage facilites and if, for example, mineral water will be available should you require it.

Testing pianos and organs

Pianists and organists need to try out the instruments beforehand. Test the speed and response of the keys, the balance and dynamic levels in the bass and treble, the potential of the instrument for *pianissimo* and *fortissimo* and for expressive, subtle tonal nuances. Test the pedals, the piano stool or organ seat and the music stand.

Nerves

Accepting that you may be nervous before a performance is half the battle in coping with general agitation. With experience, the extra adrenalin can be used to good purpose in stimulating and exciting your performance.

Everyone has their own ways of coping with nerves. In general the best way to avoid nerves getting the better of your performance is to prepare well, so that you have real confidence in knowing that you can play every part of the piece well. If there are one or two bars that have consistently posed problems during practice and that have not been totally mastered, these can be the bars that will provoke anxiety about the entire performance, endangering the security of the whole performance and are very likely to go wrong during the performance.

Allow plenty of time to prepare yourself prior to performance in a calm environment. Many performers find taking a few deep breaths helpful while others have particular tried and tested routines that they know work effectively. Above all, try to think of the performance as an enjoyable, even exciting experience.

Presentation

Your performance begins from the very moment you walk into the room or on to the stage. Your appearance and how you walk on is important, as well as setting up, and tuning. Consider your own responses when watching a performer walk on stage and start tuning up. There is much you can assess as to how they are going to play, simply by how they conduct themselves as they prepare to perform. It is always important to position yourself appropriately in relation to the audience and also to the accompanist or others in the ensemble.

Different genres demand different presentation styles. Many pianists, for example in a formal setting take a great deal of time adjusting and settling themselves on the piano stool before beginning to perform. For a guitarist accompanied by a rock band it may be more appropriate to play a few random notes or chords before giving a deliberate one bar count in. This builds up a sense of anticipation and prepares the audience as well as you for the performance.

Consider whether or not you are going to introduce the pieces yourself. If you are, make sure that you have rehearsed what you are going to say in each introduction. If any selected composers have names with difficult pronunciations, practise saying these names clearly beforehand and projecting your voice at the same time.

Remember to have practised page turns, preferably memorising the first few bars over the page. Organise a page turner if you need one. Only play from memory if you are entirely confident and have practised playing from memory in front of an audience. However, it is often expected that singers sing from memory.

Assessing performances
What a performance is marked on
All performances are generally marked on accuracy, interpretation and communication.

Accuracy
Accuracy generally includes pitch, intonation, pulse, rhythm, note values, observation of given dynamics, ornamentation, tempi and changes of tempi. As you prepare your performance all these aspects need to be practised thoroughly, until they are absolutely accurate, present no difficulties and do not hamper fluency.

To give a good performance you need to be able to show competent technical control and accuracy. To give an excellent performance your playing should display excellent accuracy with no slips or blemishes, or ones that are so small that any tiny slip is well covered.

Interpretation
Interpretation includes style, dynamic range and shading, phrasing, articulation, variety and evenness of tone; also factors specific to particular instruments, such as string bowing, breath control, wind tongueing and pedalling. A good performance will show a well-balanced understanding of how the music should be interpreted and a real sense of style throughout. This means giving full attention to the musical detail, demonstrating an ability to show musical sensitivity and, where appropriate, *rubato*, and to really 'feel' how the music should be played. Mechanical or dull performances lack this sensitivity and show little stylistic understanding. Good performances will show real musicality perhaps even with some tiny notation or rhythmic slips but these will be overridden in an overall musical performance.

Communication
A significant part of performing to an audience, small or large, is communicating your performance of the music. Communication includes rapport with the audience, commitment and involvement and being at one with the music. Genuine communication gives the feeling of the performer having an air of confidence, of someone who is in complete control of the instrument and who has that indefinable quality of being able to hold the attention of the audience and make the music his or her own.

Performing improvisations
If your performance includes an improvisation section, you may find the following points of benefit:
- Your improvisation must be fluent and consistent.

- It needs a sense of direction with points of climax or tension and repose, and it must have a clear overall shape. This means working out a structure to determine the shape. Structural designs for an improvisation section can be many and varied. Some approaches could be:

  - a straightforward ternary form, with a contrasting middle section – ABA
  - one long *crescendo*, built up from start to finish
  - an arch form as in some works of twentieth century composers such as Bartok – ABCBA
  - beginning in a simple way, building from a particular fragment, increasing in complexity towards the middle and then returning to the more simple structure of the beginning.

- You need to be imaginative in your improvisations, using the melody or rhythm or some other fragment in ways which both unify and vary the original. The section could also involve new material in which you introduce and subsequently show a range of improvising techniques, always demonstrating appropriate awareness.
- Like any other aspect of performing, improvising needs to be practised. Listen to the improvisation styles of those artists that you admire. Start with small fragments or figurations over a small harmonic scheme and build up the complexity as you progress and gain confidence.
- A good improvisation will also involve a range of and variety of dynamics and tone. It should show that you know your instrument well and can exploit its full tonal, dynamic and timbral potential.
- Finally, to be fully successful, the improvisation needs to convey a sense of conviction and involvement.

Performance investigation
Integration
To develop fully as a performer it is important to investigate the wider horizons of the performing canvas. This involves evaluating performances, responding to different interpretations and performing styles, and building up your knowledge of professional performers and performance practices. It also involves integrating your knowledge and understanding of music and your composing and listening skills with your performing activities as a soloist, in small ensembles and in large ensembles, such as bands, choirs and orchestras.

History and analysis work can help you define the styles of your pieces and understand how the structure and the tension and resolution points work in terms of tonal and harmonic directions. Similarly, listening to your intonation, tone quality and phrasing will also help to develop your aural skills in listening work. Singing in choirs can help your understanding of harmonic lines, part movement and progressions.

Repertoire
Build up your knowledge of the repertoire for your instrument through both study and practice. Assess the contribution of particular composers for your instrument from the Renaissance period, if appropriate, to the twentieth century. You might want to focus particularly on a specific time period. For example, if you were investigating the contribution of twentieth century, composers to the repertoire of the viola, you could explore the Bartok and Walton concertos, Milhaud's *Quatre Visages*, Hindemith's *Traurmusik*, or *Sonata for viola d'amore*. Explorations into chamber music could include Shostakovich's *Quartets* and Debussy's *Sonata for Flute, Viola and Harp*, for example.

Performers
Find out who the authoritative performers are

for your instrument. Listen critically to their recordings, noting the characteristics of their individual interpretative styles. It is a good idea to listen sometimes with a score, looking particularly at the technical expertise, phrasing, dynamics, articulation and different tone qualities used. Study the repertoire choices and the contribution that eminent performers have made to performing techniques or repertoire. Note the make of instrument they play.

Explore the contextual background of the music you enjoy playing. Assess the importance of particular soloists in context. Find out who they were influenced by and who they subsequently have influenced. For example, as a guitarist you could assess the contributions of Jimi Hendrix, Frank Zappa, Eddie van Halen or Pat Metheny. Not only has Frank Zappa a unique performance style, but he is also a prolific composer and writer who was influenced by the composers Boulez and Varèse. He considers himself a composer who happens to play the guitar. His heavy right hand techniques have been much imitated, as has his concert programmes which he developed into tightly arranged sequences of songs. Although it is useful, and even revealing about the character of the man, to know that he once defined rock journalists as 'people who can't write interviewing people who can't talk for people who can't read', such details are useful only in so far as they help give the broad picture. It is the contribution to the overall development of the genre that counts.

Evaluating performances

Set up formal and informal performances in your own music group. Then discuss interpretation points such as *rubato*, dynamic shadings or articulation. Explore interpreting pieces in different ways, with different dynamic shadings, tempi, phrasing and articulation. Play pieces devoid of all interpretative shadings. Such explorations will expand your understanding of different interpretations of different styles on a range of different instruments and can also help your composing.

Listen to and evaluate professional and amateur performances both live and recorded, in terms of accuracy, interpretation and communication. Record your own performance, then listen and critically evaluate. As a group assess and mark performances using the same criteria. This can give you an insight into performance assessment and also shed light on your own performance.

To be able to communicate to your audience is paramount to success and performances. This is best assessed by going to see performances in a variety of formal and informal settings and assessing how performers respond, both in terms of their communication and in their programme choices to the different venues, environments and atmospheres. Television can be a source of further inspiration as performances of varying character are featured nightly.

Writing about music

Writing about music is a skill that needs to be practised. Practise reading short extracts about music you are particulary interested in before progressing to more complex reading. Look at the different writing styles, from reviews of CDs in magazines to broadsheet reviews of performances ranging from opera to jazz and rock. Try reading the reviews written by established music critics.

When following analyses, make sure that you have the music score to hand to be able to understand fully the analysis. Evaluate your own writing, making sure that your judgements are supported by the music and that you have made your points succinctly and clearly.

Discussing music

Develop your ability to discuss your responses to music, articulate your perceptions clearly and make judgements. Take opportunities to give short presentations and lead discussions on your musical experiences. For example, many brass band players lead a very active, musical life outside school, particularly those involved in brass band competitions or playing at prestigious venues nationally and even internationally. If you are a member of a local balalaika group or have formed or play in a band, for example, integrate your musical experiences and acquired knowledge with your music coursework in discussions or presentations.

There is much to be gained from developing an ability to critically discuss your evaluations of performances. Watch programmes such as the *BBC Young Musician of the Year*, in which those judging the competition are often interviewed in the process of their evaluations. Distinguished musicians frequently support such programmes by defining what counts as a good performance, how they evaluated particular performances and their views on the pieces chosen.

Discussion topics

A stimulating and interesting way of developing your ability to discuss music is to set up informal discussions on music in your group. Some topic suggestions are given below:

Authenticity

This issue concerns the question of giving authentic performances as a concept in itself, choice of instrument, playing techniques such as *vibrato*, ornamentation, realisation of figured bass, cadenzas, choice of edition, number of players/singers to a part, treatises and venues.

New ways of notating music since 1945

Your discussion could include graphic scores, notation of extended or unconventional techniques, aleatoric music and problems of interpretation, the intricate detail of a Boulez score, or the quarter-tone clusters and *glissandi* in a Penderecki score. Various composers may indicate the same effect in different ways, or might use the same symbol to mean quite different things.

Commercial sponsorship in music – the advantages and disadvantages

Discussion on this topic could include advantages being that commercial sponsorship might

be the only lifeline for many activities if state funding is not forthcoming. Many minority genres would not be able to survive without sponsorship. Without sponsorship, choice in the arts could be reduced to only the most popular and commercially viable genres surviving, leaving on the fringe the vast range and potential for expansion of less popular but perhaps more innovatory initiatives. Many education projects exist solely through commercial sponsorship.

Disadvantages could include sponsors' powerful control over repertoire, stifling creativity and freedom. The topic could cover sponsorship for concerts, education projects, recordings and tuition.

Ensemble playing and recitals

In order to successfully perform in an ensemble, it is essential to practise regularly as part of the ensemble, whether it will be performing with an accompanist or in a larger ensemble.

Accompanists

Always choose your accompanist carefully, being aware of the technical demands and musical complexity of the accompaniment. It is important to know the accompaniment part of your pieces well. An ensemble put together just prior to performance in which co-ordination relies solely on the soloist counting the bars with little or no knowledge of the whole musical integration will not work well. The music will only work if it is played as an integrated whole.

As you rehearse, work on the following:

- The balance – different pieces require different balance perspectives. Some are 'more equal' than others. Those accompaniments which are clearly playing a supporting role for the most part can leave the way clear for the soloist to take the lead role. However, many pieces require a genuine ebb and flow between soloist and accompaniment which needs concentrated practice together to reach its full interpretative potential.

- The tempo must suit the soloist and not be too quick or slow. A performance will suffer if the soloist allows the accompanist to dictate the tempo, the *rits*, *accelerandos* and dynamics. Watch that your interpretation as the soloist is not compromised by a weak accompanist who perhaps is not up to playing at the speed you wish to play, or is not reacting with enough sensitivity to those particular moments which require subtle musical expressiveness. Subtle nuances such as pauses, short lingers and other expressive moments need to be worked at together.

- Dynamic shadings need to be practised together to ensure that both parties are creating the same degree of dynamic shading. For example, if the soloist is building to a strong *fortissimo* while the piano accompaniment supports only with a mediocre *mf*, then the effect can be very unfulfilling musically and frustrating for both the solo performer and the listener. Accompanying throughout at *sotto voce*, playing as two separate performers is as poor as over powering the soloist.

- A good accompanist will enhance the performance, actively supporting the rise and fall of the musical shape. Always bear in mind that it is the soloist who has the overall negotiating control.

Backing tapes

It is always possible, and indeed sometimes preferable, for some instruments to use a recorded backing tape instead of an accompanist. However, one of the drawbacks of using backing tapes is that they can diminish expressive possibilities in performances. As the soloist you are subject to keeping absolute time with the tape, and as such there can be little room for subtle nuances of extra length lingers, or pauses, or spontaneous, intimate interaction.

Ensembles

You may need to direct your own ensemble in rehearsal as well as being the soloist. If you are performing as a soloist in an ensemble for four or five musicians or more, note the directing skills of conductors in large ensembles such as bands, orchestras and choirs that you may be involved in. Note particularly how ensemble accuracy, musicianship and communication is achieved. What is the approach to improving balance, intonation, unanimity of phrasing and articulation, changes of tempi, co-ordinating syncopated rhythms? How are imperfections of pitch, rhythm, balance and intonation identified and corrected?

In all ensemble playing, the following points are important:

- Assess how your part as the soloist fits into the whole.
- Work on developing a high level of musical sensitivity within your ensemble. Ensemble players need to know one another's roles in the ensemble and what each player is playing. It is very much a collective musical relationship which requires sensitivity, balance, ability to complement each other on the most musically intimate level through blending and contrasting interpretative shadings, tone colour and ornamentation.
- Explore the repertoire for your ensemble by listening to and playing through a range of different styles.
- In rehearsal, always work out at the beginning exactly what you want to achieve, so as to avoid just playing through pieces with no justifiable reason.
- Promote good preparation, with all players in the ensemble learning the detail of the music.
- Cultivate an awareness of the capabilities and limitations of your ensemble.
- Develop how to set and change tempi so you can stop and restart the music at different points quickly.
- Be able to communicate your intentions effectively to the rest of the group, showing a sense of friendly authority, some imagination and some humour.
- Convey the stylistic and interpretative demands of the music.

Performing your own composition

Nowadays, many rock and pop compositions are sequenced by the composer/s and never performed live – save, perhaps, for the vocal tracks. Even they are sometimes pre-recorded and mimed to! Of course, as an AS/A Level music student you would agree with the maxim 'Keep Music Live' although, as we have seen, computers can be useful in the process of composing.

Working with your musicians

When you want to have your work performed live, there are a number of things you can do to ensure that justice is done to your work and that your musicians act positively towards your composition. In all cases, your attitude should be 'preparation, preparation, preparation'.

- First, before you rehearse your music with other people, you must know your piece inside out. You must be sure in yourself what your work is about – how it starts, how it progresses, how it ends. You must have in your mind exactly the end result that you want. You must know exactly how you want your piece to be performed, and you must be prepared to explain to individual players the effect and style that you want from them.
- Preparing accurate scores and parts is part of this process – when your musicians arrive, the parts that they receive must contain as much information as possible. This does not necessarily mean stave notation – you might give a guitarist a TAB part, or chord symbols. You must also have a full score to work from, so that you can refer to every performer's part in rehearsal. Have pencils ready so that everyone can write in notes or changes in light of the rehearsal – including yourself.
- Where there is equipment required by your score and performers, make sure that it is available, in good order, and set up in advance of the rehearsal. This may mean liaising with your performers.

Recording rehearsals of your compositions is a good way of reviewing and improving your work. In the heat of a rehearsal – especially if you are one of the performers yourself – it can be hard to listen as objectively as you can do on your own.

Taking advice from others

Remember that playing through your work with live musicians is an important part of the compositional process, and that you should be prepared to go away from the rehearsal and amend your composition.

Sometimes, you will want other musicians to advise you as you work. A more collaborative style of working is common in pop and rock music. At AS/A Level, your work must be all your own, though. If you are advised by any other musicians – for example, a drummer might advise you on technical matters or might even develop some new ideas during a performance that you subsequently incorporate into your piece – it is important that you log this process. It should be mentioned in any descriptive report that you submit with the score and recording of your composition. This will not necessarily be disadvantageous to you. If you can show the rehearsal and collaborative working as part of the compositional process in which you provided the initial ideas and impetus and which you subsequently developed, then it will be to the good.

Notes

Notes

Notes

CDs produced by Andy Murray
CDs manufactured by Thamesdown Software Fulfilment

CD1

Track 1. *'Dixit Dominus'* from *Messa e salmi parte concertati* by Rigatti. Courtesy of Deutsche Grammophon. Licenced by kind permission from the Universal Film & TV Licencing Department.

Track 2. *The Silver Swan* by Orlando Gibbons. Used by permission of EMI Records UK.

Track 3. *'Philou'* from *Terpsichore Dances* by Praetorius. Courtesy of Decca. Licenced by kind permission from the Universal Film & TV Licencing Department.

Track 4. *This is the Record of John* by Orlando Gibbons. Performed by the Choir of the Trinity College Cambridge. Original sound recording owned by BMG Entertainment International UK & Ireland.

Track 5. *'Recitative'* from *L'Orfeo, Act I* by Monteverdi. Used by permission of HNH International Ltd.

Track 6. *'G minor Fugue'* from *The Well Tempered Clavier, Book 1* by J.S. Bach. This recording is used with the permission of ASV Limited, 1 Lochaline Street, London W6 9SJ.

Track 7. *'Duo Poppea/Nerone'* from *The Coronation of Poppea* by Monteverdi. Used by permission of EMI Records UK.

Track 8. *'Duo Poppea/Nerone'* from *The Coronation of Poppea* by Monteverdi. Used by permission of EMI Records UK.

Track 9. *'Comfort Ye'* from *The Messiah* by Handel. Courtesy of Deutsche Grammophon. Licenced by kind permission from the Universal Film & TV Licencing Department.

Track 10. *L'Egyptienne* by Rameau. Courtesy of Decca. Licenced by kind permission from the Universal Film & TV Licencing Department.

Track 11. *'Gigue'* from *French Suite No. 4* by J.S. Bach. Courtesy of Decca. Licenced by kind permission from the Universal Film & TV Licencing Department.

Track 12. Overture from *The Messiah* by Handel. Courtesy of Deutsche Grammophon. Licenced by kind permission from the Universal Film & TV Licencing Department.

Track 13. *Brandenburg Concerto No. 4, BWV1049, 3rd movement* by J.S. Bach. Courtesy of Decca. Licenced by kind permission from the Universal Film & TV Licencing Department.

Track 14. *Cello Concerto in G major, RV414, 3rd movement* by Vivaldi. Courtesy of Decca. Licenced by kind permission from the Universal Film & TV Licencing Department.

Track 15. *La Serva Padrona (The Maid as Mistress)* by Pergolesi. Original sound recording owned by Arte Nove Musikproduktions Munich GmbH.

Track 16. *Sinfonia in G Major, No. 13, 1st movement* by Sammartini. From the CD *Symphonies of the Italian Baroque*, CHE 00992-2, Christophorus Entrée. More information can be obtained from MusiContact GmbH, Heuauerweg 21, 69124 Heidelberg, Germany.

Track 17. *Symphony No. 6, 'Le Matin', 1st movement* by Haydn. Courtesy of Deutsche Grammophon. Licenced by kind permission from the Universal Film & TV Licencing Department.

Track 18. *Symphony No. 3 in E♭, 'Eroica'* by Beethoven. Public Domain.

Track 19. *Piano Sonata in C minor, K457* by Mozart. Courtesy of Philips. Licenced by kind permission from the Universal Film & TV Licencing Department.

Track 20. *Piano Concerto No. 21 in C, 3rd movement* by Mozart. Courtesy of ECM Records/Decca. Licenced by kind permission from the Universal Film & TV Licencing Department.

Track 21. *Symphony No. 5, 1st movement* by Beethoven. Courtesy of Philips. Licenced by permission from the Universal Film & TV Licencing Department.

Track 22. *String Quartet Op. 76 No. 2, 1st movement* by Haydn. Courtesy of Philips. Licenced by kind permission from the Universal Film & TV Licencing Department.

Track 23. 'Le Nozze di Figaro', Cherubini's aria, 'Non Si Piu Cosa Son' by Mozart. Used by permission of EMI Records UK.

Track 24. 'Appassionata' Sonata Op. 57, 1st movement by Beethoven. Courtesy of Deutsche Grammophon. Licenced by kind permission from Universal Film & TV Licencing Department.

Track 25. String Quintet in C major, K515, Finale by Mozart. Used by permission of HNH International Ltd.

Track 26. Requiem 'Kyrie Eleison' by Mozart. Courtesy of Decca. Licenced by kind permission from the Universal Film & TV Licencing Department.

Track 27. Excerpt from Prussian Sonatas, catalogue number KTC 0011, from Etcetera Record Company BV, The Netherlands.

Track 28. Symphony No. 9 'Choral', Finale by Beethoven. Used by permission of HNH International Ltd.

Track 29. Symphony No. 45, 1st movement by Haydn. Courtesy of Deutsche Grammophon. Licenced by kind permission from the Universal Film & TV Licencing Department.

Track 30. String Quartet in F major, Op. 18 No. 1, 1st movement by Beethoven. Used by permission of HNH International Ltd.

Track 31. Piano Concerto in D minor, K466, 1st movement by Mozart. Courtesy of ECM Records/Decca. Licenced by kind permission from the Universal Film & TV Licencing Department.

Track 32. The Creation No. 3 by Haydn. Courtesy of Decca. Licenced by kind permission from the Universal Film & TV Licencing Department.

Track 33. Symphony No. 5, 2nd movement by Tchaikovsky. Used by permission of HNH International Ltd.

Track 34. Overture to The Barber of Seville by Rossini. Used by permission of HNH International Ltd.

Track 35. 'When the foeman bares his steel' from The Pirates of Penzance by Gilbert and Sullivan. Courtesy of Decca. Licenced by kind permission from the Universal Film & TV Licencing Department.

Track 36. Symphonie Fantastique: Reveries-Passions by Berlioz. Courtesy of Philips. Licenced by kind permission from the Universal Film & TV Licencing Department.

Track 37. Symphonie Fantastique: Un Bal by Berlioz. Courtesy of Philips. Licenced by kind permission from the Universal Film & TV Licencing Department.

Track 38. Symphonie Fantastique: Songs d'une Nuit du Sabbat by Berlioz. Courtesy of Philips. Licenced by kind permission from the Universal Film & Licencing Department.

Track 39. Les Préludes: bars 47-53 by Liszt. Used by permission of HNH International Department.

Track 40. Les Préludes: bars 344-356 by Liszt. Used by permission of HNH International Ltd.

Track 41. Les Préludes: Bars 405-end by Liszt. Used by permission of HNH International Ltd.

Track 42. Kinderszenen No. 11, Fürchtenmachen by Schumann. Courtesy of Deutsche Grammophon. Licenced by kind permission from the Universal Film & TV Licencing Department.

Track 43. Violin Concerto in E minor, Op. 64 by Mendelssohn. Used by permission of EMI Records Ltd.

Track 44. String Quartet in C major, D956, 1st movement by Schubert. Used by permission of HNH International Ltd.

Track 45. The Rite of Spring (Opening) by Igor Stravinsky. Performed by Yuri Temurkarnov. Original sound recording owned by BMG Entertainment.

Track 46. The Rite of Spring (Ending) by Igor Stravinsky. Performed by Yuro Temurkarnov. Original sound recording owned by BMG Entertainment.

Track 47. 'Trio' from Suite für Klavier, Op. 25 by Schoenberg. Courtesy of Deutsche Grammophon. Licenced by kind permission from the Universal Film & TV Licencing Department.

Track 48. Symphony No. 1, 3rd movement by Prokofiev. Performed by Eugene Ormandy. Original sound recording owned by BMG Entertainment.

CD2

Track 1. *Rósza Sándor szereti a táncot/Párhuzam*, traditional Hungarian. Track taken from *Songs and Dances from Hungary* courtesy of Arc Music Productions International Ltd.

Track 2. *Dance Suite* by Bartók. Recorded by Hungaroton. Licenced by Hungaroton Records Kft.

Track 3. *Symphony Op. 21, 1st movement* by Webern. Courtesy of Deutsche Grammophon. Licenced by kind permission from the Universal Film & TV Licencing Department.

Track 4. *Kontakte* by Karlheinz Stockhausen (WER 6009 2). Courtesy of WERGO/Schott Music & Media GmbH, Mainz, Germany, e-mail: wergo@schott-musik.de.

Track 5. *Sequenza I for Solo Flute* by Lucian Berio (WER 6021 2). Courtesy of WERGO/Schott Music & Media GmbH, Mainz, Germany, e-mail: wergo@schott-musik.de.

Track 6. *Ging heut'Morgens Ubers Feld* by Mahler. Courtesy of Deutsche Grammophon. Licenced by kind permission from Universal Film & TV Licencing Department.

Track 7. *Symphony No. 1* by Mahler. Courtesy of Deutsche Grammophon. Licenced by kind permission from the Universal Film & TV Licencing Department.

Track 8. *Symphony No. 2* by Sibelius. Used by permission of Chandos Records Ltd.

Track 9. *Symphony No. 2, 3rd movement* by Sibelius. Used by permission of Chandos Records Ltd.

Track 10. *Symphony No. 2, 3rd into 4th movement* by Sibelius. Used by permission of Chandos Records Ltd.

Track 11. *Muzyka Zalobna* by Lutoslawski. Used by permission of EMI Records UK.

Track 12. *Cantus in Memory of Benjamin Britten* by Arvo Pärt. Used by permission of HNH International Ltd.

Track 13. *'Nuages'* from *Nocturnes* by Debussy. Used by permission of Cala Records Ltd, 17 Shakespeare Gardens, London N2 9LJ.

Track 14. *'Sirenes'* from *Nocturnes* by Debussy. Used by permission of Cala Records Ltd, 17 Shakespeare Gardens, London N2 9LJ.

Track 15. *'Petrouchka'* from *Petrouchka* by Stravinsky. Recorded by Hungaroton. Licenced by Hungaroton Records Kft.

Track 16. *'Dance Russe'* from *Petrouchka* by Stravinsky. Recorded by Hungaroton. Licenced by Hungaroton Records Kft.

Track 17. *Spitfire Prelude and Fugue: Prelude* by Walton. Used by permission of Chandos Records Ltd.

Track 18. *Spitfire Prelude and Fugue: Fugue* by Walton. Used by permission of Chandos Records Ltd.

Track 19 and 20: *La Creation du Monde* by Milhaud. Used by permission of EMI Records UK.

Track 21. *'Intermezzo'* from *The Háry János Suite* by Kodaly. Used by permission of Sanctuary Records Group.

Track 22. *Henry VIII* from *As Others See Us* by James MacMillan. Performed by Evelyn Glennie. Original sound recording owned by BMG Entertainment.

Track 23. *T.S. Elliot* from *As Others See Us* by James MacMillan. Performed by Evelyn Glennie. Original sound recording owned by BMG Entertainment.

Track 24. *Ndenduele/Jarawa* by Adzido. Courtesy of Arc Music Productions International Ltd.

Track 25. *Mean Old Bed Bug Blues* performed by Bessie Smith. Public Domain.

Track 26. *St Louis Blues* performed by Lena Horne and the Dixieland Jazz Group. Original sound recording owned by BMG Entertainment.

Track 27. *One Note Samba/Samba de Una Nota So* by Antonio Carlos Jobim. Courtesy of Polygram. Licenced by kind permission from the Universal Film & TV Licencing Department.

Track 28. *Hound Dog* performed by Elvis Presley. Original sound recording owned by BMG Entertainment.

Track 29. *Higher and Higher*. Words and Music by